P9-DTS-003

MA`

WITHDRAWN
UTSA Libraries

WITHDRAWN
UTSA Libraries

Therapy in Motion

EDITED BY
MAUREEN NEEDHAM COSTONIS

Therapy in Motion

UNIVERSITY OF ILLINOIS PRESS
Urbana   Chicago   London

© 1978 by the Board of Trustees of the University of Illinois
Manufactured in the United States of America

"Case Study of a Puzzling Child," © 1974 by Maureen N.
Costonis. This essay was originally published in the
Proceedings of the Eighth Annual Conference of the
American Dance Therapy Association.

"How I Learned to Wall-Bounce and Love It," © 1975
by Maureen N. Costonis. This essay was originally
published in the Proceedings of the Ninth Annual
Conference of the American Dance Therapy Association.

title page and cover illustrations from Gilliom,
Basic Movement Education for Children, Reading, Mass.:
Addison-Wesley, 1970

Library of Congress Cataloging in Publication Data

Main entry under title:

Therapy in motion.

   Includes bibliographies and index.
   1.   Dance therapy.   1.   Costonis, Maureen.
RC489.D3T48   616.8'91   77–9077
ISBN 0–252–00586–4

LIBRARY
The University of Texas
At San Antonio

To John
May I return the compliment?

Foreword

It is a pleasure for me to introduce this diverse collection of papers gathered from a variety of obscure journals and now presented by a scholarly press to the reading public. This collection is unique in that it is an interdisciplinary group of articles designed to both interest and instruct the reader, covering such a wide range of topics that it can be used as a set of supplementary readings for an academic course in dance therapy or a psychiatric residency program. In addition, the comprehensive bibliography contains four hundred additional sources for the student who wishes to explore any particular area in greater depth. I believe this is the first time that there has been a reasonably comprehensive reader in dance therapy available and certainly this is the only time that I am aware of an exhaustive bibliography being made available to students and practitioners alike.

Dance therapy has had a hard time achieving respectability in the twentieth century in large part due to its informal, apprentice-type training that could hardly be called academic. In recent years various ruses have been used to change the designation from dance to movement in the hope, I imagine, that movement implies something more measurable, countable, clockable in some way that could seem more scientific. I have always leaned toward keeping the term "dance" because it has some implication of joy, abundance of energy, and well-being that I think is an integral part of the achievement of dance therapy. It would be too much of a price to pay if we exorcised the memory of schools of ballroom dancing at the expense of forgetting Martha Graham, the Denishawn School, and Marian Chace.

Dance has had a long and respectable natural relationship to healing going back to prehistory. It is true that we are being more scientific about it today, but its roots still lie in the achievement of integration of the psyche through bodily expression.

It is true that the capacity for language distinguishes man more sharply from other animals than any other characteristic. It is also apparent that our most unambiguous communications and our finer discriminations require that capacity. Thus it is no wonder that talk-

ing therapy has held first place in our interest for so many generations
of the "helping professions." But man does not live by words alone.
Our lives are lived by a pattern of synchronous melody lines that
have much to do with our well-being but little to do with our awareness, until stress of one sort or another puts them out of synchronization. Sometimes it is a flaw in the design, but far more commonly it is
a functional failure which may be either acute or chronic. One might
say this asynchrony is a style of living unsympathetically with one's
body.

For some people talking may be the optimum point of entry into
their system of distress. For others, as you will see in the chapters
which follow, we must recognize that re-establishing a flow of "body
language (or music)" should properly come first, or as it often happens, concurrently.

JARL E. DYRUD, M.D.

Contents

Preface

Movement therapy, similar to other emerging disciplines, is groping for self-definition. Abetted by the increasing attention of students and professionals from allied disciplines, the search intensifies. Regrettably, the American Dance Therapy Association (an organization whose membership has swelled from thirty to over 900 since its founding in 1966) has hindered rather than aided the search by defining dance therapy as "the planned use of any aspect of dance to aid in the physical and psychic integration of the individual."[1] Bewildering in its vagueness, this definition encourages formless conceptions of the field and its applications. Consequently when asked, "What is movement therapy?," movement therapists typically throw up their hands and respond, "I don't know; I just do it!"

A serious impediment to defining movement therapy lies in the lack of available literature. The scattered publication of research studies executed in isolation only contributes to ignorance of the field's breadth. A large number of articles are unobtainable. As Dr. Martha Davis laments, "many of our best works are rare, unpublished, or out of print."[2] In *Understanding Body Movement; An Annotated Bibliography,* twenty-four references are made to writings about movement therapy. Of these, four concern books which were out of print, ten represent unpublished articles, and eight represent specialized periodicals which dated as far back as 1941.

A clear-cut distinction between movement therapy and other therapeutic techniques which use movement is made difficult by the rapidity with which methods arise and become incorporated into another camp's bag of tricks. Movement therapy, sensitivity training,

1. In November of 1975 were issued conference proceedings which announced a new version of the official definition. The American Dance Therapy Association (hereinafter referred to as ADTA) presently defines dance therapy as "the psychotherapeutic use of movement as a process which furthers the emotional and physical integration of the individual." American Dance Therapy Association, *Proceedings of Ninth Annual Conference* (New York, 1974), iv.

2. Martha Davis, *Understanding Body Movement: An Annotated Bibliography* (New York: Arno Press, 1972), p. viii.

tai'-chi, bio-energetics, Alexander technique, psychomotor training, structural analysis, postural integration, body ego technique, encounters—if not the name, what is the same? Not one of these categories encompasses "dance" within its title, yet its adherents regularly employ techniques compatible with or even derivative of that medium. Dance therapists return the favor by borrowing in kind. No one of these groups could be excommunicated as heretical by the American Dance Therapy Association; each falls within the fuzzy outlines of the official definition.

The preferred term in this volume, "movement" rather than "dance" therapy, attempts to subsume these factions. "Movement therapy" implies use of a broad range of movement styles which are rhythmic extensions of the client's everyday movements. The specific behavioral changes for which therapy is sought are not limited to dance skills based on Western aesthetic standards. Last and least important, this choice of terminology avoids two bugaboos of American culture—the puritanical view that dance is downright immoral and the warped notion that dance is somehow incompatible with masculinity.

It is more likely, however, that the label "dance therapy" will retain its predominant usage. Two popular reference works—*Psychological Abstracts* and the *Subject Guide to Books in Print*—acknowledge the category of "dance therapy" rather than "movement therapy."[3] The American Association of Health, Physical Education, and Recreation as well as the National Therapeutic Recreation Society tend to favor that term in their literature. Perhaps this trend is all to the good. As Dr. Dyrud points out in the foreword, "movement therapy" is a rather dry term and neglects the inherent joy suggested by the word "dance."

The selection of terminology can evade certain difficulties, but more basic choices remain. In order to define movement therapy, it would be tempting to construct a theoretical model which might accommodate itself to factional divisions. Each reader must judge for himself, but I question whether or not a true synthesis of theory is possible. There are advantages to organizing a broad consensus of themes taken from the literature. We can better clarify the personal systems which undergird our practice and research. Furthermore, we can share our insights and mutual interests with workers in the mental health and special education fields.

3. *Psychological Abstracts* are published periodically by the American Psychological Association, Inc., Washington, D.C. *The Subject Guide to Books in Print* is published yearly by R. R. Bowker Company of New York.

Hence the need for this volume. In seeking to delineate the con-
tours of this problematic but increasingly popular field, I have chosen
four principal themes to serve as the framework for the essays which
have been selected: Communicating through Expressive Movement
(Part 1), Expanding the Movement Repertoire (Part 2), Enhancing
Body Awareness (Part 3), and The Creative Interface (Part 4). A comprehensive bibliography of writings about movement therapy is included in the appendix. References to sources about recreational
or social dance for the handicapped are omitted except if they are
deemed of special interest. For example, Recreation for the Handicapped or "Wheelchair Square Dancing" would be invaluable guides
to those who work with the orthopedically handicapped.[4] Sources
concerned with general teaching techniques for special populations
are included if the author specifically discusses dance activities for
these groups. Also included are references to major works by non-
dance therapists whose original techniques have since inspired numerous adaptations.

Part 1 develops the thesis that movement therapy can reorient a
client whose nonverbal communication system has somehow gone
askew. The first selection investigates how perfect synchronous movement, a heightened form of nonverbal communication, is learned
by an autistic child. In "The Case Study of a Puzzling Child," I explore
the mirroring technique designed for this type of withdrawn, nonverbal child and trace the evolution of moving in synchrony by
therapist and client. Dr. Adam Kendon, in "Movement Coordination
in Dance Therapy and Conversation," categorizes synchronous forms
of interaction; the kinesiologist emphasizes movement's interrela-
tionships with verbal communication. One of the purposes of movement therapy, he suggests, is the opportunity to practice moving
together. Shared movement is seen as necessary for social interaction
even beyond the confines of dance. An original application of Dr.
W. S. Condon's influential research, Janet Boettiger's concise study
evaluates the progress made by an autistic child who participates in
no other form of therapy. In "The Study of an Autistic Child," she
notes decreased use of bizarre gestures and increased use of touching gestures. The child also shows an improved ability to move
synchronously. Marian Chace, the grande dame of movement therapists, is the original advocate of creative movement for the purpose
of tapping the communicative potential of institutionalized adults.

---

4. Valerie Hunt, Recreation for the Handicapped (New York: Prentice-Hall, 1955).
Delta Sigma Omicron, "Wheelchair Square Dancing" (distributed by the University
of Illinois Rehabilitation Center, Champaign, Ill., undated).

She, together with Dr. Jarl Dyrud, mines a rich vein of wisdom and experience concerning "Movement and Personality." "The Frames in the Communication Process" rounds out the discussion. Anthropologist Ray Birdwhistell asserts that nonverbal forms of communication are culture-bound, learned behaviors significant for the individual's healthy functioning within society.

In Part 2 researchers focus on movement from another perspective. They emphasize movement therapy's ability to expand the individual's movement repertoire. Observers from many cultures are struck by the powerful impact of dance upon group behavior. Repeatedly noted by practitioners but virtually unsubstantiated by research is its astonishingly rapid impact upon certain clients. In "How I Learned to Wall-Bounce and Love It!," I describe the radical transformation of the range and type of movements performed by a severely retarded boy. Within ten minutes of the first as well as second movement therapy session, the child alters his bizarre style of walking, gesturing, and running. He models his movements on those of the therapist.

The other two essays in this chapter illustrate the more traditional approach of the major researchers in movement therapy. Concerned with the behavioral changes of clients in the movement therapy setting, these researchers have originated a well-defined vocabulary of movement for use in research. Their method of movement analysis, based upon Rudolf Laban's effort-shape principles, was introduced into the United States by the influential Irmgard Bartenieff. Arlynne Samuels utilizes this tool in describing the evolution of a varied movement repertoire by a depressed and retarded client in "Movement Change through Dance Therapy—A Study." Dr. Martha Davis expands on effort-shape theory to devise a movement assessment scale. "Movement Characteristics of Hospitalized Psychiatric Patients" is a seminal investigation of the similarity of movement patterns among institutionalized adults with similar diagnostic labels. The roles of practitioner, researcher, and theorist are admirably combined by these individuals—and the many others—who apply effort-shape principles to movement therapy.

In Part 3 movement researchers explore the effects of movement therapy on the body percept. Franziska Boas was first to recognize the importance of the client's newly found confidence in his physical well-being. She formulates the original application of movement therapy techniques based upon Paul Schilder's body image construct in her essay "Creative Dance." The theory was generally neglected until Wilhelm Reich rose from obscurity in the 1940s to popularity in the 1970s. This newly awakened interest is partly attributable to research in body image stimulated in the 1960s by aerospace and sensory deprivation studies.[5] Dr. Alexander Lowen deserves a great deal of the credit for his skillful translation of Reich's thought into best-sellers.[6] Today, a whole new generation of movement therapists emulates Lowen's use of a psychiatrist's couch for enacting fantasies with tennis rackets rather than with words. Reich's influence is also evident on the notices posted along Berkeley's Telegraph Avenue which announce "Neo-Reichian (Orgone Yoga) Bodywork Class" next to the listings for "Psychic Therapy" and "Massage Therapy."

Undoubtedly, the body percept is a complex subject. The object studied is dynamically variable with environment as well as past and present self-perception. Nevertheless, researchers generally agree that movement training has noticeable effects upon an individual's attitudes toward his body. Two invaluable research studies are Helen Christrup's "The Effect of Dance Therapy on the Concept of Body Image" and Dr. Philip May, Dr. Milton Wexler, Jeri Salkin, and Trudi Schoop's "Nonverbal Techniques in the Re-Establishment of Body Image and Self Identity." Both persuasively establish movement therapy's role for this key issue. "Personality, Body Perception and Body Image Boundary" is written by two psychologists whose names are synonymous with body image research: Dr. Seymour Fisher and Dr. Sidney Cleveland. In light of their experiments which relate perception of body boundaries to personality characteristics, future movement researchers can evaluate and clinicians can develop efficient techniques to heighten body awareness.

The last and longest part, "The Creative Interface," samples various therapists' styles of interaction. With the exception of Dr. Alma Hawkins, the creativity of the movement therapist has received little mention.[7] Marshall McLuhan claims that fish are last to comprehend that the water in which they swim is their environment; it would seem that movement therapists likewise neglect the crucial role played by their chosen medium. Readers unacquainted with the

5. The best-known exposition of Wilhelm Reich's point of view is found in his *Character Analysis* (New York: Orgone Institute Press, 1949).

6. Alexander Lowen, *Betrayal of the Body* (New York: Macmillan, 1967); see also *Love and Orgasm* (New York: Signet Books, 1965).

7. Alma Hawkins, *Creating the Dance* (Englewood Cliffs, N.J.: Prentice-Hall, 1964); "Dance Therapy Today—Points of View and Ways of Working," American Dance Therapy Association, *Proceedings of Seventh Annual Conference* (Los Angeles, Calif., 1972); "The Preparation of Dance Therapists for the Future," address presented to the Third Midwestern Regional Conference of Dance Therapists, Urbana, Ill., March 9, 1974.

practice of movement therapy might prefer to browse in this section
before going on to the research articles found in Parts 1, 2, and 3.
The five selections are representative of but a fraction of the range
of movement therapy techniques. Methods are generally eclectic in
origin; they may vary from ancient hula forms to ballet or "gestalt" to
"occupational therapy." These essays are merely samplers and not
definitive statements of the individual movement therapist's clients,
concepts, and clinical practice. Borrowing equally from Freud,
Skinner, and Rogers, the same clinician might deal with handicapped
children in a public school, with drug addicts in a half-way house, and
with adults in a mental institution or nursing home. His goals and
techniques differ in each environment. The visually handicapped
learn to leap without fear of space, the deaf-blind to communicate
expressively with their bodies and without reliance on eyes or ears.
In group energy, rhythm, and movement, the aged discover creative
outlets similar to those that delight any age. The disaffected and
withdrawn find unique avenues for communication with another
human being.

Certain key elements, then, differ. Movement therapists' styles
are distinctly influenced by dance orientation as well as by adherence to specific psychological tenants. Movement therapists sub-
scribe to different methods depending upon the environment in
which they work; the type and number of clients in their sessions;
the goals for the clients with whom they interact; and their roles as
clinician, consultant, researcher, or educator. I would suggest that
all these ingredients boil down to individual styles of interaction. It
is style and not fundamentals which divide movement therapists into
separate camps.

The basic leitmotiv running through Part 4 is the authors' unflagging
zest for movement as a creative medium. Movement therapists, by
and large, are dancers first—dancers who teach the individual and
not the skill.[8] To achieve this high purpose, movement therapists
consciously alter the elitist art form in which they once trained long
and hard. Intricate technical exercises traditional to contemporary
dance are jettisoned in favor of building on what the client has to
offer. Movement used by the client is not judged by the aesthetic
standard of a Louis XIV or a Martha Graham. No matter how primitive, bizarre, or fragmented, the client's present movement repertoire

8. See Mary Whitehouse, "Reflections on a Metamorphosis," in *Extensions of
Dance: Impulse 1969–70*, Marian Van Tuyl, ed. (San Francisco, Calif.: Impulse Publications, Inc., 1970).

forms the basis of the therapist's accommodating movements with him. Movement therapy virtually guarantees a successful experience for even the most uncoordinated.

In order to so transform an art form, dance is used as the creative interface between client and therapist—that is, the boundary shared in common between the two individuals ignites the creative spark. Using their bodies as artist's tools, the unity of self with another comes in their dance. Their transcending moment of total involvement is best expressed by the poet Yeats:

> Labour is blossoming or dancing where
> The body is not bruised to pleasure soul,
> Nor beauty born out of its own despair,
> Nor blear-eyed wisdom out of midnight oil.
> O chestnut-tree, great-rooted blossomer,
> Are you the leaf, the blossom or the bole?
> O body swayed to music, O brightening glance,
> How can we know the dancer from the dance?[9]

Therapist and client are as integrated as Yeats's dancer in his dance. There is a fundamental difference. The end product of dance therapy is not a work of art reproducible on stage at demand. The process of spontaneous, creative ordering is an end in itself.[10]

A great deal of literature from this new field reflects the movement therapist's self-imposed burden to "prove" movement therapy's place among the mental health professions. The clinicians of Part 4 are persuasive by dint of observable results. The skeptic has only to see blank faces and unfocused eyes come alive with smiles and sparkles in order to be convinced.

A most important foundation for any therapy, after all, is the pleasure it brings as it helps. When the aspiring student asks movement therapist Mildred Dickenson "how to do it," she booms out her pithy advice: "First of all, honey, it's gotta be fun!" It is this shared pleasure in dance that underpins our successes.

This observation releases a flood of memories. One session with a group of severely retarded and emotionally disturbed children stands out:

9. William Butler Yeats, "Among School Children" from *Collected Poems of W. B. Yeats* (New York: Macmillan, 1958), p. 214. © 1928 by Macmillan Pub. Co., Inc., renewed 1956 by Georgie Yeats, quoted with their permission and that of M. B. Yeats, Miss Anne Yeats, and Macmillan of London and Basingstoke.

10. See Paul Schilder, "The Art of Children and the Problems of Modern Art" in Dr. Lauretta Bender's *Child Psychiatric Techniques* (Springfield, Ill.: Charles C. Thomas, 1952), p. 308.

I remember one pig-tailed girl almost falling out of her wheelchair in her eagerness to touch and tag the hands of a staff member during this class. As one person pushed Janie around the room in her wheelchair, another ran backwards but facing her with arms outstretched. As Janie reached to chase her partner, her posture improved dramatically. She no longer slumped listlessly in her chair. Her brown eyes shone and she laughed delightedly.

I remember a very withdrawn boy who ordinarily moved as slowly and stiffly as an old man, if he chose to move at all. We danced as a group, quickly rising to our full heights and slowly shrinking back to our original positions. Dancing "big" and "little," we called it. I glanced over to Kevin. He had stopped his vacant staring and habitual frozen posture. At snail's pace, Kevin and his partner were mirroring the group's movements. He was dancing.

I remember that we all held hands in a great circle and rushed inward to each other. We piled twenty hands in the center of our now miniature circle. Then we gently touched and patted each other's hands. Janie, Kevin, and the other children laughed aloud each time that we repeated this sequence. And the staff members laughed, too.

A child who reaches eagerly toward a stranger. A lonely child who joins us in our dance. A group of adults and children warmly laughing and touching together. A kaleidoscope of simple events, yes. Yet they are significant in the lives of those who participate in them.

I do not wish to gainsay these shared pleasures or to denigrate the creative role of the clinician when I question whether or not we as movement therapists can go beyond the immediacy of the creative experience. The creative interface is the source of movement therapy's greatest strength as well as weakness. In order to win eventual recognition as a discipline, movement therapists must squarely face this paradox.

A leader's spontaneous reactions keyed to the client's creative involvement cannot lay the foundation for a replicable technique. Creativity cannot be taught; the artistic personality who also demonstrates mature compassion, insight, and personal warmth cannot pass on these qualities to the initiate.[11] Creativity is unreproducible for experimental purposes; research literature therefore leans heavily

11. In a study of the backgrounds of twenty-five movement therapists, Miriam Puder noted these common factors in their professional development: extensive training in dance, formal study in psychology or special education, and participation in some form of personal psychotherapy. See Miriam Puder, "Dance Therapy for Emotionally Disturbed and/or Neurologically Impaired Children," Master's thesis, Newark State College, Newark, N.J., 1972.

on anecdotal case studies.[12] Furthermore, the creative experience cannot be mandated; the client must consciously choose it as outlet. The role of movement therapist in this respect is not unlike Socrates' description of the philosopher as "midwife of ideas." He inspires the individual but cannot labor for him.

I remain optimistic, nevertheless, about future growth of movement therapy into a discipline. Parts 1, 2, and 3 indicate that the field is well on its way to the nurturing of a specialized body of knowledge. Researchers investigate how clients communicate through expressive movement, how individuals expand their repertoire of movements, and how participants develop an awareness of their own bodies. The role of dance is no longer taken for granted. Innovative research methods are used to explore replicative techniques basic to the movement therapy experience.

It is my hope that this book will stimulate others to continue what these authors have commenced. The conflicts inherent in the field make definition difficult, yet the similarities in principle are more striking than the stylistic differences. There are common themes that bind us all.

I owe a great many thanks to many individuals. I would like to express my appreciation to Norma Canner, Jean Lokke, Bruce McDaniel, Deborah Mellette, Dr. George Patrick, and my colleagues and students at the University of Illinois.

MAUREEN NEEDHAM COSTONIS

12. An exception to this generalization is Elizabeth Rosen's *Dance in Psychotherapy* which systematically records a movement therapist's clinical experiences in two mental hospitals. Rosen analyzes the group dynamics of the movement sessions, placing emphasis on the individual relationships to the leader. She categorizes six forms of client reactions to the experience: the withdrawn, self-conscious, aggressive, exhibitionistic, intellectual, and voyeuristic (nonparticipant observer). *Dance in Psychotherapy* was published by the Bureau of Publications, Teachers College of Columbia University in New York, 1957.

Communicating through Expressive Movement

Fie, fie upon her!
There's language in her eye, her cheek, her lip!
Nay, her foot speaks. Her wanton spirits look out
At every joint and motive of her body.

Troilus and Cressida
William Shakespeare

MAUREEN NEEDHAM COSTONIS

Case Study of a Puzzling Child

Variously called "tuning in," "reflecting," "mirroring," or some other name, synchronous movement is used by movement therapists to indicate rapport with the client. Janet Boettiger describes the process:

> I begin there, by reflecting her world, primarily on a body level. I try to "speak" her language by moving with her, as she moves in space. In the beginning, there is much direct imitation, which by definition means delayed response on my part. However, as she permits my presence, and as the trust develops, I find that the one-sidedness falls away and a more mutual dialogue begins to creep into being; we become synchronous.[1]

Starting with the nonverbal technique of mirroring movement, self-isolated behaviors are expanded into expressive dance gestures and eventually shaped into social actions.

The Synchronous Movement Profile (SMP) is my proposal for sketching one aspect of this process. This essay describes the rapid development of perfect interactional synchrony between myself as movement therapist and an autistic child. Over the course of four months, a 60.5 percent increase in the amount of perfect interactional synchronous movement was accompanied by a 40 percent decrease in the amount of time taken to establish synchrony. These figures demonstrate the client's ability to benefit from practice in synchronous movement. Janet Boettiger's description of the mutuality of movement dialogues is thus substantiated.

Perfect interactional synchrony differs from the form of synchronous movement discussed later in this chapter by Janet Boettiger. It is more than the sum of one person's facial, postural, and gestural reactions to exterior stimuli. Perfect interactional synchrony is defined as identical and simultaneous use of separate body parts along similar movement pathways when the angles of limbs of client and therapist are compared.

---

1. This quotation is taken from Janet Adler Boettiger's essay, *The Study of an Autistic Child,* which is the third selection in this chapter.

Dr. Jarl Dyrud, professor and associate chairman, department of psychiatry, University of Chicago, reports that he achieves high inter-rater reliability using the SMP with graduate students and nurses as the observers. He comments further:

> Her units (the Costonis SMP) are larger than in kinesics, but her units are based on larger concepts of interaction which is observed rather than inferred. This is a measure which dips into the development of empathy. We can shrewdly conjecture into body image, ego-feeling, but I think the payoff area is in the interactive area, where we are getting close to having a system in which we can work and research.[2]
>
> M.N.C.

Patricia

Patricia was an unusually beautiful five-year-old, but her actions belied her appearance. While living at Adler Zone Center, an Illinois residential short-term treatment center for children, Patricia quickly trained the staff members to keep a respectful distance from her. She had tantrums in ear drums, yanked hair, and left behind two-week-old bruises as souvenirs of her ability to bite. She squealed in shrill delight when she "got" her victim.

In April, 1973, when I first began working with her, the average daily frequency of these aggressions toward staff members numbered fourteen. This measurement included her pulling hair, blowing or spitting in faces, climbing inappropriately, and jumping on people.

The staff members of Adler Zone Center are proud of their pioneering work in management techniques. By the use of behavior modification and token economy systems, they have dealt successfully with other troublemakers talented at playing the classic game of "Uproar."[3]

Patricia, however, puzzled them. Possibly she interpreted the non-verbal signals sent out by each staff member. At any rate, she seemed to know when and where each individual would draw the line. The ultimate point reached, Patricia acquiesced or defied, according to reasons known only to herself. She performed nothing whatsoever with one person. With another, she managed the assigned tasks for all of ten minutes; most reported that she consistently worked with them for three or four minutes at a time and no more. Her baseline

2. Dr. Jarl Dyrud, "Movement and Language," paper presented to the Third Midwestern Regional Conference of Dance Therapists, Urbana, Illinois, March 9, 1974.

3. Eric Berne, *Games People Play* (New York: Grove Press, 1964), pp. 130–131.

in April was 47 percent for compliance to assigned tasks (given a ten-second deadline to perform).

Testers finished frustrated and puzzled when they attempted to gauge her present functioning levels and her potential. In the Fine Motor Assessment Report, one tester noted that Patricia refused to follow a moving object with her eyes, catch a ball, copy with a crayon, or play appropriately with specified toys. She hazarded a guess that Patricia possessed these capabilities. In assessing her gross motor skills, a different tester noted that "Patricia would not look at nor imitate any actions."

Attempts to measure her language skills were also subject to Patricia's unpredictable behavior. She refused to speak for the speech therapist. Even with the family's assistance in recalling her vocabulary and speech pattern, she was placed at a ten-month-old level of language development. Patricia's speech backslid even further after she was enrolled at Adler.

Patricia, it would seem, had her own pride. Throughout four months she managed to remain her noncompliant self in the face of a massive onslaught by child care workers, psychologist, teacher, speech therapist, social workers, and family.

Her admission to Adler was based on the hopes of getting a handle on her unmanageable behavior. The primary admission goals were: "to increase compliance and attention to task skills and implement a program for shaping language behavior." Some four months after her entrance, Patricia did not choose to respond along these lines.

Indeed, her unpredictable behavior called into question an original diagnosis of early infantile autism. No one was certain whether or not she should be labeled autistic, neurologically impaired, mentally retarded, emotionally disturbed, or just plain ornery. All of these diagnoses were investigated at one time or another.

The staff was reluctant to push Patricia to the limits when the boundaries of her skills were not defined, so they decided to begin at the beginning. Speech development and behavioral changes are predicated on the ability to imitate as part of the learning process. It was of utmost importance to determine whether or not Patricia possessed this basic capability. Her teachers, counselors, therapists, those professionals who had attempted to assess her skills, as well as myself, were all equally uncertain whether or not she could learn.

The psychologist in charge of Patricia's case asked me to observe if Patricia were capable even of imitation. There were several advantages to requesting that I collect impressions on this subject. First,

Patricia was highly motivated to succeed in this area. She favored daring activities which involved gross motor skills.

Second, dance is primarily a nonverbal activity. It seems suited for the nonverbal child whose level of language development may be so low as to preclude ordinary verbal comprehension. Caught up in the contagion of rhythm, the intimacy of touch, and the joy of moving, the child may be drawn unaware into learning.

Patricia had responded well to the four dance sessions previously held. It was hoped that a more accurate picture of her potential might prove possible during dance therapy sessions than anywhere else, because there she performed at her best.

The Adler staff had remarked that Patricia was not aggressive toward me and, in the main, surprisingly agreeable to my requests. Her compliance score was 87.5 percent. This contrasted sharply to the 64.3 percent baseline score of compliance which she had obtained in the cottage during this period. Furthermore, her attention span was noticeably longer in this activity than in others in which she engaged for a period of three to four minutes at most. She persevered for some twenty to thirty minutes per dance session. (In fact, I was the one who had to call it quits for lack of breath!) The most important advantage for my assessing her had to do with an unmeasurable quality: Patricia and I had established instant rapport.

Synchronous Movement

I chose to evaluate Patricia's imitative behavior in terms of a method uniquely employed by dance therapists. The diverse techniques of dance therapists are drawn from eclectic sources, ranging from t'ai-chi to gestalt. Yet synchronous movement is one tool that is common ground for us all.

Forms of synchrony may differ. There are the "mirroring" movements of Janet Adler Boettiger with an autistic child which may be seen in her movie, "Looking for Me." Within a group situation, there are synchronous variations on a particular movement category. For example, participants might simultaneously engage in all kinds of jabbing motions as they shout out angry feelings.

Not only found in dance, synchronous movement marks the interactional sequences of everyday life as well. Researchers in kinesics have theorized concerning its true significance.[4] They have noted that

---

4. See Ray Birdwhistell, *Kinesics and Context: Essays on Body Motion Communication* (Philadelphia: University of Pennsylvania Press, 1970). Marian Chace and Jarl Dyrud, "Movement and Personality," American Dance Therapy Association, *Pro-*

conversation, for example, is invariably accompanied by the synchronous actions of its participants: heads nodding in unison, simultaneous gestures, and synchronous directional changes in the posture. Studies show that the opening and closing of dialogues are punctuated with a great deal of synchrony. In a speech to the Committee on Research in Dance at a 1968 Workshop in Dance Therapy, Dr. Adam Kendon suggested that synchronous movement is a key to increasing the listener's and speaker's sense of empathy and rapport.[5]

In dance therapy sessions, heightened awareness develops as therapist and client move together. I would submit that this rapport, as expressed through movement, can be captured. By means of the proposed Synchronous Movement Profile (SMP), a change in the amount of perfect synchronous movement over a period of several sessions or during each session is charted.[6] The data are indicative of the growing ability by an alienated and disaffected client to establish contact with another person. Measuring changes in the amount of synchronous movement during dance has the advantage of describing this quality in an environment most conducive to its employment.

Charting the Synchronous Movement Profile

The Synchronous Movement Profile is designed for ease of application as well as reliability of observation. All that is needed are: the SMP chart, a pencil, and a watch with a second hand. The observer needs little training; even a dance background is unnecessary for his part.

In order to chart a Synchronous Movement Profile (see Table 1), the subject's body is divided into five areas for observation: head, torso, hands, arms, and legs. If the subject's angles of rotational or plane movement of any of these body parts are virtually identical to

ceedings of Third Annual Conference (Madison, Wis., 1968). William Condon, "Linguistic-Kinesic Research and Dance Therapy." American Dance Therapy Association, Proceedings of Third Annual Conference (Madison, Wis., 1968).

5. Adam Kendon, "Movement Coordination in Dance Therapy and Conversation," Committee on Research in Dance, Workshop in Dance Therapy: Its Research Potentials. Proceedings of a Joint Conference by Research Department of Postgraduate Center for Mental Health, Committee on Research in Dance, and American Dance Therapy Association (New York, 1968).

6. The original 1971 study upon which this investigation is based was supported in part by Title I Project #5612–1(5) at the Adler Zone Center in Champaign, Illinois. My thanks to Dr. George Patrick, Director of Activity Services at Adler, for valuable suggestions and support in implementing the Synchronous Movement Profile study. Dr. Ron Nelson of Adler was also of great assistance in reviewing the data.

Table I

SYNCHRONOUS MOVEMENT PROFILE

NAME: _____

DATE: _____

OBSERVER: _____

CODE:
MOVEMENT IN SYNCHRONY = 2 points
APPROXIMATION (up to a 45 degree angle from the above) = 1 point
NON-APPROXIMATION (more than a 45 degree) = 0 point
SYNCHRONOUS MOVEMENT PROFILE (SMP) = Total of Time Units

TIME UNITS*	1	2	3	4	5	6	7	8	9	10
HAND										
ARM										
HEAD										
TORSO										
LEG										
SMP										

SMP Total _____

* Observer charts during a 10-minute period. 5-second units are used for observing; 55 seconds or the duration of the minute are spent in notating results of the observation.

those angles of the dance therapist's, then that movement is adjudged "synchronous." If a body part is within a forty-five degree angle but not moving in the identical pathways of the dance therapist, then the term of "approximate synchrony" is applied. If the subject's and dance therapist's angles of movement are differentiated by more than forty-five degrees, this is adjudged to be "nonsynchronous" movement even though the subject might later attain the identical position.

Numerical weighting was assigned for each term: identical synchrony was weighted two points, approximate synchrony one, and none for nonsynchronous movement.

The observer watches the movement of client and therapist for a five-second period out of every sixty seconds. At the conclusion of that five seconds, the observer has fifty-five seconds left in which to chart his judgments.

The perfect score for each of the minute units would be ten—two for arms moving in identical synchrony, two for torso, and so on. Growth in synchronous movement over the course of the session is obtained by comparing the changes in the SMP minute units from beginning to end. A total score or profile may be obtained by adding up the SMP units for the period of ten minutes. Perfect rating for ten minutes would be 100. That total score may be used for comparison with other scores obtained on previous occasions.

Measurements can be made even more refined with the use of videotape and its stop-the-action possibilities. Synchronous movement of right or left upper legs, lower legs, hips, forearms, and so on, can also be analyzed. Synchronous movement of facial expressions or hand gestures could also be fruitfully studied in this manner.

The second application of this method necessitates the use of video equipment. Viewing videotapes has the advantage of breaking down motion into stationary shapes defined in 1½ second fractions. Instant replays are an added bonus.

Detailed observations by video are, of course, more reliable than observers can be in a real-life situation. Correspondence under these circumstances is remarkably high. Two observers (one experienced and one inexperienced) separately charted the films of Patricia and me. Out of the twenty profiles which they scored, nineteen were in perfect agreement. The index of correspondence is .95 in a scale where .9 is accepted as highly reliable. This figure demonstrates that the SMP may prove an accurate method whose reliability is not dependent upon prolonged training procedures. The other widely used alternative for reliably measuring change in dance therapy sessions involves the use of Effort-Shape techniques.[7] Observers trained in this methodology require at least two years of study.

A Description of the Dance Therapy Sessions with Patricia

Perhaps at this point the dance therapy techniques used with Patricia had best be clarified. While it was intended that her imitative abilities be tested, she was not taught to mimic. A great deal of Patricia's training at Adler consisted of situations where she was given simple verbal commands, such as "Do this!," and a demonstration was performed. She was allowed ten seconds to respond and, if she did not, was assisted manually. Someone manipulated her through the task as Patricia passively acquiesced.

In contrast, dancing was not considered to be a skill that I, as dance teacher, imparted to Patricia. (She danced rings around me in terms

7. Penny Bernstein and Enzo Cafarelli, "An Electromyographical Validation of the Effort System of Notation," American Dance Therapy Association, *Monograph Two* (Columbia, Md., 1972), p. 85.

of daring and endurance, anyway.) Although synchronous movement with me was the key to the measurements taken, I verbally reinforced any creative, albeit nonsynchronous, contributions on her part. I did not intend to turn Patricia into a windup dancing doll.

Patricia and I danced together; it was mutual moving. On one level it could be described as simply as that. But, as Patricia's ability to move in synchronous harmony grew, the rules of the game changed somewhat.

In the first session, I mirrored her actions in order to out-maneuver her negativism. Whatever she performed—however withdrawn or rejecting or "socially unacceptable"—I did so also. When she kicked the floor in anger and screeched, I cheerfully termed it a kicking dance and joined her.

I suspect that, when she understood what I was attempting, she deliberately held herself motionless for a prolonged period. She curled on her knees on top of a chair and faced the wall away from me. Her arms covered her face; only her backbone was visible. Except for bursts of stereotyped gestures, she sat as still as it is possible for one to be. Twelve motionless minutes is a long time for an active five-year-old.

From her curled over position on the chair, Patricia suddenly darted out her arm toward me. She briefly touched my arm and held her hand out for me. I was puzzled. Up to this point in this first session, she seemed hostile and withdrawn. All of her nonverbal signals had made it clear that she did not seek or allow touch. But, there the hand was! I reached mine toward hers in a tentative, slow manner. She quickly withdrew.

However, after that dramatic invitation, we began to dance. By the end of the class, she was climbing all over me and laughing gleefully. She hugged me and allowed me to chase her. I twirled her in my arms, although she seemed hesitant about the experience. Her exuberance contrasted sharply with the stereotyped and frozen kind of movement predominating at the beginning of the session. At its finish, she refused to stop. In various ways—pulling, dancing, jabbering, cuddling—she pleaded for more. It would seem that the technique of synchronous movement cut through her usual noncompliant behavior.

Patricia's ability to move synchronously definitely improved with practice. This is as true of her overall skill in attaining synchronous movement as it was true for her learning to leap in synchrony. In our first session, I did my utmost to move exactly as she moved. Nevertheless, it took a full eight minutes before we achieved a fully synchronized movement. I would suggest that synchronous movement implies consent on the part of both parties rather than mimicry on the part of one.

In session number five, I attempted to "lead" Patricia in order to determine whether or not she could imitate my behavior. She imitated my actions far more than she refused to comply with my invitations. I did not verbally command her. I performed the dance movements and verbally reinforced her if she attempted them. At times I twirled her about as reinforcement for imitative behavior or pulled her across the floor—whatever she requested. As a consequence of this reinforcement, it seems, she often repeated the original movement sequence.

The SMP Analysis of the Dance Sessions

Patricia's SMP unit score for the first minute of the session was five. Her score six minutes later was ten, which is perfect synchrony. From that point on, she achieved perfect synchronous movement scores of ten in three of the next five minutes (minute units 6, 9, 10). Slightly over 33 percent of the total scores measured within that ten-minute period were judged as perfect synchrony. Even though Patricia was asked for the first time to follow me, she adjusted to the new rules within six minutes. This figure is only two minutes more than her average time for achieving synchronous movement (as measured from the start of the session).

Our synchronous movements stand out in dramatic clarity if films of our movements are analyzed in units of one and a half seconds. In the following example, it is difficult to believe that the synchronous movement examined was more than an isolated incident. I should stress that movement in synchrony was a regular feature of all our dance therapy sessions.

Patricia, soon after I started with her, performed a small running jump with both legs thrust forward in the air. It characteristically occurred after she turned out the lights and raced across the room. I exaggerated this small jump into the dancer's split-legged leap, the *grand jeté*. Ordinarily a five-year-old is not capable of performing such a difficult feat. Patricia admired the spectacular, and it was not long before she achieved an equivalent. What is surprising is not that she copied me; incredible as it may seem, we performed the rapid running and leaping sequence in perfect synchrony.

In a split second analysis of this phenomenon, it is possible to see our movements in extraordinary unity. As we begin the running take-off, both her arms swing at the same angles from the body as mine; her same foot reaches forward just as the upper leg bends from the body at identical angles to mine. As we leap high together, her legs do not seem to stretch as long as mine. The angle between the two upper legs, however, approximates that of mine. As the ball of my foot descends barely to touch the floor, hers, too, arrives at the same point. Her other leg is still thrust backward in the air, as is mine. Both of my arms move away from the body at identical angles to each of hers. As we land with full weight on the floor and continue our running sequence, the identical synchronous movement likewise continues.

It made no difference that she had short legs and I, long; she lacked a dancer's training whereas I had the advantage of twenty-some odd years; her motor maturation was that of a five-year-old and mine of the over-thirty generation. Even if Patricia started late and trailed along after I had begun to run across the room, it did not prevent our moving in perfect unity.

This phenomenon is not a one-time fluke. Expanded sequences of synchronous movement are repeated time and again. For example, in session nine, four of the eleven-minute units measured reflected SMPs of ten each as we performed running leaps (units 4, 6, 10, 11). Within an eight-minute period, we ran and leaped in identical synchronous movement exactly half of the time measured.

In comparing this same running and leaping sequence of session eleven to its earlier form in session three, we can measure the effects of practicing synchronous movement. This analysis will be described in terms of one and half-second units.

At one point in session three, Patricia and I were running and jumping as we held hands. The hand-holding would likely have heightened the synchrony of our shapes and movement paths. The sequence starts with our flipping the light switch on and off. The SMP was seven. We start to run and achieve the same score. One and half seconds later, we are running full-out, again with a score of seven. As we leap holding hands, the SMP drops to five. It rises to a nine as we land exactly at the same time and prepare to continue running.

We achieve a high SMP rating up to that point. This score is nowhere near the SMP of ten for the full fifteen seconds, as seen in session eleven and repeated many times on other occasions. When we compare the two events just analyzed, Patricia shows a 30 percent increase in her ability to perform a similar movement sequence in a more synchronous manner.

I will continue to discuss this particular movement sequence in light of a dramatic drop in SMP from nine to zero. The analysis demonstrates that, even though engaged in the very same activities, a high SMP rating is not necessarily the correlate of similar movement sequences.

As you recall, Patricia landed in almost perfect unity with me and was assigned the SMP score of nine. One and one-half seconds after an SMP rating of nine, however, the SMP dropped to zero. This sharp decline occurred simultaneously with Patricia's decision to reach for the trampoline. It was territory forbidden to her because of its fragile mooring to the wall. Exactly as she reached forward to climb on it, I reached forward toward her. Her SMP score was zero. The ratings for the next four units also changed abruptly from the previous five. We both walked toward the Time-Out chair where she was to sit, but we were out of step even though we moved in the same direction. Her scores during this three-second sequence were three and five respectively. We both stood side by side as she defiantly refused to sit for one brief second (SMP = 4). She then acquiesced. (SMP = 2). Until she sat, we were both nominally engaged in the same activities—reaching, walking, standing—during the same time sequences. There the similarity ended. As the SMP analysis reveals, our movements are not performed in tandem.

Within that fifteen seconds, Patricia moved abruptly from high to low synchronous movement—from a total of thirty-five for the first five units as compared to a score of fourteen for the last five. This is a drop of 60 percent in the SMP scores. Once again the data supports the notion that synchronous movement stems from a willed mutual effort to move in tandem.

Results of the Dance Sessions

Our dance developed into a form of mutual interchange. Our repertoire today is not so one-sided as formerly, for the movements do not totally originate with Patricia. Sometimes I begin the dancing games. Or I twiddle my fingers and jabber and flop on the floor beside her. Often I expand into dance form a movement which she has begun. At times she imitates what I do, dances synchronously, pulls me into position for a favorite activity, or she just watches.

At beautiful moments we slide without broken rhythm, hand in hand around the room. Or we run and leap from corner to corner— completely in synchrony. It is at these moments that we say something special to one another—something untranslatable except in the joy of performing the movement together.

Patricia's ability to move in synchrony dramatically improved over the entire ten sessions. Identical synchrony now averaged 4.8 minutes for us to achieve instead of eight minutes. This represented a 40 percent decrease in the amount of time needed to establish identical synchronous movement. The scores of unit SMPs throughout the session showed progressive growth from March to May. The average SMP score for the first minute of each session was 5.2 out of a possible ten. The average for the tenth minute was 8.6. This figure represents an average increase of 60.5 percent from the start to the midway point of each session.

Other figures reflect significant change on Patricia's part. Patricia's use of language during dance therapy sessions increased markedly. Her first two sessions were dominated by "Phetuh-phetuh!" noises accompanied by stereotyped gestures. The number of words ranged from zero to as many as seven per dance session when she began to speak. More than two words are used on the average for each dance session by Patricia. The cottage staff workers reported no use of language whatsoever during that time.[8]

An intriguing sidelight to Patricia's use of language was her high SMP score previous to her utterances. The one exception to this generalization occurred when she spoke the word "No!" Her actions seemed to parallel her words, for the SMP score was comparatively low—three out of a possible ten.

Another measurement which paralleled the changes noted in Patricia's SMP and use of language was that of the number of Time-Out's. At Adler, the child who misbehaves is removed from the circumstances of his action as well as from any social reinforcements. Patricia was made to sit in the corner.

The first time this program was instituted, Patricia scored five Time-Out's. She quickly changed her tune. Two weeks later, she chose to misbehave only after the session had ended. She sidled over to the trampoline when the record stopped and signaled the end of the session. This pattern continued for weeks. Eventually that behavior, too, was extinguished. At the cottage, she averaged a daily frequency of ten Time-Out's per day as measured over a month's time. Patricia was not once Timed-Out during our dance sessions that same month.

---

8. In another study of an autistic child, it was similarly noted that his language usage, as well as other affective responses, increased during dance therapy sessions. The results of this study were incorporated in the author's master's thesis entitled "Expanding Stereotyped Object Manipulation into Expressive Dance Movement: Dance Therapy with an Autistic Child."

Conclusion

The Adler staff gained confidence in her abilities. As a result, Patricia was placed in a community school in July of 1973. There she presently continues to learn and to speak. Adler staff workers, unsolicited by me, have also noted an increase in use of gesture and in general imitative behavior around the cottage.

To sum up the results of this study of synchronous movement with this puzzling child, the analysis strongly supports that Patricia is indeed capable of imitation. Perhaps unusually so. She can not only accurately perceive changes in her environment; also, she is able to perform complex actions as she simultaneously accommodates herself to the movements of another person.

A 60.5 percent increase in the amount of synchronous movement within a ten minute period of time combined with a 40 percent decrease in the amount of time taken to establish synchrony is an indication of Patricia's ability to learn. The analysis of her synchronous movements during our running and leaping also demonstrates her ability to learn synchronous movement.

According to Adam Kendon, dance therapy gives its participants practice in moving together. If perfect synchronous movement is a learned form of behavior benefitting from practice, I would like to propose use of the Synchronous Movement Profile as an evaluation tool of the client's progress in this form of interactional synchrony.

Bibliography

Bernstein, Penny, and Enzo Cafarelli. "An Electromyographical Validation of the Effort System of Notation." American Dance Therapy Association. *Monograph Two.* Columbia, Md., 1972.

Berne, Eric. *Games People Play.* New York: Grove Press, 1964.

Birdwhistell, Ray. *Kinesics and Context: Essays on Body Motion Communication.* Philadelphia: University of Pennsylvania Press, 1970.

Boettiger, Janet Adler. "The Study of an Autistic Child." American Dance Therapy Association. *Proceedings of Third Annual Conference.* Madison, Wis., 1968.

Chace, Marian, and Jarl Dyrud. "Movement and Personality." American Dance Therapy Association. *Proceedings of Third Annual Conference.* Madison, Wis., 1968.

Condon, W. S. "Linguistic-Kinesic Research and Dance Therapy." American Dance Therapy Association. *Proceedings of Third Annual Conference.* Madison, Wis., 1968.

Costonis, Maureen. "Expanding Stereotyped Object Manipulation into Expressive Dance Movement: Dance Therapy with an Autistic Child." M.A. thesis, University of Illinois, 1972.

Dyrud, Jarl. "The Meaning of Movement: As Human Expression and as an Artistic Communication." Panel discussion with Marian Chace and Jean Erdman. American Dance Therapy Association. *Proceedings of Third Annual Conference.* Madison, Wis., 1968.

Kendon, Adam. "Movement Coordination in Dance Therapy and Conversation." Committee on Research in Dance. "Workshop in Dance Therapy: Its Research Potentials." *Proceedings of a Joint Conference by Research Department of Postgraduate Center for Mental Health, Committee on Research in Dance, and American Dance Therapy Association.* New York, 1968.

Laban, Rudolf, and F. C. Lawrence. *Effort.* London: MacDonald and Evans, 1965.

Ruesch, Jurgen, and Weldon Kees. *Nonverbal Communication.* Berkeley: University of California Press, 1966.

Stern, Edith. "She Breaks through Invisible Walls." *Mental Hygiene.* July, 1957.

Dr. ADAM KENDON

Movement Coordination
in Dance Therapy and Conversation

Dr. Adam Kendon lives in a rarified world where units of 1/24th of a second are cultivated as are orchids in a greenhouse. Movement patterns so analyzed reveal a subtle but orderly interaction between listener and speaker. The listener coordinates his movements to those of the speaker; motion and speech serve as shared rhythmic cues. In this selection, Kendon suggests that variations in listener-speaker movement patterns have to do with their respective communicatory roles as much as with their idiosyncratic style of movement.

The terms "synchrony," "self-synchrony," and "dyschronous" originated with Dr. W. S. Condon. "This harmony existing between the speech and body motion of the speaker is tentatively called 'self-dysynchrony.' The further harmony existing between speaker and listener(s) is tentatively called interactional synchrony."[1] These modes are observable, Condon claims, in all films of interaction between normal subjects. This orderly sequence is fragmented in special cases. In one film of a schizophrenic, the right arm and leg do not coordinate synchronously with the other body parts (left arm, leg, head), nor with his speech. Further, all but the left side of the body coordinate their movement flow and rhythms with those of the therapist.[2]

Researchers in kinesics often compare gestural movement during speech to rhythmical dance movement. Condon states that the "startling rhythmical and participant nature of human communication . . . suggests that human interaction may be inherently dancelike

Previously published New York, Committee on Research in Dance, 1970, pp. 64–69, *Workshop in Dance Therapy: Its Research Potentials* (Proccedings of a Joint Conference by Research Department of Postgraduate Center for Mental Health, Committee on Research in Dance, and American Dance Therapy Association).

1. W. S. Condon and W. D. Ogston, "Sound Film Analysis of Normal and Pathological Behavior Patterns," *Journal of Nervous and Mental Disorders,* Vol. 143 (4) (1966), p. 342.

2. *Ibid.,* 344.

in form.[3] The nonverbal gestures and body movements that ordinarily accompany conversations also are described in terms of dance movement by Dr. Adam Kendon: "The listener dances with the speaker to show he is 'with' him, receiving him; he then gets the speaker to dance with him as a way of heightening the synchronization between them, so they can both reach the point of disengagement at precisely the same moment."[4] The synchronized movement forms the unspoken part of the dialogue. It is necessary, according to Kendon, in order to heighten rapport and increase both listener's and speaker's sense of identification, particularly at the beginning and end of dialogues.

Movement therapy, knowingly used as communication, makes it possible to give practice in interactional movement to many of those emotionally disturbed who have difficulty in expressing themselves intelligibly. The client is assisted in making order out of his jumbled or incomplete forms of nonverbal responses. It has been suggested that schizophrenics, for example, reveal a deficit in motor agility as a "result of insufficient practice in personal nonverbal interaction during infancy."[5] He must perforce develop an awareness of his own body's signals as well as those of others. Kendon concludes his essay with the observation that "through this practice, a participant's capacity for coordinating his movements with others may be enhanced and thus may, at least for some individuals, be of importance for his competence in handling the tasks of social interaction. This is because a capacity for moving in coordination with others is a fundamental one for face-to-face interaction of any kind." Nonverbal communication does not seem to be a purely natural or intuitive form of expression. Even the significance of a smile must be learned by the infant. According to Dr. Birdwhistell, expressive movement is taught within certain prescribed forms by each and every society. If "body motion is a learned form of communication," as he asserts, then movement therapy logically follows as a viable method for teaching nonverbal communication to those who need practice in moving

3. W. S. Condon, "Linguistic-Kinesic Research and Dance Therapy," *American Dance Therapy Association, Proceedings of the Third Annual Conference* (Madison, Wis., 1968), p. 22.

4. "Movement Coordination in Dance Therapy and Conversation" was first published in *Workshop in Dance Therapy: Its Research Potentials. Proceedings of a Joint Conference by Research Department of Postgraduate Center for Mental Health, Committee on Research in Dance, and the American Dance Therapy Association* (New York, 1968), p. 67.

5. Jurgen Ruesch and Weldon Kees, *Nonverbal Communication* (Berkeley, Calif.: University of California Press, 1956).

together.[6] Any resulting moments of shared synchronous movement are the stuff of future dialogues.   M.N.C.

The Workshop Conference on Dance Therapy was an exciting occasion. As one who has done some research in body motion and its place in social interaction, I was especially glad to attend, for I had for some time been curious about dance therapy, though I had not had any previous contact with it. Reflecting upon what I had learned at the conference, it seemed to me that some of my own work might be quite closely related to some of the questions raised by dance therapy. In the following I shall summarize some of my recent findings, and link them with a suggestion about what seemed to me to be one of the most central functions of dance therapy.

It is my suggestion that in dance therapy one gives participants practice in moving with other people. Through this practice, a participant's capacity for coordinating his movements with others may be enhanced and this may, at least for some individuals, be of importance for his competence in handling the tasks of social interaction. This is because a capacity for moving in coordination with others is a fundamental one for face-to-face interaction of any kind, or so I believe, for, as I shall try to explain, it is through such joint movement that people signal to one another their readiness to begin an encounter, and their continued mutual openness, and it is through joint movement, also, that they attain the precise coordination necessary for smooth disengagement. In addition, in any successful encounter, the actions, such as utterances, which constitute the transaction are smoothly exchanged, and this presupposes that the participants are rhythmically in accord with one another. It seems likely that such rhythmic accord is mediated partly by coordination of movement between the participants. Movement coordination undoubtedly occurs in social interaction, as I shall try to show. I suggest that this is a fundamental feature of the process, and someone who cannot achieve it will be faulty in his capacities as a social performer.

Face-to-face interaction is, of course, possible where a participant is not fully "in time" with another. However, where this happens we may expect that the others will be distracted from the business of the encounter and become concerned about the behavior of the others, or with his own behavior. To the extent that this happens, participants are likely to find the encounter lacking in ease, or liveli-

6. Ray Birdwhistell, *Kinesics and Context* (Philadelphia: University of Pennsylvania Press, 1970). p. xi.

ness or interest; it may seem boring, awkward, or frustrating.[7] Perhaps for relatively uninvolving encounters this may not matter, though even in something as noninvolving as buying a newspaper, if the news vendor is slow, preoccupied, or in some other way "out of time," the transaction can be very annoying. If someone is persistently "out of time" with others, other people will always find interaction with him unrewarding, or disturbing, and he may as a result become the target of hostility or indifference and he will, less and less often, be sought out for social engagement. The isolation from others that this may lead to, with its consequences of loss of practice in the skills of interaction, and of the effectiveness of social controls on his behavior, will only add to his impairment as a social performer. Add to this his own anger and frustration at being excluded repeatedly from social life, and perhaps patterns of behavior will begin to develop which others would label as psychotic. Restore, then, to such a person a capacity for moving in time with others, and you may give back to him a skill of central importance to his capacity as a social interactant.

Direct evidence that movement coordination is fundamental to skill in face-to-face interaction is lacking, so far as I know. However, there is reason to believe that it occurs as a rule, and from the few detailed observations of it that are available, its probable importance is apparent.

First, consider the process by which an encounter is established. As we all know, when two people meet and talk about some topic, they almost all go through some ritualized verbal exchange, even if this is very brief. Yet even before this, it is to be noted, there are certain conditions which must be met. Each must perceive that the other is ready and "open" to the other's messages. Typically, this appears to involve three steps: a meeting of the eyes, a mutual adjustment of the speed of movement, and the establishment of a particular distance between the participants. The importance of the meeting and holding of the gaze is fairly well known,[8] though there are complexities here that have never been fully described. Mutual coordination of speed of movement is less well known, but I believe it is an important indicator of the mutual willingness of persons to remain "open" to one another, after the initial exchange of glances. This

7. See E. Goffman, "Alienation from Interaction," *Human Relations* 10 (1957), 47–59.

8. For a good account of the role of gaze in the initiation of interaction see E. Goffman, *Behavior in Public Places* (New York: Free Press, 1963), pp. 83–104. See also A. Kendon, "Some Functions of Gaze Direction in Social Interaction," *Acta Psychologica* 26 (1967), 22–63.

may be observed most easily in open settings, such as squares, hall-
ways, or wide corridors, where people meet and talk. Two people
who approach one another may be seen to adjust their speeds of approach, so that they come to halt simultaneously. Where there is not
more than a greeting, however, there is an exchange of glances, but
there is no mutual adjustment of speed of movement.

The importance of the adjustment of movement speed in the
process of engagement easily may be tested by an experiment which
anyone may try, if he is brave enough. If you are walking along a
street, catch up with another pedestrian who is walking in the same
direction, draw abreast of him, and then adjust your speed of walking
to precisely that of his own. This will almost certainly produce some
reaction in your "victim," who may speed up, or drop behind, or find
something interesting to look at in a shop window, or he may even
look at you and talk to you. Whatever his precise reaction, it may be
seen as a response to a situation you have created in which some
kind of social engagement is expected. It is one that the "victim" will
find extremely difficult to ignore. It is, indeed, almost as provoking
as the situation that is created if you catch and hold the gaze of
someone on the street.

Careful analysis of films of social interaction has shown that there
is continuous and microscopic coordination in the movements of the
participants.[9] In some work of my own, that will be published in detail, I have examined how the pattern of movement coordination
changes as an engagement progresses. The film[10] that was examined
for this study was of an informal gathering of eleven people, one of
whom (B) was acting as a kind of chairman, conducting a discussion
on family life. He would turn first to one, then to another, to evoke
from each some account of his experience in his own family. The
particular sequence that was most fully analyzed included B asking a
question of T, one of the participants; T's reply, which lasted about
thirty seconds; a further question and a much shorter reply from T;
with B finally turning to address another participant. In this sequence,
then, we were able to examine in detail the establishment and termination of an axis of interaction, within an ongoing gathering.

The findings from this analysis can be briefly summarized. When B
puts his first question to T, he faces him and points at him with an ex-

9. W. Condon and W. Ogston, "Sound-Film Analysis of Normal and Pathological
Behavior Patterns," *J. Nervous and Mental Disease* 143 (1966), 338–347.

10. The film used is known as TRD 009 "English Pub Scene." It was made by Ray L.
Birdwhistell and Jacques Van Vlack and produced by the Commonwealth of Pennsylvania, with assistance from the Institute for Intercultural Studies.

tended arm. T is sitting forward in his chair. At the precise moment that B finishes his question, T leans back in his chair, and it is only two seconds later, when he is sitting with his back fully in contact with the back of the chair, that he begins to speak. His posture shift is the first and immediate response to B's question, a response which probably marks the change from his position in the interaction as a listener, to that of a speaker.[11] Concurrently with this shift of posture by T, B also moves. He leans back slightly and lifts his head. He then becomes still, and remains still until T begins to speak. As T utters the first two phrases of his speech, he moves his left hand out to his left, then back to his lap, and he then tilts his head to his left. Precisely in time with these movements, B moves his right arm, which is still extended toward T, out to his right, and then back again, and then he tilts his head to his right. After this he puts his pipe in his mouth and holds it there with his right hand and, until the last two phrases of T's discourse, he remains still, except for movements in his eyes, mouth, and fingers of the right hand. It will be seen, then, that from the time T begins to respond to B's question, until the point where B puts his pipe in his mouth, B is moving in time with T, and the movements he makes amount to a mirror image of the movements of T. B moves in step with T, and in the same fashion. He dances T's dance.

This mirroring by the listener of the movements of the speaker in this instance lasted for about five seconds. In other examples of the establishment of interactional axes that we have examined, the mirroring of movement is again found, though it is rarely as extensive as in the example just described. But in all the cases we have observed, the mirroring of movement occurs only between the speaker and the person he addresses directly. Other participants may move concurrently with the movements of the speaker, but their movements have quite a different form from those of the direct addressee. By mirroring the movement of the speaker, the addressee at once differentiates himself from the others present, and at the same time establishes an overt bond between himself and the speaker. For the speaker this can serve as visual confirmation that his speech is being received by the person he is directing it to, and for the others present it can serve to clarify their own expectations in the situation.

For most of T's discourse, as we have already said, B remains more or less still, though he looks at T, and T continues extensive movement as he talks. Over the last two phrases of T's discourse, however,

11. A. E. Scheflen, "The Significance of Posture in Communication Systems," *Psychiatry* 27 (1964), 316–324.

B begins to move again. Here he tilts his head forward and to the left, and this coincides precisely with a movement of T's head in the opposite direction. B then tilts his trunk to the left, and lowers his head still further. Coincident with this, T moves his trunk and head to the right. Here it appears that B initiated the movement, which T then came to follow. Whereas over the opening section of T's discourse B danced T's dance, here B begins a dance with T, then picks up. It seems probable that with these movements of head and trunk, B is giving advanced warning to the speaker that he has something to say after the speaker is finished. In addition, it may be that B is overtly beating time to the rhythm of T's speech, and he may thereby facilitate the precise timing of his own entry as a speaker, much as a musician may begin to move conspicuously with the music, as he readies himself to enter with his part at the right moment.

Immediately after the end of T's speech, B puts another question to him. T's answer is short: "Well, I tried to," with the primary stress of the utterance falling on "tried." As T gives this reply, B turns his head to face another participant whom he will shortly engage. This head turn is timed to take exactly as long as T's reply, and as B turns his head, he lowers it and raises it again in a slight nod, which coincides precisely with the stressed word "tried." Here, evidently, B, in one movement, signals his disengagement with T but, as he does so, because of the way his movement is timed and shaped, he also acknowledges his receipt of T's reply. Perhaps this kind of compounding of movement function is the mark of a good chairman, who manages to keep moving business forward without, at the same time, actually cutting anybody off.

In the instances we have described then, as well as in others that have been analyzed, we have seen that the listener's movements are closely coordinated with the behavior of the speaker, and we have noted in particular that in engagement and disengagement this coordination, both in terms of rhythm and of form, is particularly conspicuous. Perhaps we have exemplified here on a small scale the heightened rapport and increased sense of identification between participants in an encounter at its initiation and termination, a feature of greeting and parting rituals that has been noted by some writers.[12] The listener dances with the speaker to show he is "with" him, receiving him; he then gets the speaker to dance with him as a way of heightening the synchronization between them, so they can both reach the point of disengagement at precisely the same moment.

12. E. Goffman, "On Face-Work," *Psychiatry* 18 (1955), 213–231.

The phenomenon of "dancing together," as we have referred to it, has been occasionally described by other writers[13] though of course we need descriptions of many more examples before we can draw firm conclusions about its occurrence and function. However, such examples as we have do suggest that coordination of movement between interactants, often of quite a subtle kind, is part of the process of interaction, and that it appears heightened at moments of engagement and disengagement indicates that it may play an important part in the process by which encounters are established.

To return, now, to dance therapy, I have already suggested the idea that here one gets people to move together who are not normally capable of it. It may be noted how simply rhythmical music is often used, and how the movements employed are simple, repetitive, and rather gross. Circumstances are created, thus, in which coordination of movement with others is relatively easy to achieve. It would be very interesting to know if, over the course of time, this coordination improved and became more subtle and if, in those in whom this change occurred, it could be shown to have occurred in other kinds of encounters less stylized than the dance.

I am suggesting, in short, that dance therapy be viewed as a kind of behavior therapy, one in which one gets patients to actually engage in a kind of behavior which they need practice in, and in doing this one may be said to be engaged in a kind of social skills training.[14] I am further suggesting that a profitable line of research would be to look at the effectiveness with which movement coordination between persons is achieved in dance therapy, and whether this has any effect upon the participant's ability to coordinate his movements with others in more everyday social settings.

13. Besides Condon's work, see also J. A. Meerloo, *Unobtrusive Communication: Essays in Psycholinguistics.* Assen, The Netherlands: Van Gorcum, 1964.

14. M. Argyle and A. Kendon, "Experimental Analysis of the Social Performance" in L. Berkowitz, ed., *Advances in Experimental Social Psychology,* Vol. 3 (New York: Academic Press, 1967).

JANET BOETTIGER

The Study of an Autistic Child

Janet Boettiger was fortunate to have Dr. W. S. Condon's assistance in filming and analyzing her movement therapy sessions with an autistic girl. In turn, it is our good fortune that she shares her research efforts in this essay as well as in her profoundly moving film "Looking for Me."[1]

After immersing herself in repeated viewings of films made during twenty-six movement therapy sessions, Boettiger notes Amy's patterned responses of synchronous, self-synchronous, or dyssynchronous movement. These terms are derived from Condon's research. She observes "a sharing of the same body parts, moving in the same direction, with the same point of change in direction" and labels it "symmetrical synchrony." She also observes an overall increased tolerance for physical proximity and body contact with herself. As Amy's usage of autistic gestures decreases in number, the formerly withdrawn girl develops a wide repertoire of communicative gestures. A remarkable breakthrough has occurred.

Boettiger's concise essay is significant for the wealth of implications suggested by its data. Movement therapy research on the subject of autism is rare compared to the number of other kinds of studies about early infantile autism. Yet those few research studies which are to be found in the literature seem to bear out her observations. Furthermore, the direction taken by certain researchers, including myself, owes a great deal to her original analysis of movement therapy sessions with Amy.   M.N.C.

I would like to discuss both aspects of my work in dance therapy, the therapy and the efforts in research. Both areas for me are exploratory, especially the latter, as I have resisted any opportunity to objectively

Reprinted by permission from the American Dance Therapy Association, Third Conference Proceedings (1968), pp. 43–48. All rights reserved.

1. This essay was first published in the American Dance Therapy Association, *Proceedings of Third Annual Conference* (Madison, Wis., 1968).

evaluate my work, assuming that research in such a realm as dance therapy would automatically require compromise. Also, I was hesitant to demand of myself any "laboratory" discipline, as I knew it would involve a new kind of work in which intuitive response would not be helpful.

First, I will briefly describe my therapy. I am impressed with the simplicity of Ronald Laing's statement: "The sense of identity requires the existence of another by whom one is known." For a severely disturbed child, I can only be effective in helping her develop her identity if I am genuinely reflective of what she knows best—her tiny, perseverative, intensely physical world. At this time, I am concerned with providing an opportunity for a disturbed child to be herself literally, with all of her "bizarre" and "crazy" mannerisms and expressions. I begin there, by reflecting her world, primarily on a body level. I try to "speak" her language by moving with her. In the beginning there is much direct imitation, which, by definition, means delayed response on my part. However, as she permits my presence and as the trust develops, I find that the one-sidedness falls away and a more mutual dialogue begins to creep into being; we become synchronous.

In terms of research, I have a strong personal need to move from an intuitive to a more reflective level in understanding my own work. I also feel that dance therapists, as a group of people, need to begin to look at their work, even though it is, for many of us, a very personal kind of work because it is so heavily dependent on intuitive response. Practically, if we are going to survive as a group with something to offer, we need to communicate, first with each other and then with the mental health professions. We have no finished research, per se, and we need to begin, no matter how crude our initial efforts might be.

I began on a very small scale. I studied one patient, in a controlled situation. I studied simply what was happening within the dance therapy experience. I studied a child called Amy, age 3.9, diagnosed as autistic after an intensive diagnostic work-up at Children's Hospital. Amy had had no schooling or therapy and her parents had had no attention from any agency or clinic when the recommended dance therapy was begun.

I saw Amy in a large empty room, three times a week for thirty-minute sessions for an eight-week period. During this time neither Amy nor her parents saw any other therapist, counselor, or psychiatrist.

Dr. William Condon, a man sensitively skilled in observing body movement, observed each session. Each session was audiotaped and afterward the observer and I discussed what occurred, on tape. I also made personal notes after each session. A professional photographer was in the room for the first, ninth, sixteenth, and twenty-sixth sessions making video tapes. He came once prior to each filming session and took still photographs. Films for analysis were made from only the first and last sessions.

At the end of the two-month (research) period, I began to study the films. I used the natural history approach which entailed only looking for approximately eighty hours until the natural patterns of the experience began to emerge. Analysis ultimately occurred on four different levels:

1. Study of closeness—distance patterns based on offer and touch sequences.
2. Study of dyssynchrony, synchrony, and symmetrical synchrony.
3. Study of autistic gestures.
4. Study of Amy's patterns of expressive communication.

The first level of analysis revealed the most striking parameter, that of closeness—distance. In the first session, Amy approached or allowed me to approach her, then made a highly stylized autistic gesture or series of these, permitted touch, or moved away into the space of the room. By the ninth session, her distancing revealed new aspects; more space and few gestures. For example, once, in this session, she ran back and forth the length of the room ten consecutive times, each time coming closer to me (I was stationary at one end) and finally touching, more mutually and spontaneously initiated, and much wanting to be held. When she was ambivalent about touching, at the moment of touch she pulled back, did not circle, did not gesture, and did not leave. She paused, often looking at me, and then tried again, usually the second time sustaining contact.

Intensive study of this pattern revealed: an increase in the number of touches tolerated by Amy (Table 1); an increase in the average duration of touch sequences, not only as session 1 and session 26 progressed, but also between the two sessions (Table 2).

The second level of analysis, unlike the first which demanded counting, or a macro look, involved a micro study of the movement patterns. (It is beyond the scope of this paper to describe the phenomena of synchrony and dyssynchrony.[2]) I found that Amy and I

2. W. S. Condon, "Linguistic-Kinesic Research and Dance Therapy," American Dance Therapy Association, *Proceedings of the Third Annual Conference* (Madison, Wis., 1968).

Table 1

Offer and Touch Sequences

	Therapist Offers	Amy Permits	Percentage Total Permit / Total Offer
Session 1	39	19	48.7
Session 26	9	6	75.0
	Amy Offers	Amy Permits	Percentage Total Permit / Total Offer
Session 1	0	0	0
Session 26	7	6	85.7

Table 2

Average Duration of Touch Sequences

	First 5 Touch Seq.	Last 5 Touch Seq.
Session 1	241.6 frames	838.2 frames
Session 26	400.0 frames	3889.8 frames

were synchronous (we initiated and sustained directionality of change of body parts at the same 1/24 of a second) always when touching. Amy became dyssynchronous (moved arhythmically in such a way so that I could not "tune-in") usually after touch sequences. When this happened, as she distanced herself physically and emotionally, she would become self-dyssynchronous almost always within an autistic gesture.

Symmetrical synchrony (which is my own label) occurred when there was a sharing of the same body parts, moving in the same direction, with the same point of change in direction. These were beautiful moments in which this heightened form of synchrony was not only felt within the experience but also verified on the film.

The third level of analysis involved a study of Amy's autistic gestures. An autistic gesture is a movement repeated consistently, difficult to imitate, reflect, or become synchronous with, highly individualized with formal structure, and utterly unique. A study of several of these isolated gestures revealed a decrease in occurrence within the sessions (Table 3).

In the fourth level of analysis, developing patterns of expressive communication were studied. For purposes of consistent recordings, I studied only overt gestures. Eye contact only existed in the begin-

Table 3
Frequency of Autistic Gestures

	Session 1	Session 26
Teeth banging	53	10
Leg thrusting	49	1
Head shaking	27	11
Hitting back of hand or record	17	4

ning when Amy was physically distant from me. By the final session, eye contact was occurring consistently when we were extremely close physically (that is, face to face). She finally was gesturing with her arms extended toward me for me to pick her up frontwards, and by scooting into me backwards and taking hold of my hands and putting them on her ankles for me to pick her up backwards. She pulled me up when I was sitting and she wanted me to be up and holding her. When I held her and she wanted to gallop, she bobbed up and down, pushed my hand with hers in a "steering" position, and often moved her lips and looked at me, as if she were imitating talking.

Finally, Amy's development within the total dance therapy experience of two months is reminiscent of the developmental stages of the first nine months of an infant's life. For example, she began to explore my body just as the infant explores the mother's body. Then she explored her own body (not a new experience for her as it is for an infant developing at age appropriate levels). She then began to imitate me.

In summary, from a therapeutic perspective, perhaps as trust developed, this child slowly and safely regressed (within the sessions) and then gradually began to grow through the pseudo-infancy stages, experiencing herself for the first time as one of two people in relationship. Or, from a more purely research perspective, as there was an increase in touch tolerance and touch duration, there was concomitantly a decrease in autistic gestures.

JARL DYRUD, M.D., AND MARIAN CHACE

Movement and Personality

Young professions in their formative stages lionize other fields which are endowed with firmly established theoretical bases, training curricula, and research techniques. Movement therapy is no exception; the sheer number of collaborative ventures published attests to the desire to borrow expertise from authorities. Attention from such personages, while flattering, tends to overemphasize the science rather than the art of movement therapy.

One of the most fruitful collaborations found in the literature is that of Dr. Jarl Dyrud and Marian Chace. Both have a healthy respect and understanding for the other's point of view as artist and scientist. Both authors exert considerable influence on movement therapists through a large network of personal contacts as well as by virtue of the profundity of "Movement and Personality."[1] With clarity and grace, it articulates a persuasive rationale for the use of creative dance as therapy.

Dr. Jarl Dyrud was inspired to collaborate as a reminder to members of the American Dance Therapy Association about the nature of Chace's contributions at a time when her intuitions were considered old-fashioned. The article, however, is more than a defensive summary of her scattered writings. A sophisticated theoretical niche is hewn out for dance therapists that distinguishes them from other mental health workers.

The first president of the American Dance Therapy Association, Marian Chace, was the *grande dame* of movement therapists. The 1942 date of her invitation to join St. Elizabeth's staff is regarded as one landmark in the earliest stirrings of the profession. More than clinician, she was teacher to all who sought her out—and a staggering proportion of prominent movement therapists claim some kinship today. Chace was a catalyst to the profession; she encouraged aspir-

Reprinted by permission from the American Dance Therapy Association, *Third Conference Proceedings* (1968), pp. 16–20. All rights reserved.

1. "Movement and Personality" was first published in the American Dance Therapy Association, *Proceedings of Third Annual Conference* (Madison, Wis., 1968).

ing students and interpreted the field to those of differing orientations.

Even after an article featured her in *Time* magazine, she remained modestly unsusceptible to claims of innovative psychic techniques or of mystic sources of healing energy.[2] "I just dance," she replied, and that settled the subject.   M.N.C.

As dance therapist and psychotherapist, we agree that movement and personality are closely interrelated from infancy onward throughout life. As therapists, we are primarily concerned with those people who need help from us, because either their private misery or their public eccentricity has reached such proportions that something has to be done. In either case, we see our task to be one of confronting a problem in the field of expressive behavior. By expressive behavior, we mean that which the patient does or does not do to communicate, and his intended or unintended effects upon his environment.

It has long been recognized (at least since Darwin's "The Expression of Emotions in Man and Animals") that human expressive behavior takes many forms beyond the spoken word. The gifted clinician is distinguished from his less gifted colleagues by his ability to understand more than what is said. As Freud said, "he that has eyes to see and ears to hear may convince himself that no mortal can keep a secret. If his lips are silent, he chatters with his fingertips; betrayal oozes out of him at every pore." In spite of this fact, we in the psychiatric field have for years done our teaching and published reporting and research largely in terms of verbal behavior. It is true that speech behavior is one of the most outstanding characteristics which distinguishes man from other animals. It is also true that the range of verbal expression that man is capable of leads to the possibility of ease in identifying response units and discriminating variations and classes of verbal behavior, which when examined even in terms of ordinary grammatical speech has a high degree of precision compared to the study of nonverbal behavior.

There is, however, considerable reason to think that our emphasis on the spoken word has defensive qualities as well as the convenience of specificity.

The linguist, Mario Pei, wrote of his fantasy about the origins of language as follows: "In the beginning men had no need for language because they could read each other's minds. When the need

---

2. *Time* magazine, "Dance Therapy," 73 (Feb. 23, 1959), pp. 60–62.

arose to conceal what one thought, language developed, along with tacit agreement to ignore the other evidences of expression."

Whether this is historically true or not, we do know that nonverbal behavior can be communication of a very direct form. We also know that it is an expression of emotion rather than of thought, at times in harmony with the spoken word, at other times at variance with it; but at all times requiring a "response" to be understood in contrast to our ability to "track" another person's verbalizations with such responding. When one stays removed from the transaction, as so often happens with verbal communication, understanding of the nonverbal communication will be vague and uncertain. Participation in dialogue which includes the nonverbal elements requires an awareness of our own body responses and those of the other person. Then the vagueness and uncertainty diminish, but the price is greater emotional involvement.

A common denominator of those people designated as mentally ill is failure to sustain participation in just this sort of dialogue. The reasons range from the schizophrenic's intense awareness of and misreading of the signs, to the hysteric's indifference to the subtleties of a relationship. In the terms of Jacques Lacan, one might say that in all cases the dialogue is interfered with by the patient's reluctance to speak of himself (resistance) and his reluctance to speak to the therapist himself (transference).

The reluctance manifests itself at times in the verbal content, but is most strikingly and reliably observed in distortions of expressive motility. A depressed person, for instance, may show either lassitude or extreme tension, but in either case expressive motility is restricted.

Interestingly enough it has been found in psychopharmacology that the usual initial effect of antidepressant drugs is apparently not a central effect on affect per se, but a stimulation of the patient to put out more motor behavior. Thus, the agent of change operates directly in the field of expressive movement. An hour of dance exercises preceding a therapeutic hour may have as dramatic an effect on the patient's capacity to express himself as the most potent antidepressant drug. It has the added features of organizing the response in a social context which maintains and reinforces such expressive motility. This is not to say that such drugs are unnecessary, but rather that when they are indicated, dance therapy can have an additive effect to channel the new drug-induced propensity to respond rather than leaving its organization and reinforcement to chance.

This organization and reinforcement of expressive movement as an opening move in the development of dialogue has struck us as being more fundamental to dance therapy than the cathartic notion of using it to simply "get out affect." Perhaps the best reason for our preference for calling this work dance rather than movement therapy is that the word "dance" emphasizes the expressive aspects of movement. It is true that initially what is important is for some movement to come under the control of the environmental stim- ulus—the rhythmic beat of the music. Very soon, however, the movement can be related to the therapist's movement also in syn- chrony with the music, at which point we may say that a truly human relationship is beginning. Often long before the regressed schizo- phrenic patient comes under the influence of his therapist's spoken word, the outlines of dialogue can appear in his hesitant responses to movement with the music and the dance therapist. It may also occur that his earliest organized verbal responses come in the dance therapist's studio. Conversely in the psychotherapy sessions, gestures or even a change in posture often appear to be the first evidence of remembering an experience which is then followed by the verbaliza- tion of it.

At this point, we could develop a series of case histories to illustrate this fact, but let us assume that it is established. The question is really, "why has the development of psychotherapy proceeded along such verbal and intellectual lines?" Why has our psychology tended to be mental rather than biobehavioral?

The mind-body dichotomy is as old as Western civilization, and though it was challenged from time to time by a few offbeat mystics, such as Blake or St. Theresa, the major challenge was Freud's insight into mind as metaphor for the experiencing self which was body. The major and popular deviations from Freud were naturally those which reinstated the dichotomy by de-emphasizing the irrational and expanding the rational functions of man as mind. The popularity of the various systems of psychoanalytic psychology over the years has seemed to vary directly with the extent to which this exclusion of the body is maintained and people perceived, or conceived of as disem- bodied ideas.

An unfashionable deviation in the opposite direction was that of Wilhelm Reich. At the time when Freud was being experienced as quite unbearable, Reich not only persisted in emphasizing physical functioning at a conceptual level, but also compounded his obnox- iousness by actually involving the body in the psychiatric process. In his book *Character Analysis*, he described how muscle tension is often a resistance blocking the expression of affect. He also described how working directly to release the muscles gave access to a richness of expressive behavior. His work lost much of its professional audience in his later years, yet it has relevance. The expressive behavior which was released by muscle relaxation may very well have been of particular value, because it occurred in a context of beginning dialogue, re-establishing patterns of motility which could then logically extend from motor, to affective and cognitive sequences of increasing adequacy in the dialogue between patient and therapist.

Much of the current literature on child development suggests that this route from motor to affective to cognitive is the normal pattern of growth and development. It is now recognized that the psychomotor development of the child provides the action which is subsequently internalized as thought and feeling. Watching a group of nursery school three year olds, it becomes apparent that their dialogue is in large part one of movement. Verbal behavior is simply less reliable at three. The troubled child moving through a group of children moves asynchronously with them in crossing the room and simply bumps into more of them than the child who fits into the group and moves with them in an easy and comfortable way. In a subtler way, the same is true of adults, if we bother to notice.

In summary, we would like to suggest the following train of thought. Expressive behavior in its entirety is the substance of human interaction. The infant's patterns of movement, of action upon and reaction to his environment, gradually become internalized to form his mental and emotional life. In psychiatry there has been a long period of concentration on the verbal aspects of expressive behavior. Now recently, we have come to see more and more interest shown in its nonverbal aspects. Let us hope that this new interest in nonverbal behavior will not be treated like the weather which everyone talks about, but no one does anything about. Counting it or charting it is no substitute for responding to it. Dance therapy is an appropriate way to do something about it. That is, to bring expressive behavior into a more sensitive relationship with the environment. Perhaps it is appropriate to recapitulate the developmental scheme by leading a person deeply alienated from himself and others into dialogue by steps which begin as simply as daring to stretch and daring to move in relation to the dance therapist.

RAY BIRDWHISTELL

The Frames in the
Communication Process

Anthropologist Ray Birdwhistell, as did the media medium Marshall McLuhan, coined a new realm of inquiry to suit his fancy. Other thinkers preceded him, but many more were stimulated to follow his example. Today kinesics is considered a branch of science separate unto itself, even though its adherents spring from widely divergent backgrounds, such as mathematics, dance, or psychology.

Dr. Birdwhistell set the guidelines for looking at movement. Movement (particularly facial expression and gesture) is studied primarily as it relates to speech. Curiously enough, the linguistic frame of reference is transported *in toto* to nonverbal forms of communication. Minute sequences of movement are correlated to spoken syllables. While intellectually intriguing and potentially significant in its implications for neurological research, an analysis of speaker as soloist neglects a basic necessity: it takes two to communicate as well as to tango.

Birdwhistell's later work broadens its range to include analysis of "pure" movement. Each culture strictly prescribes appropriate rules for predictable interaction. As Birdwhistell points out, he who does not practice them is shunted aside.[1] He suggests that the movement alphabet of the emotionally disturbed person is every bit as normal as that of the community in general.[2] What strikes us as foreign may be the inappropriate setting or timing or range of these so-called bizarre movements.

Persons visually handicapped since birth will never learn the intricacies of nonverbal communication, and consequently their social isolation is compounded. For example, the blind youth who twists his upper torso perpendicular to the person whom he greets thereby

Reprinted with permission of The University Press, University of Pennsylvania.

1. Ray Birdwhistell, *Kinesics and Context: Essays on Body Motion Communication* (Philadelphia: University of Pennsylvania Press, 1970), from which this essay is taken there entitled "Age of a Baby."

2. *Ibid.,* "Becoming Predictable," 24.

throws a stumbling block into further communication. Because blind infants do not respond with smiles and wriggles to their mothers' open, extended arms, some parents imagine that their babies have "rejected" them.[3] When the visually handicapped child rocks and flaps his hands, casual onlookers note the "crazy" actions and vacuous face. The violation of these rules of social interaction is not to be taken lightly: hence the concurrence of the Wisconsin Supreme Court with a school board ruling that a handicapped child of normal intelligence could be refused admittance to school because his presence had "a depressing and nauseating effect upon the teachers and school children."[4]

A movement therapist's intervention helps to sensitize the visually handicapped to the importance of the sighted person's communicatory signals. Young adults learn the significance of many signals and add them to their own narrow repertoire. Blind toddlers learn how to communicate their response to the sound of their mothers' approaching footsteps. Visually handicapped children expand their blindisms into the socially acceptable form of rhythmic movement to music. As Birdwhistell points out in this selection, adherence to predictable rules for interaction makes the participants feel at ease, a prerequisite for a continued relationship.   M.N.C.

Traditionally, we have regarded communication as that process by which one individual imparted knowledge to another. Many scholars have felt that an exhaustive measurement of communication could be accomplished through so-called black box research. By this procedure one subject is given a set of clearly limited pieces of information which he is instructed to impart to another. It is recognized that there are certain external interferences in this process. These interferences, called "noise," are kept in mind when the receiver subject is tested to determine the proportion of the original message which he has received. The data derived from this kind of research are not what I am talking about when I discuss communication. The universe to be measured by such a methodology, however brilliantly conceived and executed, properly belongs to the informational theorist or researcher. The anthropological linguist or kinesicist utilizes a

3. Working with parents of visually handicapped infants is discussed in Selma Fraiberg's "Intervention in Infancy: A Program for Blind Infants" in *Journal of the American Academy of Child Psychiatry* 10 (3) (July, 1971).

4. *State ex rel. Beattie* v. *Board of Education* 169 Wis. 231, 172 N.W. 153 (1919).

different method to deal with phenomena he feels are too complex to be reduced to such a formula.

Few serious students of information theory lay claim to their methodology as a technique for unraveling the intricacies of social interaction. All too often, however, the dilettante finds in the exquisite clarity of the information model a familiar and attractive construction which permits a simple and mechanical "explanation" of human interaction. The term "interaction" is the significant concept here. The order of phenomena we are tracing, analyzing, and describing cannot be reduced to the familiar action-reaction formula.

When we talk about communication we are not talking about a situation in which John acts and Mary reacts to John's action and in turn John reacts to Mary's action in some simple, ongoing, one-after-another sequence. Essentially, we discuss communication as a complex and sustaining system through which various members of the society interrelate with more or less efficiency and facility. According to communication theory, John does not communicate to Mary, and Mary does not communicate to John; Mary and John engage in communication.

Now there is a good reason, or rather, there are a plethora of reasons, why the action-reaction formula feels so familiar. Most of us who engage in extended cogitation about such an abstract conception as communication are literate, even educated, men. Our special conception of interaction, modeled on the relationship between the teacher and the taught, the physician and the patient, the demagogue or the plutogogue and his followers, serves to reinforce our earliest learning. Our memories of our earliest interactions are full of situations in which our parents told us what to do. And, for many of us, infancy and childhood was a period in which we acted and they, the parents, reacted.

The introspective view of the natural course of experience was further shaped by our experience as readers. In the novel, and even more clearly, in the drama, we find individuals who speak politely in turn. And, if we really accept the literary model of social interaction, we would be convinced that most people speak in complete sentences, and more important, that they listen with awareness to what the other person says—most of the time. One day in the average home or office reveals how poetic is such a conception. Parenthetically, many avid and otherwise sophisticated readers become so impressed with literary reproductions of social interaction that they give these a special historical significance and grieve loudly and evangelically that "the art of conversation is lost." It seems doubtful that, except in highly stylized imitations of the written language, there ever were conversations of the kind we grieve for. Certainly, we have no records on tape or in sound movie form which would indicate that in this, or in any of the societies which we have studied, such conversations ever take place except in ritualized circumstances.

Gregory Bateson, in a brilliant article on what he describes as "deutero-learning," points out that human learning is patterned, that we learn to learn, that we learn to learn to learn, and that we also learn to learn not to learn. We perceive in pattern, and we remember in pattern. Only in this way are we able to incorporate our society's way of viewing and testing the universe.

This problem of patterned remembering constitutes one of the most difficult barriers to communication research. When we take a tape recording and turn it over to a secretary for typing, her patterned memory, her belief that human beings speak in turn, and her belief that most human beings, on paper at least, speak in complete sentences leads to a situation in which she hears this kind of material on the tape. By actual count, even skilled secretaries working from unstructured interviews make about one mistake every five words. Thus a typescript may contain a good record of what the discussion or the interaction was about, but it is very inaccurate as a record of the actual behavior in the interaction. Lest we get some ideas that this is a disease which is peculiarly secretarial, let me add that our experience, utilizing the ears of some of the best linguists in America, has shown that even these experts, when working with shapes of material larger than a word or simple syntactic sentence, give us records with errors every ten to fifteen words. By careful cross checking, with independent recording, and, finally, with group assessment, we have been able to reduce the error to one in every twenty-five to thirty words.

One last remark about theoretical or practical impediments to communication research: until very recently, most of us, if we accepted the theory of evolution at all, saw evolution as a process which could be schematized as development from the inorganic to the organic to the higher organisms to man and finally to society. The work of the last quarter century of the ethologist, the comparative psychologist, the information theorist, and the anthropologist has led the student of communication to the overwhelming conviction that such a reconstruction is faulty and misleading. It has long been clear that a complex organism is not merely an assemblage of cells each of which independently becomes a part of the complex system.

The cell components of a complex system are, rather, by the very dynamic of their genetic selection and development absolutely *dependent* for life upon the activities of the other cells within the organism which have other kinds of specialized jobs to do. Comparably, the more research we have done into animal, fish, and bird behavior (and I stress the word "behavior"), the more we have become convinced that society is absolutely necessary for the maturation of the given animal individual. Most students of animal or human behavior are now prepared to agree that social life, or society, to put the statement in a different form, is absolutely an adaptive necessity for human existence. Communication, in this sense, is that system of coadaptation by which society is sustained, and, which in turn, makes human life possible.

Viewed from this perspective, communication is that system through which human beings establish a predictable continuity in life. Far from being a process centrally devoted to change, most of social interaction is concerned with maintaining an ongoing equilibrium. We are aware of the change points, but this awareness should not delude us into limiting communication to these points of stress in the system. We must remember that the system, as an essentially steady-state organization, operates to inhibit as well as to permit parameters of change in interpersonal activity. While the study of change is rewarding, research on communication if it is aimed at understanding its processes cannot be limited to parametric aspects of interaction.

In order for us to deal with other human beings in any systematic and comfortable way, they must behave in a predictable manner. In turn *we* must behave predictably if we are to comprehend ourselves, much less be predictable to them. Being in some measure predictable constitutes the *sine qua non* of sanity and humanity. However, it must be kept in mind that, while communication is necessary for life, all people who do not communicate precisely as we do do not immediately die. As we grow up, we learn that other people may speak different languages, and we can learn that it is possible, if not necessary, to learn how to translate these differences.

As we grow up we may become so sophisticated as to realize that the other man's language is just as natural as ours. If we are to live in a complex society, we must learn that even within a given language, within a given communication system, people from different regions of the country and with subcultural backgrounds different from ours do not communicate exactly like us. To successfully operate we must internalize the fact that there are systematic variations in the way in which a child, or an adolescent, or an aged person engages in communication. A few even become so sophisticated as to realize that the male and the female subcultures are sufficiently different that there can be imperfect understanding between male and female. As we mature, we become socialized. This is just another way of saying that we learn that many of the differences in the way in which people communicate or respond to our communication reveal the differences between their roles, their social position and activity, and ours.

If the communicational behavior of an individual is sufficiently unexpected and idiosyncratic as to be beyond the range of our previous experience, we may be unable to relate to him successfully. We can bear inappropriate behavior only if we can anticipate its inappropriateness. Undiagnosed unpredictability in others leaves us with doubts about ourselves. So, the definition of others as insane permits us to deal with them. There is nothing novel about the recognition that insanity is a state which evidences itself in distortions of the communication process. It is possibly somewhat less commonplace to recognize that many of those whom we call insane are not as chaotic or disordered in their communication behavior as we, the observers, would like to believe.

Our preliminary but intensive investigations into schizophrenia have convinced us that the schizophrenic is not chaotic or disordered in his communication; rather, he has a different pattern, a different system of communication. It is probably the systematic distortion of what still appears familiar to us that makes us feel so distressed. We are forced to describe as chaotic or fragmented that which under analysis can be seen as a perfectly understandable but still distorted system. As a systematic disturbance schizophrenia becomes a comprehensible phenomenon. We are now engaged in trying to find out how the pathological system differs from that employed by those we characterize as "normal." We must know much more about both to make efficient comparison possible.

If we recognize that our communication system is not something we invent but rather something which we internalized in the process of becoming human, we must study the socialization process if we are to isolate those factors which contribute to mislearning or misusing this system.

Although the line of approach which I, as an anthropologist and as a student of communication theory and research, must follow is concerned with the communication process, I do not believe that *the* cause of mental illness is so simple as "bad communication." I think that as research proceeds we will continue to discover genetic, chemical, and organic factors in mental illness. It is already clear from preliminary research that even the most severe social environmental influences do not necessarily create serious mental illness. However, what I am concerned with is the delineation of those factors in the early incorporation of the communication system which leads the child to be inadequately prepared to deal with life as a maturing human. If his system is different from that of the group in which he grows up, he will consistently feed his parents and peers distorted information about himself and his state of mind. He will receive from the outside world information that cannot help but lead him into further distress or privacy.

The child, in order to communicate, must learn to comprehend and enunciate a complex hierarchy of systems which makes up the language.

Out of the thousands of possible sounds that can be made with the so-called vocal apparatus, which can be heard by that intricate organization, the human ear, only certain of these provide the significant particles of his vocalic system. Each society chooses certain classes of sound, some fifteen hundredths of a second in duration, and assembles them in its own special way. Through these assemblages special orders of experience that stand for experience can be transmitted to others. It is not difficult for us to comprehend that the sound *d o g* is not a four-legged canine. It is somewhat more difficult for us to comprehend that these pieces of assembled sound, regardless of how intricately combined, do not have meaning in and of themselves. It is not easy to appreciate the fact that each piece of experience (of whatever duration) exists in a larger context which structures its function in the communication system. That is, while we can hear that the *p* in *pit* differs from the *b* in *bit*, it is somewhat more difficult to comprehend that, without context, *pit* does not have a meaning in itself other than that it is different from *bit*. A little thought will tell us that we must look at a larger context to find out whether a *pit* is a hole in the ground or the hard core of a peach. *Bit* can be a tiny particle, a piece of iron in the horse's mouth, or a part of a drill. Even such a limited exercise makes us recognize that these words are not absolute carriers of meaning. They can be comprehended only by reference to their context.

As we move to the analysis of the sentence, a special assemblage of these things called words, we discover that there are communication signals designed to cover larger and larger, meaningful stretches of material. To steal one of Professor Henry Lee Smith's favorite exam-

ples, any normal child of six will recognize that, though they are
made up of the same words, he has no difficulty in distinguishing between "She is a nice girl" and "She is a nice girl." Or to put it differ-
ently, although he cannot tell you exactly how it is done, any normal
American informant will tell you that you have given quite a different
message when you say "She is a nice girl?" # and "She is a nice girl."‖
The difference between those two sentences takes place in about 3 to
5 milliseconds. The way in which the terminal pitch of the two sentences is handled makes the first what we might call a declarative
statement and the second an interrogatory or doubt statement. The
more acute observers will note that when one speaks, he is not simply presenting data which linguists term phonetics or phonemics or
morphology or simple syntax. When these linguistic particles are put
together in a communicational frame, in actual speech one does a
series of things with one's body. In speaking these sentences, I do not
have very much choice about which movements I make. Each of
these sentences, within its context, requires a very special set of
movements. To review, "She is a nice girl" is marked by a set of head
movements which take place over the *She*, the *nice*, and the *girl*. In
this example I mark the sentence by lowering my head. I can just as
easily do this with my eyelids, with my hand, or even with my entire
body. These kinesic markers, as we have termed them, can be seen,
too, in the contrast sentence ⌒ "She's a nice girl #" in which I cross-
reference with the markers just as I can with drawl in my voice over
the "she's," the "nice," and the "girl." I could vary this, but, essentially, the "sweep" marker over the "nice" indicates that I am not
totally enthusiastic about the young lady. Comparably, the example,
"She is a nice girl"‖ contains a series in which I may knit my brows
over "nice" and make a slight lateral and upward movement over
"girl." Obviously, this does not exhaust the possibilities. In actual
practice, I can vary this in a number of ways—the meaning varying in
a consistent manner with each significant vocalic or kinesic shift.

I am trying to demonstrate the necessary interdependence of the
kinesic and linguistic; without going into an extensive course in
kinesics, we can see that in communication we handle an extensive
number of signals which all of us have learned, but only after such
signals are abstracted can they be taught. The duration and velocity
—that is, the timing—of each of these is significant and important.
There is clearly a difference between the order of statement which
I make about myself when I close my lids with no perceptible duration of holding at the point of closure, and when I close the lids at
the same rate of speed, allowing about a quarter of a second duration

of the closure. Or again, contrast these with the situation in which I close my eyelids much more slowly, leave them closed for a duration, or close them slowly and leave them closed for a hardly perceptible duration.

Practiced observers will recognize that the remainder of my face cannot remain immobile in an actual speech situation. Necessary shifts take place in the remainder of my physiognomy and my head as well as in the positioning of my body and hands. A series of movements in any part of my body could have changed the nature of the communication in a manner analogic to the shifts which occur if I change the quality of my voice, the words, or the phonemes in the verbalized material. These are only a few of the communicational particles which must be understood if we are to comprehend the complex phenomenon of communication. Only extended research can reveal the full structure, traces of which we can now detect.

In kinesics we engage in experimentation in the British sense. That is, we look at phenomena to trace what is happening, rather than attempt to control the variables and make something happen in an artificial situation. This is the natural history approach. For years a group of linguists, Norman A. McQuown, Charles Hockett, Henry Lee Smith, Jr., and George Trager, the ethnologist Gregory Bateson, the psychiatrists Henry Brosin, and, for an unfortunately limited period of time, Frieda Fromm-Reichmann, and myself as the anthropological kinesicist studied a series of family films taken by Mr. Bateson at Stanford in research on schizophrenogenic families. We continually asked ourselves the question: What is it about the communication between these disturbed families that is somehow different, either in quality or in intensity or quantity, from that which we have seen in other families of comparable social station in which there is no mental disturbance? What we are seeking at present are hypotheses, propositions, and working models upon which further research in normal and pathological family situations can be based.

The family in this study is made up of a middle-class father and mother and three children. We originally studied the mother as an ideal type for what we were calling self-containment—that is, she had a minimal response to the messages being sent to her by others within her family. This unhappy woman has three children. The first, already in school, has shown serious disturbance. The diagnosis of the child's behavior by skilled child psychiatrists ranges from a statement of "schizophrenic-like" to "seriously disturbed." The second child, whom we see at four and a half, seems, at first glance, to be hopefully healthy. Sustained consideration of this complex

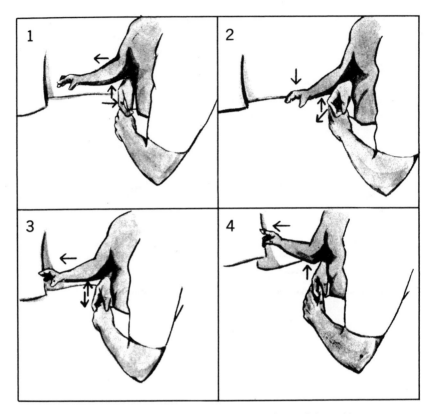

Mother changing baby's diaper. Illustrations are derived from film sequences 0–42. Frames 0, 3, 6, 9 of film sequence.

family situation makes us wonder whether this child's adaptation to *this* family will equip him for adaptation to families whose messages are somewhat less contradictory. For present purposes, however, we shall largely ignore these older children and pay special attention to the relationship between the mother and the third child, an infant, who is at the time of the filming about seven months old.

Running through the film we made of the family would make it possible to see the adjustment pattern of these families. Following this exercise we can examine the relationship between the mother and the baby, a little girl.

Any sustained interaction between mother and baby may be used to assess the structure of the social relationship. What we have chosen to look at is that situation in which the mother changes the baby's diaper—a task which she will perform several times a day

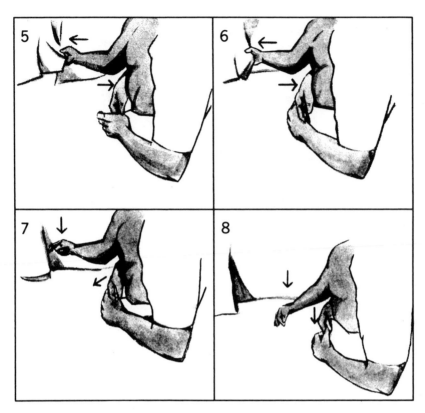

Frames 12, 15, 18, 21 of film sequence.

for eighteen to thirty months. The structure imposed by the task seems to eliminate some of the intrusions occasioned by the presence of the researchers. That is, a familiar task (with regularized component behavior) resists observer intrusion.

The onset of the film shows the mother with her left arm supporting and balancing the baby's weight. The mother's left hand assists her right in the removal of the diaper. It is to be noted that the mother's right hand, at the wrist, is pressed against the extended right arm of the baby. Simultaneously, the lateral aspects of the thumb side of the mother's right hand press against the baby's body in the lateral abdominal region.

In the next pictograph we see that the baby's hand has started to move down. Mother continues her pressure on the baby's upper arm, but she moves the thumb aspect of her right hand away from the baby's body and directs it in the removal of the diaper.

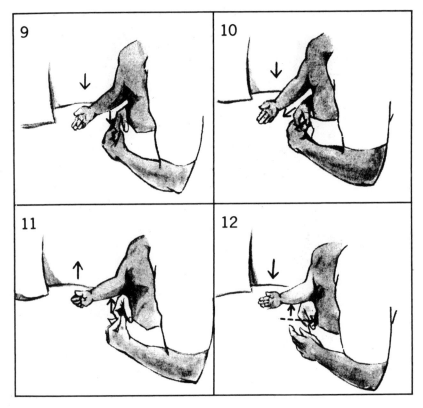

Frames 24, 25, 27, 28 of film sequence.

The third pictograph is a continued movement on the part of both which extends into the next picture.

In the fifth pictograph, as the infant's hand makes contact with the curtain, mother presses against the body of the infant with her right wrist, an action which she continues in the sixth picture.

In the seventh pictograph the baby relinquishes its hold on the curtain and begins to move its hand down. At the same time, the mother moves her hand away from the child's body and turns her attention completely to the task of removing the diaper.

In the eighth, ninth, and tenth pictographs we see the continued progress of the infant's hand down while mother continues to busy herself with the diaper.

In the eleventh pictograph, mother presses against the upper arm of the infant and reverses the movement of the infant's arm.

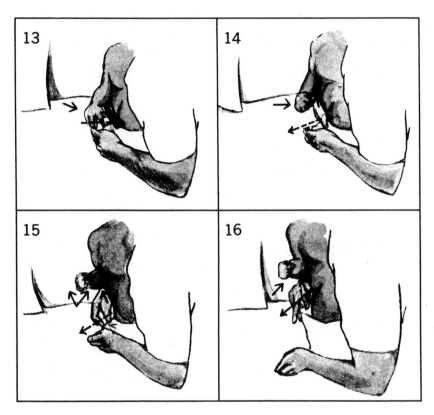

Frames 32, 35, 38, 42 of film sequence.

By the twelfth pictograph we see something entirely different. Now, she pushes not only up but toward the baby's body.

To review, in the first series, she pushed upward to extend the baby's arm, she pushed against the body to push it down. In the second instance the pressure against the baby's body indicated that the hand should come down and toward the body either of the mother or the child. Pictures twelve and thirteen are critical. She now sends both messages at once, seemingly emphasizing one of the messages somewhat more strongly than the other. This time she uses not only the wrist but she curls her thumb against the baby's body. At the same time, she thrusts her wrist against the child's upper arm. Thus, the child is in what Gregory Bateson has called the double-bind—neither of the messages can be obeyed without disobeying the other. In picture fourteen mother presses upward again against the arm, relieves the pressure against the body, and pushes the baby's hand and arm toward a lateral position. By the sixteenth picture we see that the baby's hand is moving again toward an outstretched position. Following this sequence the baby waves its arm up and down in the air.

It would be easy to dismiss this scene as, on the one hand, a way in which a mother protects the baby from being stuck with a pin while she removes the diaper. On the other hand, it is all too easy to be horror-struck by the inevitable confusion which the baby feels, or at least we feel, in such a situation. It is clear that only extended further research will let us know the significance of small portions of times like this. However, if we place this scene in the larger context of the family, this scene gains new significance as an item in the complicated situation of communication within this family. Thus, this small scene, 1¾ seconds in duration, becomes exceedingly important. The exact nature of its significance must wait for future research.

When one thinks how many 1¾ seconds of interaction there are in the socialization process of this or any other infant, it is clear that by the time babies become children they are very old indeed. If, as we suspect from the observation of extended contact between this mother and this infant, this 1¾ seconds contains within it a micropattern which is duplicated many times in a scope of minutes, hours, and weeks, we have come close to the problem, or at least near certain problems, of the relationship between human learning and human health.

PART 2

Expanding the
Movement Repertoire

All the world's a stage,
And all the men and women merely players.
They have their exits and their entrances,
And one man in his time plays many parts,
His acts being seven ages. At first the infant,
Mewling and puking in the nurse's arms.
Then the whining schoolboy, with his satchel
And shining morning face, creeping like snail
Unwillingly to school. And then the lover,
Sighing like furnace, with a woeful ballad
Made to his mistress' eyebrow. Then a soldier,
Full of strange oaths, and bearded like the pard,
Jealous in honour, sudden, and quick in quarrel,
Seeking the bubble reputation
Even in the cannon's mouth. And then the justice,
In fair round belly with good capon lin'd,
With eyes severe and beard of formal cut,
Full of wise saws and modern instances;
And so he plays his part. The sixth age shifts
Into the lean and slipper'd pantaloon,
With spectacles on nose and pouch on side;
His youthful hose, well sav'd, a world too wide
For his shrunk shank; and his big manly voice,
Turning again toward childish treble, pipes
And whistles in his sound. Last scene of all,
That ends this strange eventful history,
Is second childishness and mere oblivion,
Sans teeth, sans eyes, sans taste, sans every thing.

As You Like It
William Shakespeare

MAUREEN NEEDHAM COSTONIS

How I Learned to Wall-Bounce and Love It!

Movement therapists posit that each client moves in a distinctly idio-syncratic style which may be modified through movement therapy. This hypothesis is key to one rationale for the use of dance as therapy. Many institutionalized persons, for example, employ bizarre gestures or inviolable rituals. Movement therapists assist their clients to transform these solitary, fixed movement sequences into expressive dance movement.

Since expansion of movement repertoire is considered to be an important goal of movement therapy, the movement researcher is faced with the difficulties of measuring ephemeral alterations. The Movement Range Sampler (MRS) is my proposal for a quantifiable technique to measure two interrelated aspects of movement: the range of motion for each body part and the path sculpted in space by each movement.[1]

The case of a wall-bouncing boy will be used as an example of how the MRS may be applied. Data from the MRS reveals that the boy's bizarre style of running and walking was significantly modified within the first ten minutes of the first movement therapy session. The amount of rotational movement in the torso, for example, decreased by two-thirds. The run observed in minute 10 was consequently less jerky and more efficiently tailored to the forward thrust of the energy flow than that of minute 1.

The child developed a significantly expanded movement repertoire in the second session. His movements demonstrate a greater variety and an increased range when minutes 1, 5, and 10 are compared. His stereotyped gestures were seven times less numerous at the conclusion of this session than at its beginning. Bizarre gestures with the right arm ceased, and free-flowing dance movement developed. The number of stereotyped gestures with the left hand decreased, al-

---

1. With apologies to Ms. liberationists, the Movement Range Sampler will be referred to as MRS.

though that arm remained frozen in place. In minute 10 a variety of movements occurred which had not been previously observed: throughout minute 1, only two units of rotary were noted; in minute 5, five units of vertical; in minute 10, twelve of vertical, two of rotary, and one of intermediate plane were simultaneously performed. Both range and variety of movement can be said to have expanded considerably.

Data from the Movement Range Sampler suggests that selected aspects of a client's movement repertoire can be modified with surprising rapidity.   M.N.C.

Case of the Wall-Bouncing Boy

A nine-year-old boy entered Adler Zone Center, an Illinois short-term residential treatment center for children. When I scanned the admission records, I noted that Mickey was reported to explode in tantrums and refuse to eat. This behavior is not unusual for the children who come to our center. The third reason cited for Mickey's admission, however, caught my eye: there was a cryptic reference to his "wall-bouncing." My curiosity piqued, I continued to read. Considered severely mentally retarded with secondary emotional and behavioral problems, a psychiatrist diagnosed him as suffering from "nonpsychotic organic brain syndrome with convulsions, speech impairment, exotropia, and mental retardation." No other references were made to the briefly mentioned wall-bouncing rituals.

I ambled over to the cottage playroom and picked out a tall, handsome lad among the clutter of toys and active children. I watched Mickey stride purposefully to the wall, clap the palms of his hands sharply on it while violently snapping his torso and head backwards. Simultaneously, he performed a balletic *demi-tour en l'air* and ended facing the opposite direction. It was at this point that my idle curiosity turned to active involvement. I volunteered to take Mickey for individual movement therapy sessions once per week.

Therapy for Mickey seemed particularly urgent. His family threatened to institutionalize him permanently if his bizarre behavior did not cease and his language usage increase. My goals as movement therapist with Mickey were: (1) to shape language behavior, and (2) to shape stereotyped behaviors into expressive dance movement.

In terms of the results for the first goal cited, Mickey employed more frequent language during movement therapy sessions than elsewhere at Adler. Over a two-month period, his average number of words per ten-minute session was four. A correlation was noted for instances of proximity and language utterances. With one exception, each session that language usage increased in frequency, so did the occurrences of body contact between us. Each session that verbalizations decreased from the previous week's score, so did the instances of physical contact. No significant correlation was found for moments of perfect synchronous interaction and language usage.[2]

Shaping stereotyped behavior into expressive dance movement was the second goal of our movement therapy sessions. In retrospect, it seemed an overly ambitious goal because Mickey possessed a rare talent for bizarre mannerisms. Dramatic gains were noted over the course of the next two months, nevertheless, and even within the limited confines of the first session.

At home, Mickey upset his family with his continual wall-bouncing. They lived in a small trailer, and it rocked from side to side each time that he performed this ritual. His family's overwrought reaction was thus understandable.

Mickey's repertoire of mannerisms was considerable in both frequency and variety. Mickey sucked his thumb vigorously, ground his teeth, rolled his eyes upward and back, drooped the upper half of his body to the left side, clasped his hands, snapped his head backward, fixed on lights, stared into space—I cannot begin to enumerate them all. The sheer volume of these mannerisms boggled the mind. During our third movement session, for example, forty-seven head-snapping actions were clocked in six minutes.

Within the two weeks following the third movement therapy session, certain of these behaviors ceased. Operant learning procedures were applied on the cottage to five categories of stereotyped gestures, including head-snapping and wall-bouncing. The technique was almost immediately effective.

Even though these same stereotyped gestures (such as wall-bouncing) continued to be expanded into dance gesture, it was my experience that the original bizarre forms never returned. Many administrators of institutions express reluctance when the movement therapist requests permission to "mirror" bizarre mannerisms. The staff members fear that such behavior will thereby increase. I believe that the movement therapist's mirroring techniques are not sufficiently reinforcing to cause or encourage this behavior in other situations. In fact, the benefits in gaining rapport outweigh any disputed dis-

2. Perfect synchronous interaction is defined in "Case Study of a Puzzling Child," Part 1.

advantages. Furthermore, as the data from this article indicates, dance is an important substitute for bizarre mannerisms.

Mickey ceased performing these five ritualistic forms within a two-week period. This progress is comparatively simple to illustrate by counting and charting the frequency of specific gestures performed: from forty-seven head-snapping actions within a six-minute movement therapy session to none during any following sessions.

That kind of negative fact is demonstrable, but other developments are more subtle to trace. At the end of the first movement therapy session, both I and the observers spontaneously commented on a changing quality in the movements used by Mickey.[3] Ordinary actions, such as running and walking, seemed more normal in appearance than ever before. Something had happened to Mickey's characteristic style of running and walking in this ten-minute period. But what?

This paper explores a method for specifying these changes. The proposed Movement Range Sampler (MRS) describes two interrelated aspects of movement: the range or scope of movement path of each body part and the type of movement path sculpted in space. Data from the MRS substantiates change in the client's use of movement during each session. Within ten minutes of the first movement therapy session, Mickey was seen to increase both the scope and variety of his movements. In the second session, stereotyped gestures were transformed into flowing dance movements. Over the course of many months, subtle changes noticeable only after repeated viewings of these early videotapes became pronounced in real life. A year later, graduate student Peggy Brown reported that Mickey's repertoire of movement patterns and choice of dance activities continued to expand in sessions with her as therapist.

The Difficulties of Describing Movement

Mickey's ordinary actions such as running and walking were as weird as his gestures. Effort-shape followers would have called his movements fragmented and bound. Perceptual-motor adherents might have pointed to his loping walk and twisted run. Such movements could be termed inefficient, unbalanced, poorly coordinated, or awkward. These adjectives were all accurately applied. Descriptive labels, however, lacked the researcher's precision in any attempt to define Mickey's style of running and walking.

3. My thanks to Deborah Mellette who first noted this change. Thanks also to Jessie Coven and Susan Burton who assisted as observers.

Movement therapists are caught on the horns of a dilemma. On the one hand, they concur in their assumption that each client moves in an idiosyncratic manner that may be modified as a result of movement therapy. On the other, they cannot agree upon how any such modifications are to be described. In order to substantiate their effectiveness as change agents, they must pinpoint the kinds of changes that occur during or after treatment. Up to this point, the movement researcher is faced with the complexities of measuring ephemeral alterations, yet he has only descriptive adjectives as his tool.

Effort-shape techniques tend to dominate research literature. Many practitioners couch their movement assessments in the objective language of effort-shape. Movements are categorized into eight dimensions: bound or free, direct or indirect, quick or slow, strong or light. Directions are termed as downward, upward, across to side, out to the side, backward, or forward. There are also six shape categories: retreating or advancing, narrowing or widening, sinking or rising. In addition there are symbols for four motion factors. The motion factors are force, space, time, and flow.[4] Establishing a common vocabulary of thirty movement terms is no small chore for researchers, yet others are still more ambitious. They hope to transform the system into a viable method of observation integrated with therapeutic techniques.

Descriptive profiles of client's movement patterns abound, a substantial number of which are based on effort-shape principles. Martha Davis, Arlynne Samuels, and Sharon Chaiklin have each developed observational checklists; explanations of their work are found later in Part 2. Beth Kalish reports that research continues on the development of an objective rating instrument to evaluate atypical body movement. Her *Behavioral Rating Instrument for Autistic and Other Atypical Children* will be forthcoming shortly. Dr. Judith Kestenberg, Penny Bernstein, and Marian North also are highly regarded for their research. Yet up to this point only one study has been published which compares observer scorings in order to derive a reliability index of these techniques, and its author calls for more rigorous testing of observer reliability.[5]

Even though many clinicians employ its terminology, relatively few use effort-shape in their research. Why this disparity? Effort-shape requires over two years of intensive training to develop into a quali-

4. See Cecily Dell, *A Primer for Movement Description* (New York: Dance Notation Bureau, 1970).

5. See "Movement Characteristics of Hospitalized Psychiatric Patients" later in this part.

fied observer, and advanced training is available only at the Dance Notation Bureau in New York City. Videotape viewing is considered unacceptable for research purposes. Therefore movement research which utilizes effort-shape entails a highly skilled observer present for each session. Due to the high probability of human error, several observers must participate. Only one such study—that of Dr. Martha Davis previously mentioned—meets these requirements.[6]

In searching for an alternative to describe selected aspects of movement repertoire, the technique should first of all be available to those who must learn it from books. It should be equally adaptable to live and video research. It should be a precise and replicable method which is easily comprehended by the movement researcher and his colleagues from related fields.

The Eshkol-Wachmann Movement Notation System

I feel that the proposed Movement Range Sampler is an option that fills these needs and provides other advantages as well. It should be stressed that the MRS is an alternative or supplement to, not a rejection of, effort-shape contributions to movement research.

The MRS is derived from concepts of Noa Eshkol and Abraham Wachmann's movement notation system. Remarkably compact, a full explanation of Eshkol-Wachmann notation consists of thirty-two pages in their text. The entire system requires thirty-one symbols, including the numerals 0 to 9. The manuscript consists of horizontal divisions which represent separate body parts and the vertical which stands for time divisions.

A serious drawback to effort-shape is the difficulty of deriving quantifiable data from qualitative descriptions. As Irmgard Bartenieff puts it, effort-shape deals with the "how" of movement as opposed to the "what." A limited variety of descriptive adjectives is extremely useful for certain purposes; they lack the researcher's precision for other purposes.

The MRS does have the decided advantage of quantifiable accuracy in describing "how." The mathematical basis of Eshkol-Wachmann makes possible computerization for research and teaching purposes.[7]

6. Marian North's pioneering work is flawed in this respect. Upon completion of the observational session, Miss North and each observer discuss their findings with the others. At the next observation of the same child, it would not be unlikely if interobserver correspondence were affected. Lecture by Marian North at Urbana, Illinois, March 30, 1973.

7. Dr. Annelis Hoyman of the University of Illinois, Department of Physical Education, is engaged in adapting the system for computer learning.

The system has been investigated for inclusiveness. No other movement notation system claims the ability to describe the full potential range of body movement. The University of Illinois computer (Plato, as it is affectionately called), under the direction of Professor Heinz Van Foerster, has verified such capability.[8] Eshkol-Wachmann is not limited to movement of the human body. It has been used to notate movement of gymnasts and viruses; the courtship dances of jackals and the choreography of "Swan Lake"; the stereotyped behaviors of neurologically impaired rats or of severely retarded children. Its potential application seems unlimited.

The Movement Range Sampler

The Movement Range Sampler is the author's proposal for a quantifiable technique to measure two interrelated aspects of a client's movement: the range of motion of each body part and the movement path sculpted in space by each part. It owes its inspiration to the Eshkol-Wachmann movement system. The MRS, however, is not a true system for notating movement. The body's exact position in space is omitted. The MRS is unlike the effort-shape profiles because specific paths of individual body parts are required for the observation. An impression or gestalt of body efforts and shapes may be utilized in effort-shape.[9]

To explain the MRS, it is unnecessary to go into details about the Eshkol-Wachmann system. The reader is referred to *Moving, Reading, Writing* for further investigation.[10] The MRS is based upon Eshkol and Wachmann's notion of measuring the angles of body parts as they move separately in spatial pathways. Each body part is scored independent of any other on a separate line. A full circle swing that originates in the right upper arm, for instance, describes a circle or an angle of 360 degrees. For convenience in scoring the MRS, each forty-five degree angle arbitrarily equals one unit. Therefore, the movement range is written as a total of eight (45 degrees $\times$ 8 = 360 degrees). Assuming that the lower arm and hand passively follow the

8. N. Eshkol, P. Melvin, J. Michl, H. Von Foerster, and A. Wachmann, *Notation of Movement* (Urbana, Ill.: Biological Computer Laboratory Report, Feb. 15, 1970).

9. If describing "effort" is ever to be more than an observer's rough estimate, other techniques ought to be experimented with to supplement our descriptions. Perhaps the oxygen analyzer backpack of the anthropologist might be useful in correlating actions with energy use.

10. Dance Mart of Brooklyn distributes some of the Eshkol-Wachmann texts, or write to: Movement Notation Society, 75 Arlozorov Street, Holon 58327, Israel, for information.

upper arm as it swings, it is necessary to notate only the movement of the upper arm. The reader will notice that the MRS (unlike Eshkol-Wachmann) ignores the starting position of the movement and its exact placement in space at the finish. The concern is "How much?" and not "Where?"

Similarly derived from Eshkol-Wachmann principles of movement analysis, the types of movement paths employed are categorized as the following: rotary (written as ⌒), conical (written as (∧), and plane. Plane movements are subdivided into vertical (↑), horizontal (→), and intermediate (↗).

Rotary movement, for example, is noted in the ballerina who plants her feet parallel on the stage and rotates to the right clockwise and the left counterclockwise to the traditional first position. The movement originates in the upper legs. In the box for right upper leg ⟨2⟩ is written and in the box for left upper leg ⟨2⟩ is notated. In rotary movement, the axis of the limb and the axis of movement coincide (the angles of movement = 0).

A straight arm describing a figure eight in the air performs two sets of cone-shaped motions—one clockwise and one counterclockwise. (⟨8⟩ ⟨8⟩). The axis of the moving limb shapes a full or partial conical envelope in conical movement (the angle of movement to the axis of the limb is less than 90 degrees).

The various categories of plane movement are easy to identify. The head waggle of the Hindu dancer is labeled horizontal plane movement of the head. (→) Without realizing it, the child who jumps for joy is engaged in vertical plane movement. (↑) Intermediate plane movement is observable in a woman using her right arm to pick up an earring and attach it to her left ear. (↘)

Time samples, a well-accepted research technique of behavior observation, are employed in the MRS because of the complexities of notating and observing an ever changing scene. For the same reason, a limited number of body parts may be selected for analysis. The chart consists of ten time frames, which may be as minute or gross as the observer chooses.[11] Time frames must be consistent for the entire chart. In a live session the observer analyzes the movements for five seconds within each minute. Then he notates for the remainder of the minute. The observer for this study was trained in the Eshkol-Wachmann notation system and reported little difficulty in adjusting to these time constraints.[12] With the advantages of video playback, she commented, such problems vanish.

11. A sample MRS chart is included in the appendix.

12. My thanks to Laurie Feldman, graduate of the University of Illinois, 1975, for her help.

In each box are listed separate body parts. The observer marks two items: the range of motion—if any—along with the category of movement path. The full circle swing of the upper arm used as a previous example would be notated as ↑ 8. At the end of ten samples, the total score for each category is added and placed in the tally box at the bottom.

Data from the Movement Range Sampler

The first walking sequence of the first minute of Mickey's first movement therapy session was selected for video analysis. This walk is not untypical of his characteristic loping movements seen on the playground, as well as in other dance sessions.[13] My assistant notated the MRS for five frames, approximately one-third of a second apart, as I scored the Synchronous Movement Profile (SMP).[14]

In these five frames, Mickey performed a total of twenty-eight units of vertical plane movement with assorted body parts. The majority of these units occurred in the leg area as he stepped forward. In addition, six units of rotational movement were noted. These occurred in the upper arm, head, and torso. For the full sequence, his upper leg remained in a rotated position. There was no outward movement noted in the upper leg as it had already occurred; therefore no rotational movement was scored for that body part. Rotational units consist of six out of thirty-four units notated, or 18 percent of all movement units noted. These rotational movements are counterproductive to the forward thrust of walking. In fact, seconds after this sequence occurred, Mickey twisted his torso so far backward and sideways that he toppled, and was unable to continue walking forward. The average SMP rating for the entire five frames was 2.8 out of a possible ten for perfect interactive synchrony.

Comparing this lope to Mickey's walk in minute 10 of the same session, I find a substantial decrease in the amount of rotational movement. Twenty-four units of vertical movement occurred in these five frames but only one of rotational. (Mickey's head turned toward mine; this is an action fully compatible with walking forward.) Instead of 18 percent of the total, the rotational is only 4 percent of all movements notated. The left arm originally was frozen in a flexed and rotated position close to his chest; it later swung freely. The SMP rating also changed. It was 7.6 out of 10, more than twice as high as the score for his first walk. As if confirming our increased

13. Conversation with Mary McCarty, March, 1974.

14. Scoring for the Synchronous Movement Profile is described in "Case Study of a Puzzling Child" in Part 1.

rapport, Mickey's face was no longer blank; he smiled broadly and looked directly at me as we walked together across the room.

The minute 10 run also differed markedly from that of minute 1; the torso rotated one full unit less (45 degrees) each running step. His first run was decidedly inefficient. Each time Mickey stepped on his right foot, his entire torso rotated 1.5 units to the right (approximately 67.5 degrees clockwise from normal standing position). The rest of the upper body—the arms, head, hands—froze into position as he twisted.

A dramatic contrast was Mickey's running posture by the end of the session. The torso rotation decreased by a 45-degree angle on each step. The total rotational movement score for all body parts also declined from 15 to 2.5. At the same time there was a small decrease of vertical plane movement from 36 to 32. No other category of movement was observed. The SMP score doubled from four to eight.

Awkward-looking rotational movements, that are inefficient and counterproductive to the forward thrust of the walk or run, were shaped into largely vertical movement. Mickey's total score for rotational movement decreased from 18 percent of all movement employed by him in the walking sequence to 4 percent. There was an overall decrease of five times less rotational movement used for the minute 10 run. In particular, the upper torso rotated forty-five degrees less on each running step. Without that rotational drag, the action was integrated with the task at hand.

The Growth of Synchronous Interaction

As Mickey changed his style of running, he was able for the first time to achieve perfect synchronous interaction with me. His angles of body parts moving in separate spatial pathways, when compared to those sculpted in space by my movements, were identical in every respect. Within the ten minute period of this first session, he doubled his SMP rating. His average SMP was twice as high both in walking and running when first instances of these actions are compared to the last. Such an increased ability to adjust to my movements over the course of the session illustrates Mickey's heightened awareness of environment.

Expanding Stereotyped Gestures into Dance Movement

Mickey's stereotyped gestures were analyzed in terms of both the MRS and SMP in a videotape taken of the second session. The first seconds of the first, fifth, and tenth minute were selected arbitrarily as samples. Nonetheless his actions were adjudged typical of others observed in this and later sessions. Each time sample extended ten frames (each approximately one-third of a second apart). Mickey's gestures during that session included the following: head-snapping, wall-bouncing, thumb-sucking, hand-flapping, arm-shaking, teeth-grinding, and eyeball-rolling. The latter two could not be viewed from the videotape and thus are not included in the following analysis.

In the ten frames beginning in the first minute, both the right and left hands indulged in continuous stereotyped gestures. The score for the gestures was assigned as 10 frames $\times$ 2 hands = 20. The only movement noted in the MRS was two units of rotary. The left hand was held frozen in a stereotyped gesture and close to the chest. The SMP for the ten frames was zero.

The ten frames of the fifth minute were marked by five units of vertical movement performed by the right hand. The left hand continued in stereotyped gestures (10 frames $\times$ one hand = 10). The SMP score continued at zero.

By the tenth minute the right hand and arm were dancing freely. They moved a total of twelve units in the vertical plane, two of rotary, and one in the intermediate plane. The left hand gestured in stereotyped fashion exactly three times. Both arms were rapidly moving in and out of perfect or approximate synchrony with mine. Because of difficulties in camera focus, an exact SMP was not possible for all of these ten time frames; the scores ranged from zero to two and one was selected as the median.

Modification of Bizarre Gestures		
Frequency	20	10	3
SMP	0	0	1
MRS	⌒2⌐	↑5	↑12 —⌒2⌐— 1↗
	Minute 1	Minute 5	Minute 10

The invariable, stereotyped gestures and frozen postures of the first interval blossomed into free-flowing dance. This was accomplished in heightened rapport with the therapist. Eye contact, laughs aloud, and broad grins accompanied this significant change.

Ritualistic movement patterns of the entire body as well as fixed hand gestures expanded into inventive forms of dance. Up until the

Copyright,
November 1974
Maureen Costonis

Name _____

Date _____

Observer _____

MOVEMENT RANGE SAMPLER

	1	2	3	4	5	6	7	8	9	10
Left Hand										
Upper Arm										
Right Hand										
Upper Arm										
Head										
Torso										
Right Upper Leg										
Foot										
Left Upper Leg										
Foot										

Time Intervals   1   2   3   4   5   6   7   8   9   10

Total Units Per Category:

(∧)   Conical Movement _____

(→)   Horizontal Plane _____

(↗)   Intermediate Plane _____

(↑)   Vertical Plane _____

(↷)   Rotary Movement _____

SCORING: Total Amount of Movement for each category = 1 unit for each 45 degree angle movement.

midway point of this second session, the observers of the videotape remarked that Mickey engaged in his characteristically twisted run. In an analysis of a run selected somewhat after that point, the break from old habits was apparent. Mickey revealed a highly expanded and varied repertoire of movement. He was dancing as he ran.

A typical run in the first minute of session one consisted of thirty-six units of vertical plane movement and fifteen of rotary. In session two Mickey ran in time to the music while swinging his arms in large circles about him. Comparing a fragment of equal duration to the previous run, Mickey scored thirty units of vertical plane, nine of intermediate plane, four of horizontal plane, twelve of rotary, and two of conical movements.

Mickey increased his range of movement and experimented with different varieties of movement. Intermediate and horizontal plane movement as well as conical were charted for the first time as he ran. As stereotyped gestures decreased in frequency, Mickey developed an ability to move with larger and more varied forms than were evidenced in the beginning of the session. The expanded variety and scope of gestural and postural movements were surprising in light of the limited time constraints unless one were to speculate on the process of psychological modeling proposed by Albert Bandura.[15]

Conclusion

The Movement Range Sampler grows out of a movement notation system that is inclusive, quantifiable, and adaptable to the diverse needs of microbiologists, neurologists, as well as movement therapy researchers. Because it is based on a precise and therefore replicable technique, I propose the Movement Range Sampler for sketching aspects of the client's changing use of movement during the dance therapy session. The limited data derived from the MRS in this initial study suggests that movement therapists may possess effective techniques for the modification of bizarre movement patterns and that within a remarkably short time even a severely retarded child may jettison his private rituals in favor of dance.

Bibliography

Bandura, Albert. *Psychological Modeling: Conflicting Theories.* Chicago: Aldine-Atherton, 1971.

Davis, Martha. "Movement Characteristics of Hospitalized Psychiatric Patients." *Fifth Conference Proceedings.* New York: American Dance Therapy Association, 1970. Pages 25–45.

Dell, Cecily. *A Primer for Movement Description.* New York: Dance Notation Bureau, 1970.

Eshkol, Noa, P. Melvin, J. Michl, Heinz Von Foerster, and Abraham Wachmann. *Notation of Movement.* Urbana, Ill.: Biological Computer Laboratory Report 10.0. Feb. 15, 1970.

Eshkol, Noa. *Moving, Writing, Reading.* Holon, Israel: Movement Notation Society, 1973.

15. Albert Bandura, *Psychological Modeling: Conflicting Theories* (Chicago: Aldine-Atherton, 1971).

ARLYNNE SAMUELS

Movement Change
through Dance Therapy—A Study

Many movement therapy researchers assert that consistent movement habits relate to personality characteristics.[1] They define these
individual patterns of expressive (nonfunctional) behavior as "movement repertoire." Arlynne Samuels assumes further that a varied
movement repertoire is essential to express a full range of emotions.
Therefore, one goal for Jay (the withdrawn client described in this
case study) is to shape an expanded movement repertoire.

Sharon Chaiklin and Arlynne Samuels have devised a movement
observation scale which describes certain qualities of the client's
original movement repertoire. The observer traces the evolution of
changes during the sessions. It is noted that Jay makes increasing
use of his body parts and of space around the body, as well as of
quick-strong-direct motions. At the end of twelve sessions, his energy
level is said to increase, and self-synchrony to appear.

The Chaiklin and Samuels scale is but one of many descriptive
checklists based on effort-shape terminology. Markedly influenced
by Laban's concepts, a number of movement therapists—notably
Bartenieff, Davis, North, Kalish, Hunt, Bernstein, Kestenberg, Weisbrod—have experimented with differing versions for research purposes. One contingent of this group suggests that diagnostic assessments of inner psychic states are derivable from these movement
observation devices. Marian North, in describing one child's abilities
to make use of shapes within large areas of space, generalizes his
deficiencies as symbolic of "a weakness in shaping the external world
to his own needs." From there, she asserts, "retardation academically
and in relationships" is a logical consequence.[2] Penny Bernstein out-

Reprinted by permission from the American Dance Therapy Association, Monograph 2, *Writings on Body Movement and Communication* (1972), pp. 56–77. All
rights reserved.

1. Gordon Allport, *Studies in Expressive Movement* (New York: Macmillan, 1933).

2. Marian North, *Personality Assessment through Movement* (London: MacDonald
and Evans, 1972), p. 45.

lines techniques to treat movements which she ascribes to specific psychoanalytic labels. For the "urethral sadistic" client, Bernstein prescribes "movement activities involving the rhythmic control of sharp reversals from free to bound-flow which start and stop suddenly both in postural and gestural patterns."[3] Dr. Judith Kestenberg relies on data from her movement observation scale in order to "describe and delineate basic differences between the oral, anal, urethral ego organization in the first few years of life."[4]

Others are critical of this trend. Dr. Martha Hargadine challenges the premise that a varied movement repertoire is a sign of mental health.[5] Bartenieff, transplanter of effort-shape to this country, implies that techniques aimed at modifying the client's effort-shape profile misconceive the thrust of her work.[6] Welding effort-shape categories to psychoanalytic labels might not only be premature but also potentially limiting. Diagnostic labeling is increasingly attacked by mental health professionals; isolation in the back waters of the labeling controversy is a serious risk.[7]

Effort-shape observational tools, however, as sensitively yielded by Samuels, are valuable. Hopefully, these will not get lost in the controversy. M.N.C.

Movement, whether it be that of the structured dance forms or of the everyday movements of the individual, communicates basic emotions. When we move we are making a statement about ourselves.

3. Penny Bernstein, *Theory and Methods in Dance-Movement Therapy* (Dubuque, Iowa: Kendall-Hunt, 1972), pp. 67–68.

4. Judith Kestenberg, Hershey Marcus, Esther Robbins, J. Barlowe, and A. Buelte, "Development of the Young Child, as Expressed through Bodily Movement: I," *Journal of American Psychoanalytic Association* 19(4) (Oct., 1971), 763. See also Judith Kestenberg, "Suggestions for Diagnostic and Therapeutic Procedures in Movement Therapy," American Dance Therapy Association, *Second Annual Conference Proceedings* (Washington, D.C., 1967).

5. Martha Hargadin, "Relationships between Measures of Self-Actualization and Evaluation of Scope of Movement," Ph.D. dissertation, University of Southern California, Los Angeles, 1973.

6. Irmgard Bartenieff, "Dance Therapy: A New Profession or a Rediscovery of an Ancient Role of the Dance?," *Dance Scope* 7 (Fall–Winter, 1972–73), p. 15.

7. For opposing views on this subject, see Edward Zigler and Leslie Phillips, "Psychiatric Diagnosis: A Critique," *Journal of Abnormal and Social Psychology* 63 (1961), pp. 607–618. Also Frederick Kanfer and George Saslow, "Behavioral Analysis: An Alternative to Diagnostic Classification," *Archives of General Psychiatry* 12 (1965), pp. 529–538. Both sides of the issue are treated in Norman Sundberg, Leona Tyler, Julian Taplin, *Clinical Psychology: Expanding Horizons*, 2nd ed. (New York: Appleton-Century-Crofts, 1973), Appendix B.

Thus, how one perceives himself and others, and experiences the world about him, is expressed through the body.

Because many patients feel inadequate in communicating their feelings verbally, they rely to a large extent on nonverbal communication as a means of expression. Body actions are often used to convey emotions which are factual or symbolic expressions. Dance used as a therapeutic tool, with its emphasis on the body as a means of expression, can aid in the integration process. It offers the individual a means to experience and express the full range of human emotions, as well as a way of relating to the environment—or to other people when he is limited in verbal communication by the dynamics of his illness. The immediate goal of the dance therapy session then is to break through the isolation of the individual patients with movement, and help them to be able to accept another person without fear, even if only for a few minutes.[8]

The dance therapist focuses on the patient's movement patterns at that particular moment in time. It is the specific movement repertoire of the patient that the dance therapist relates to and interacts with through movement. Sessions are not prestructured; the dance therapist works with what unfolds as a result of the movement interaction.[9]

Dance therapy deals with personality as manifested in movement behavior. The therapist, acting as a catalyst, incorporates into his own movements the expressed quality of the patient's movements. This results in rapport with the patient; it enlarges and develops the movements so that a full range of feelings can then be expressed. Patterns are helped to alter or expand upon the movement patterns that exist, thereby effecting change by working through the movement and developing a broader movement repertoire.[10] It is through changes in postural motility that changes in sensory experiences also occur.[11]

Many processes occur in a dance therapy session. There is body integration—a feeling of how parts of the body are connected and that movement in one part of the body affects the total body. Further-

8. M. Chace, "Dance Therapy of the Mentally Ill," *Dance Magazine* (June, 1956), p. 38.

9. Claire Schmais and Elissa White, "Introduction to Dance Therapy." *Workshop in Dance Therapy: Its Research Potentials.* Proceedings of a Joint Conference by Research Department of Postgraduate Center, Committee on Research in Dance and American Dance Therapy Association (New York, 1970), p. 3.

10. *Ibid.*

11. L. Bender and F. Boas, "Creative Dance in Therapy," *American Journal of Orthopsychiatry* 11(2) (1941), pp. 235–245.

more, by using movement to get at feelings, inappropriate behavior can be eliminated. Patients are also helped to be aware of how their movements reflect their feelings or to recall earlier emotions and experiences.

Social interaction in dance therapy sessions allows even the most regressed and withdrawn patients to feel close to one another. Those who cannot tolerate a one-to-one relationship can collectively express feelings through movement. The group experience provides a supportive basis for group and individual expression. Movement allows the acting out of feelings which are not always socially acceptable in verbal transactions. Verbalization can and often does result from movement as patients relate to the various movement patterns. Earlier experiences are often evoked by specific movement sequences.

The defense of the psychotic patient's reaction to people in the environment has been shown to be such that initial contact is oftentimes more easily established by a nonverbal method of expression. With this in mind, the present study was undertaken to assess the changes in behavior during dance therapy sessions.

This study covers a three-month period (October 20, 1971, to January 12, 1972) in which Jay, the patient, was seen for one hour, once a week, for individual dance therapy sessions (twelve sessions). Aside from these weekly dance therapy sessions, the only other treatment offered to this patient was chemotherapy.

Medical History

This twenty-one-year-old black male patient has been raised from birth by his aunt. At the age of six his speech was still very slow, having just recently begun talking. It was upon the recommendation of the school psychologist that the patient was placed in a school for retarded children, where he remained for two years. His aunt described him as being shy, quiet, neat, and high-strung prior to his illness.

At seventeen the patient experienced a psychotic episode and stopped eating and talking. He was seen by a psychiatrist who felt that state psychiatric treatment was indicated. The patient attended Phipps Outpatient Clinic once a week over a six-month period.

May 20, 1971, the patient experienced another psychotic episode and returned to Phipps Clinic. His initial diagnosis at that time indicated mental retardation with possible EEG abnormality such as psychomotor variant. At that time the patient reportedly expressed vague fears although there were no hallucinations or delusions. The psychological diagnosis was catatonic schizophrenia and mental retardation.

On June 3, 1971, the patient, Jay, was admitted to the medical and surgical unit of Crownsville State Hospital. He was withdrawn, had delusional fears, and occasional psychotic episodes, and required intravenous feeding. His diagnosis at Crownsville is that of mental retardation with catatonic episode. Shortly thereafter Jay was transferred to another unit of the hospital. At the time this study was begun, Jay was being spoon fed and would go to the bathroom if someone led him. He reportedly had not spoken since his admittance to the hospital.

Psychological Evaluation

The results from the psychological tests (November, 1971) indicate that Jay is functioning at a mental age of four years, five months. His real potentials could not be determined because of his present condition. "The general impression is that we are dealing with a case of schizophrenia, catatonic type, withdrawn. The onset of the illness probably dates from the patient's childhood. The impairment in the intellectual functions could be the result of this mental illness rather than a congenital mental deficiency."

Medication

Jay began receiving 50 mg. librium upon his admittance to the medical and surgical unit of the hospital. When he was transferred to another unit of the hospital his medication was changed to 50 mg. tofranil twice a day. This was continued until August 16, when he began receiving 8 mg. tralofon twice a day along with other medication (not specified on chart). Jay remained on this until the first week in December, when all medication was terminated until January 1. In January he began receiving 50 mg. tofranil twice a day along with 100 mg. thorazine three times a day. Therefore, sessions 1 through 7 were with medication, 8 through 10 without medication, and sessions 11 and 12 with medication.

Procedure

In order to assess the changes in movement behavior, four different methods were used.

1. Each session was briefly summarized.

2. A movement observation scale, based on effort-shape analysis, was completed for sessions 1, 3, 5, 7, 9, 11, and 12. Thus using the movement patterns of session 1 as a baseline, changes in the patient's movement behavior were recorded and compared on a bi-weekly basis.

3. The movement observation scale was used to compare Jay's movement profile with that of the general population. This was done for sessions 1, 4, 8, and 12.

4. Movement factors were evaluated according to Davis' "Movement Diagnosis Scale"[12] at the beginning of the study and at the termination.

A copy of the Movement Observation Scale and the Movement Diagnosis Scale are in the Appendix.

Summary of Dance Therapy Sessions[13]

Session No. 1, October 20, 1971:

The goals of the first session were to establish a relationship between patient and therapist and for Jay to experience the potential of the things he was able to do. It was also hoped that he would build expectations for himself. The therapist, Sharon Chaiklin, worked specifically with his immediate handicaps—trying to move his limbs, head, to free his neck from tightness, and to use breathing to develop strength.

The patient kept his eyes closed for the entire session. At the end of the session when he looked into the monitor of the videotape equipment there was real directionality outward of his vision. He seemed surprised and delighted when he recognized himself on the screen. His movements were very limited and remained close to his body. All of the movements were very controlled and tense, so tense that it caused shaking in the arms. Jay's breathing was very shallow. He was unable to make a sound as he exhaled and the therapist was unable to feel the air being exhaled. The only strength observed was when pushing and pulling with the therapist and when he was hitting the tambourine.

From the movement patterns observed, the therapist and the observer felt that the patient was a catatonic schizophrenic and not

12. M. Davis, "Movement Characteristics of Hospitalized Psychiatric Patients," American Dance Therapy Association, *Fifth Annual Conference Proceedings* (Washington, D.C., 1970), pp. 25–45.

13. This article is based on a series of therapy sessions during which Arlynne Samuels was the observer and Sharon Chaiklin the therapist.

mentally retarded. There seemed to be a connection between what Jay was thinking and what he was doing. This was an active process. He was able to make a conscious attempt to initiate movements and not to imitate them as a retarded person does. There is motor impersistence in retardates—the movement starts and suddenly becomes limp, the intensity cannot be sustained. Jay did not exhibit this or other characteristics such as hyperrotation, hyperextension, fragmentation which appears as uncoordinated and unrelated, lack of rotation of limbs.[14]

Schizophrenic movement patterns which Jay exhibited were fragmentation of movements, fixation in one plane, and reduced mobility.

Session No. 2, October 27, 1971:

Jay started the session by initiating the breathing exercise. His breathing was deeper; the therapist could feel the air being exhaled. His eyes remained closed during most of the session although this did not stop him from leading in walking forward and backward while holding hands facing each other. He was able to use a lot of strength in pushing and pulling, so much in fact, that his arms began to shake. He was unable to get his hands close enough together to clap but was able to push the therapist's hands to make hers clap. The movements still remained very close to the body. Jay was unable to move his feet while sitting in a chair; he wasn't even able to lift them. Aside from shaking it, Jay still did not consciously move his right arm. It remained bound and held rigidly.

Prior to the session Jay was helping to move a coffee table out of the room. In order to do this he had to bend down. This he did very slowly and in a fragmented way. One of the legs of the coffee table broke and Jay suppressed a laugh as the others reacted with laughter. His apparent understanding of the humorous situation prompted the observer and the therapist to request a psychological evaluation to see if it supported their feelings—that the patient was not retarded but appeared so because of lack of education and mental illness. It was felt that he had been mentally ill since childhood and that this arrested his development.

Session No. 3, November 3, 1971:

The breathing was stronger and easier to hear now, although it still lacked rhythm. At times during the session Jay was able to take deep breaths when he felt he needed it. His eyes remained open approximately one-third of the session. There was still some involuntary shak-

14. M. Davis, "Movement Characteristics."

ing of the arms. At one point in the session Jay was able to move in perfect synchrony. This happened when the therapist was playing a calypso record. His entire body was involved in the movement; his hips moved, his knees were bent, he moved his arms in perfect rhythm, and his head was relaxed. Instead of moving in a fragmented way he was able to move in unison.

Using a stretch rope Jay was able to pull his arms out to the side, away from each other. He was not able to use the same pulling movement vertically, although he did manage to twist the upper part of his body against the lower.

Session No. 4, November 10, 1971:

Jay took more initiative during this session. He was able to lead the therapist around the room. Much strength was utilized in pushing and pulling, although he favored the left hand and arm. Yet, he was able to use both hands equally. His movements are still very bound. Jay was able to use his right hand when he beat the tambourine. The movements were strong and quick and in time to the music. This was the first time that Jay had used quickness.

Jay's rhythm is improving. This could be seen in his breathing which is more continuous and even in rhythm and when swinging his arms. Here he didn't stop the flow of the movement as abruptly but was able to maintain it. When using the streamers, his right arm began to move in rhythm with the rest of his body.

Jay's walk is still very stilted although there has been a slight improvement. There is less waddling from side to side and he is able to take larger steps. He still experiences difficulty in attempting something that requires total body involvement.

Jay's eyes remained open exactly one-half of the session today. During the time that his eyes were closed it appeared to be less a means of withdrawal but rather an indulging in experiencing movement sensations. The head and neck remained rigid except when doing the calypso. There was more facial expression today. When he was pushing, his face was set in a grimace. He seemed to enjoy feeling his own strength. Toward the end of the session he was smiling and humming faintly to the music. At this time he was also able to lean against the therapist and sway with her in time to the music. When someone gave him a soda at the end of the session he said, "Thank you."

Session No. 5, November 17, 1971:

Jay's breathing has become much deeper. One can see his back ex-

panding as he sucks in the air. He was able to blow out the air with
a good bit of force. Most of the session was spent working with the
hoops. He moved with less boundness as he threw the hoops up in
the air and caught them. He was also able to push the hoops forward
for momentum. Jay's body was still very fragmented when he bent
over to pick up the hoops. It was as though he had to gather himself
together before bending.

His eyes remained open for most of the session as he had to watch
where the hoops were going.

It was during this session that he began to release the tension in
his left arm. Jay and the therapist were each holding an end of the
hoop. The therapist was twisting the hoop in order to get Jay to rotate
his arm. When he relaxed the arm and rotated it, it could be felt
by her.

Session No. 6, November 24, 1971:
Jay's breathing is much stronger now and he is able to make a loud
noise when he blows the air out. The rhythm of his breathing is still
erratic though.

Jay was beginning to assert himself during this session. He was able
to stop the therapist from moving him further than he desired, and
when she attempted to pull him over, he pulled her up as a way of
saying no.

When pushing he was able to use more strength than he has used
before. His whole body became involved as he leaned into the movement. Balloons were used to help evoke movements. The fragmentation could be observed quite clearly in his fingers as Jay attempted to
hold the balloon. His fingers were so rigid that he was unable to
curve them around the balloon in order to grasp it. When the balloon
would slip from his fingers, his body jerked as he tried to catch it.
Because of this he had difficulty in picking the balloon up when he
dropped it.

This was the first time that Jay used his right arm. While working
with the streamers, he was able to make very large circles in the air
and moved with more directionality. His body naturally moved in
synchrony as he moved the streamers around his body.

When using the hoops, Jay initiated a game with the therapist. He
kept blocking her each time she tried to get past him. He began to
use quickness as he tried to move from one side to another to stop
her. Through his facial expression one could see him trying to figure
out a way of stopping her.

Jay was beginning to use his mouth and jaw muscles quite a bit during the session. It was predicted that he would begin talking shortly.

Session No. 7, December 1, 1971:

As Jay entered the room he was smiling. The therapist said that he had good news and asked if he would like to tell what it was. He didn't respond but kept staring at the clock on the wall. After a while he said that he couldn't hear her, that her voice "passed over" him. He said that it went over his head. It was during this session that Jay began to make choices.

Another characteristic of the session which became a part of the sessions to follow was the development of a game. Jay blocked the therapist's path so that she could not get by. He had to move fairly quickly to out-guess where she would move to next.

Toward the end of the session Jay began to look depressed when the two of them were swaying to the music. His body was less rigid and his face appeared softer.

The most salient features of the session were Jay's making a choice concerning what he wanted to do and his talking.

Session No. 8, December 8, 1971:

Jay moved very little during this session when compared to the other sessions. His movements were much slower than they have previously been. There was even a change in his breathing; it wasn't as strong as it had been. In total, he seemed to be depressed.

Near the beginning of the session the therapist asked him to take her hand, which he did for the first time. She was trying to get him to take leadership. He initiated a movement while holding each other's hands and then continuing to hold hands he stopped. The two of them remained still for a few minutes and then the therapist asked, "What do you want, Jay?" One tear trickled down his face. He remained silent and let go of her hand a few minutes later. During this brief period one could see changes occurring in his body even though he was standing still. His upper back became more relaxed, his head lifted and some of the tension disappeared in his face, thus giving him a softer appearance.

Session No. 9, December 15, 1971:

Almost as soon as he entered the room Jay began to focus on the clock, and continued to stare at it for ten to fifteen minutes. As the therapist tried to divert his gaze by blocking his view, he began to laugh, suppressing it as best as he could.

As she began to get closer to Jay, he began to move back. At times he put out his hand to stop her. This became a game where he would try to sneak around her. At one point he faked her out and ran across the room. She kept confronting him and backing him up. Smiling and looking at her, he planned his next move and quickly darted to the other side of the room. Again, much of the rigidity was gone from his face.

Session No. 10, December 22, 1971:

At the beginning of the session Jay talked about going home for Christmas. When he began to talk his eyes fluttered, his mouth quivered, and his jaw moved in short, jerky movements. He focused his attention on the clock and when the therapist blocked his view he would often times startle and occasionally close his eyes.

He was handed a ball and asked to throw it. He held it for a long time and then walked over and handed it to her, thus making his decision as to what he wanted to do. They played the "space game" where the therapist kept blocking his path. His speed increased as he tried to sneak around her and outrun her. He didn't move too much during the session and seemed depressed. He became withdrawn toward the end of the session.

Session No. 11, January 5, 1972:

The salient feature of this session was Jay's manipulation of the therapist. As she tried to get him to twist his upper body by helping him to move his shoulders around, he resisted her and smiled. She continued and he, still smiling, exerted a lot of strength to move against her. Again he was consciously making her aware of his desires. At this point he was very bound and constricted as he resisted her moving him.

They played the "space game" again but this time when he got past her he ran into the adjoining room. As he tried to get around her he tiptoed about (she had closed her eyes) slowly to try and trick her. This was the first time he used the balls of his feet. Prior to this he constantly resisted moving his legs or feet. He was beginning to be spontaneous in trying to find ways of moving around her. When a chair was blocking his path, he picked up one leg and tried to step over it. He kept trying to accomplish this for a few minutes, backed away from the chair slowly as though about to give up, and then suddenly ran to the chair and jumped over it. To move that suddenly and that quickly and with that much energy was a major accomplishment for Jay. Another important fact was that he was very much aware of his subtle movements as well as hers.

Session No. 12, January 12, 1972:

Jay's body was still out of alignment with the head tilted to the left side as the body tilts to the right. He was able to sway and walk in time to the music. His breathing was much stronger and he was able to use his breath to blow the therapist out of his way during the "space game." She began imitating him by assuming the same stance and movements as him. It was apparent from observing that when feelings began to surface, he would consciously change his way of moving to stop the feelings. He was beginning to learn how to avoid certain feelings without withdrawing into himself and closing out the environment. During the follow-the-leader game, Jay seemed very much aware of his subtle changes as well as the therapist's.

Movement Observation Scale

A system of movement observation was needed in order to assess changes in the patient's movement behavior. Most of the research in body language deals with the cultural and interactional aspects of movement behavior and not the personality or character of the individual as expressed by his own particular style of movement. A system of movement analysis which would describe an individual's style of moving—its shadings and tone, the qualitative changes in movement —was needed. Effort/Shape Analysis, a notation system developed by Rudolf Laban, and expanded by his colleague Warren Lamb, offers such a system. Because of its applicability in observing, recording, and assessing changes in any aspect of human movement, Effort/ Shape Analysis is currently being used in the fields of psychology, dance, dance therapy, anthropology, and child development studies.

A scale, based primarily on the effort-shape system, was developed by Samuels and Chaiklin in order to study movement as it occurs in everyday activity, during interpersonal interactions, and during dance therapy sessions. It was during this present study that the opportunity arose to see if the scale was workable and/or needed to be refined or changed. Some minor changes were made during the course of this study. The movement variables of the scale and their operational definitions may be found in the appendix.

Changes Measured by the Movement Observation Scale

The following movement qualities, observed during the first session, were used as a baseline for comparison for the following sessions:

Effort-Flow—This was given a rating of 1 in Session 1 and remained at 1 during the entire study. Thus, Jay's movements remained very bound.

Efforts

Quick—Jay did not exhibit this element until Session 5. It increased to a rating of 3 by Session 11.

Strong—This increased from a rating of 1 during Session 1 to a rating of 5 by Session 12.

Planes—Jay was only moving in the vertical plane at the beginning of the study. By Session 3 he had begun to move in the horizontal plane also.

Kinesphere—This increased from 1 in Session 1 to the maximum of 5 during Session 5. The areas of space around the body increased from merely using space only in the middle and forward ranges to using space above, below, and to the side of the body.

Areas of Movement—This was limited to the hands and arms in Session 1. By Session 7 he was beginning to move his feet.

Eye Contact—This increased from 1 in Session 1 to 4 by Session 4.

Trunk Involvement—In Session 1 Jay was using his trunk in one unit. In Session 3 he was able to move the upper half of the trunk separately from the lower half and to move his trunk congruently.

Tension Areas—While tension still remained in the same areas, there was a lessening of tension as time went on.

Rhythm—Jay's body was dyssynchronous in the beginning session. By Session 5 he was able to move in synchrony; this further increased to a rating of 3 by Session 11.

Energy Level—There was so little movement in Session 1 that it was difficult to get a sense of any energy used. By Session 11 his energy level had increased to a rating of 3.

Amount of Expressiveness—This increased from a rating of 1 to a rating of 3 by Session 9.

Kind of Expression—There was an increase from 1 in Session 1 to 3 by Session 7.

Frequency in Spontaneity—There was hardly any spontaneity exhibited in Session 1. By Session 11 the rating had increased to 3.

Relating to Others—In Session 1, Jay was very withdrawn and was given a rating of 1. By Session 5 he was able to relate to the therapist, thus increasing the rating to 3.

During the first session he wasn't able to initiate movements, but by Session 9 this had increased to a rating of 3.

Comparison of Jay's Movements with that of the General Population

This was done for Sessions 1, 4, 8, and 12. Because of his illness, on a larger comparative scope, many of the subtle changes would not have been noted. Therefore, the previously described sessions were rated in comparison to his own movement behavior. However, when he was rated in comparison to the general population, changes in the following areas occurred:

Efforts

Quick—Increase from no use of quickness to a rating of 2.

Strong—This increased from 1 to 3.

Kinesphere—This element increased from 1 to 2.

Eye Contact—This increased from 1 to almost a rating of 3.

Energy Level—There was an increase from no energy to a rating of 2.

Amount of Expressiveness—This showed an increase from 1 to 2.

Kind of Expression—There was an increase from 1 to 2.

Frequency of Spontaneity—Increase of 1 to 2.

Relating to Others—Responsiveness to others increased from 1 to 2, initiation increased from 1 to 2.

Movement Diagnostic Scale

This movement scale is based on movement characteristics which are frequently seen in hospitalized patients and rarely seen in the general population. The scale is divided into eight factors. Using the scale, Jay was rated at the beginning and at the end of the study. While there was no decrease or increase in the number of movement factors during the twelve sessions, each of the items which were observable in Jay decreased in intensity. Thus improvements were seen in each of the individual items. A copy of the Movement Diagnostic Scale and those items observed in Jay can be found in the appendix.

Conclusion

When Jay first started dance therapy he was not talking, was extremely bound, barely moving, and kept his eyes closed about 80 percent of the time. However, he seemed to have motivation to work.

The first sessions were spent in trying to expand his movements, introduce new ways of moving, and establish some relationship built on respect. Through the use of props such as ribbon sticks, tambourine, hoops, and a ball, he began to move more and developed more eye focus. Time was spent with him to develop strength in breathing so that he could be more aware of himself, his ability to control his own body, and establish a sense of strength.

As he worked on these, his ability to keep his eyes open and not shut out his environment increased. He was able to use both arms to manipulate props. He began to show use of strength in throwing, and quickness. He also began to speak.

As the weeks passed, the sessions shifted from just movement into a responsive relationship with the therapist. He began to show initiative and spontaneity in developing games. He delighted in teasing and resisting. In pushing and pulling games he made use of a great deal of strength.

One of the unexplained events had been his great fascination with a wall clock in the room where they worked. He spent a great deal of time looking at it, trying to pass the therapist to reach it, and looking around her to see it. Some of this became a game in avoiding the therapist.

There were a few moments when intense feeling came through nonverbally. During one session tears were elicited—during another, the same feeling came close but was avoided through the use of movement.

A closer, trusting relationship between him and the therapist developed.

His sense of humor came through in frequent smiling and the teasing games he developed.

He used his strength easily, but still found it hard to move more than within a limited space, with very limited use of the body and limbs.

He needs a full program to stimulate his senses and offer situations in which he can achieve without too many demands placed on him.

Addendum (March 5, 1972)

Since the series of sessions outlined in this paper, Jay has continued the weekly dance therapy sessions. The room was changed to the dance therapy room which is more private and has mats.

During one of the sessions, the "space game" shifted when Jay decided to prevent the therapist from getting a chair which she was using to divide the room. In this situation he was forced to deal with the quickness and subtle shifts in movement of the therapist. He was successful in his quick shifts around the chair and prevented the therapist from reaching it.

The next two sessions were spent using the floor mat. It was my purpose to help him shift from the resisting games toward a co-operative effort in working toward less body tension. By initiating an entirely new approach, he had no previous set toward it. We worked on getting his head and neck to turn, his arms to swing to the horizontal in line with his shoulders, and his legs to move. This was done by both actual manipulation by the therapist and his own efforts in releasing the boundness.

After this second session the therapist told him about a proposed news videotape and asked if he would be willing to be filmed. It was explained that he would need to sign the release. He replied in a way that indicated willingness. He was able to sign his initials.

The next session was used on the mat, and using the ribbon sticks. The session after was the one taped. During it he was about as free as he had ever been in the arms, and was able for the first time to lift them longitudinally while standing. He initiated neck movements to turn the head, although on a very small scale. There was much inter-actional movement with the therapist able to move in much closer than previously.

Movement Observation Scale

Arlynne Samuels and Sharon Chaiklin

Effort-Flow (tension of the movement)

Bound _____ Free
    1   5

Free _____ Bound
    1   5

Does it change from free to bound _____

Does it change from bound to free _____

Burst flow _____

Sustained _____

Efforts

Space:

Direct (straight, undeviating, channeled) _____
                                           1   5

Indirect (spiraling, flexible) _____
                        1   5

Time:

Slow (sustained, lingering) _____
                    1   5

Quick (sudden, instantaneous) _____
                        1   5

Force:

Strong (forceful, vigorous) _____
                  1   5

Light (weightless, buoyant) _____
                1   5

Shape-Flow (movements occurring toward or away from the body)

In to out _____

Out to in _____

Shape

Rising (ascending) _____

Sinking (descending) _____

Widening (spreading, expanding) _____

Narrowing _____

Advancing (progressing forward) _____

Retreating (withdrawing) _____

Path in Space

One phasic (linear movement using only one plane) _____

Reversal _____

Two phasic (curved, uses two planes) _____

Sculptured (spiraled, three planes) _____

Planes

	Primary Stress	Secondary Stress
Vertical _____	Up and down _____	Side to side _____
Horizontal _____	Side to side _____	Forward/bkwd _____
Sagittal _____	Forward/bkwd _____	Up and down _____

Body Attitude (the qualities which are maintained in the body, out of which movement occurs)

Narrow _____

Neutral _____

Wide _____

Sunk _____

Other _____

Kinesphere (the limits of an individual's space around his body)

Small _____ Large
     1   5

Specific Areas:

High _____ Forward _____

Middle _____ Side _____

Low _____ Back _____

Gesture (movement of one part of the body)/*Posture* (movements which
      spread through and involve the entire body)

Gesture _____
     1   5

Posture _____
     1   5

Begins posturally to gesture _____

Begins gesturally to posture _____

Ratio of change _____

Area of Body in which Most Movement Occurs

Hands _____

Feet _____

Legs _____

Arms _____

Head _____

Trunk _____

Eye contact

None _____ Total
     1   5

Trunk Involvement (how trunk area is used)

One unit _____

One unit, vertical stress _____

Two units _____

Two unit-top rigid _____ Bottom rigid _____

Body axis spreading (opening, widening) _____

Upper against lower with twist _____

Upper against lower without twist _____

Is trunk being used congruently _____ Incongruently _____

Does not apply _____

Tension Areas

Face _____ Mouth _____ Jaw _____

Neck _____

Shoulders _____

Chest _____

Back _____

Midsection _____

Pelvic _____

Arms _____

Hands _____

Fingers _____

Legs _____

Rhythm (Synchrony of body parts)

Dissynchronous ——————— Synchronous
            1   5

Energy Level

———————
1   5

Amount of Expressiveness (quantitative expression of feelings through movement)

Limited ——————— Extensive
          1   5

Kind of Expression (qualitative)

———————
1   5

Frequency of Spontaneity

———————
1   5

Relating to Others

Unresponsive ——————— Responsive
              1   5

Does Not Initiate ——————— Initiates
              1   5

List of Movement Factors Abstracted from the

Movement Diagnostic Scale by Martha Davis[15]

NOTE: Items marked with an asterisk (*) were observed in Jay.

Fragmentation

1. Impulsive erratic postural shifts; starting or stopping abruptly or erratic impulses within the phrase.
2. Segmentation (use of one part, a pause or clear separation before movement in another part) which is so severe that in effect the body becomes fragmented into parts.
3. Movement occurs sporadically in different parts during a phrase with no clear sequence or fluent connections.
4. Fingers and/or palm hyperextended; flexion-extension only at the knuckles and/or wrist; with a neutral tonus.
5. Two or more parts simultaneously going in different planes (spatial fragmentation).
6. Erratic fluctuations in the effort-flow pattern.
7. Severe contradictions in the effort-flow characteristics of the body in stillness.
8. Different rhythms simultaneously occurring in movement of different parts of the body which appear unrelated.
* 9. The sequence of weight shifts is disorganized; that is, one part shifts, then another in a different direction, and so on, such that the body doesn't come to a clear balanced rest.

Diffusion

1. Movement is spatially diffuse and unclear (i.e., no clear straight, round, or three-dimensional paths, no clear transitions, difficult to discern spatial phrases) in either short phrases or long phrases.
2. Continuous diffuse effort patterns; effort-flow and possibly some effort qualities "running on," difficult to determine distinct phrases and any clear build up or decrease in intensity. No clear endings to the movement.
3. An action is not completed before person starts a new action, no pause or transition but a kind of diffuse overlapping of actions.

Exaggeration

1. Exaggerated, overstressed, too-large postural shifts.
2. More postural movements than gestures.
3. Large, exaggerated, though spatially clear, movements throughout a phrase, that is, no modulation of the size of the movement within a phrase.

15. *Ibid.*

Fixed, Invariant

1. Repetitive movement of an isolated part of the body; the dynamics are the same throughout; the body part appears unrelated to rest of the body and seems to "go by itself."
2. Movement in the sagittal plane only.
* 3. Movement in one plane only per phrase.
4. Two-phasic or cyclic movement only.
5. Repetition of one or two effort qualities in an unvarying way; the movement may stay intense but with no build up or decrease in intensity; the phrase is clear and has a clear beginning and end; it is often two-phasic. That is, there is no modulation in the intensity of the movement with only one quality at a time or a combination of two qualities.
6. Frozen gestures: an action apparently related to some expression or conventional action but highly repetitive and each time dynamically the same.
7. Ritual: an activity performed in a set order of actions; each time done dynamically the same way.

Bound, Active Control

* 1. The body attitude is rigidly held; there is some bound quality and rigid tonus.
* 2. Parts are still for long periods, actively held and restricted.
* 3. Fixed and rigidly held finger constellation or position.
* 4. The movement is too small or sparse to determine its spatial character; has an actively held and restricted quality.
* 5. The effort-flow is often bound or very bound.
6. The movement is a series of segmented gestures which are spatially clear and controlled because of even bound flow and either directness or lightness.

Flaccid, Limp

1. The body attitude is flaccid, inert, limp.
2. Hand goes limp and into "zero" flow at the end of a gesture.
3. Body parts in stillness show flaccidity, complete limpness, and giving into gravity.

Reduced Mobility

Serious Features:

* 1. Body attitude immobile and set, tonus is neutral, not clearly bound or free.
* 2. Virtually no active movement of the trunk; minimal weight shifts in standing up, sitting down, or walking; trunk only passively follows limbs in action.
3. Gestural trunk movement only.

 4. No movement in head or limbs; person barely walks.
* 5. Head absolutely still as person talks.
* 6. Head and shoulders held still, eyes fixed forward as person walks.
* 7. Little or no movement of face apart from eyes.
* 8. The movement is too small or sparse to determine its spatial character; it has an inert quality.
* 9. Fixed shape or position held against gravity for long period; it is not resting on something or holding up an object.
 10. In stillness the body parts are neutral or "zero" in flow, neither clearly limp or held.
*11. No clear grasp or closing or whole hand.

Borderline Features:
* 1. Trunk is maintained as one unit, no twist.
* 2. No active, successive spreading or movement through the trunk or part of it (that is, movement is only simultaneous).
* 3. No active initiation of movement in lower trunk.
 4. No active initiation of movement in the upper trunk.
 5. "Fleeting" postural movement only.
 6. Single phases of postural movement only.
 7. Single and double phases of postural movement only.
* 8. Only distal parts of body move (hands, feet, head, forearms).
* 9. No successive movement in limbs.

Dynamic, Vital (a high score here indicates mental health)
 1. High rate of postural movement.
 2. Spatial complexity (that is, shaping, clear directions, curved transitions, diagonal movements, and so on) occur in different body parts and throughout the body.
 3. A wide range of effort-flow within a free to very bound range; not even or neutral in character.
 4. Effort qualities frequently visible throughout the body.
 5. Presence of different effort dynamics which are clearly observable and frequent.
 6. Has clear relationship to weight in gestures of head and limbs; either strength or lightness; can give into gravity or make an active impact; varied flow patterns.
 7. Has clear placement of or relation to weight in the trunk, can give into gravity or be forceful in trunk shifts, in sitting down, and so forth.

Bibliography

Bender, L., and F. Boas, "Creative Dance in Therapy." *American Journal of Orthopsychiatry* (1941), 11, No. 2.

Chace, M. "Dance Therapy of the Mentally Ill." *Dance Magazine* (June, 1956), 6.

Davis, M. Advanced Effort-Shop Workshop. New York, April, 1971.

———. "Movement Characteristics of Hospitalized Psychiatric Patients," in American Dance Therapy Association, *Fifth Annual Conference Proceedings*. Washington, D.C., 1970.

Dell, C. *A Primer for Movement Description*. New York: Dance Notation Bureau Inc., 1970.

Laban, R. *The Mastery of Movement*. London: McDonald and Evans, 1960.

Lamb, W., and D. Turner. *Management Behavior*. New York: International Universities Press, 1969.

Schmais, Claire, and Elissa White, "Introduction to Dance Therapy." *Workshop in Dance Therapy: Its Research Potentials*. Proceedings of a Joint Conference by Research Department of Postgraduate Center, Committee on Research in Dance and American Dance Therapy Association. New York, 1970.

MARTHA DAVIS, Ph.D.

Movement Characteristics of Hospitalized Psychiatric Patients

Dr. Martha Davis, sage amongst movement philosophers, reveals a depth of scholarship and breadth of vision in her writings unequaled by other movement therapy researchers. In collaboration with Irmgard Bartenieff and other like-minded colleagues, she carves order out of the chaos which stems from our culture's neglect of movement and mind.

Davis's basic tool is developed from Rudolf Laban's effort-shape analysis. She describes effort-shape as an objective "system for observing and defining the elements of movement style."[1] This system has several advantages for her. It uses a limited number of descriptive symbols—twenty-four in all. It seems reliable for research purposes.[2] Finally, it is not incompatible with labanotation, a widely circulated dance notation system also invented by Rudolf Laban. Movement therapists are more likely to be acquainted with this observational framework than they are with schemes of Eshkol-Wachmann, Birdwhistell, Condon, Hall, Benesh, and so forth.

Davis's essay presents a sharp contrast to the points of view expressed in Part 1. She argues that "movement within the framework of effort-shape analysis is considered an organic process."[3] As does Bartenieff, she sees effort-shape analysis as "indicative of mental and emotional processes."[4] Bizarre movement is considered a symptom of mental instability rather than a distorted but learned form of behavior.

Reprinted by permission from American Dance Therapy Association, *Fifth Conference Proceedings* (1970), pp. 25–45. All rights reserved.

1. Martha Davis, *Methods of Perceiving Patterns of Small-Group Behavior* (New York: Dance Notation Bureau, 1970), p. 51.

2. This is the only study of an effort-shape movement scale which seeks to determine inter-observer correspondence. It was first published in the American Dance Therapy Association, *Fifth Annual Conference Proceedings* (Washington, D.C., 1970).

3. Davis, *Methods of Perceiving Patterns,* p. 51.

4. Irmgard Bartenieff, *Effort Observation and Effort Assessment in Rehabilitation* (New York: Dance Notation Bureau, 1965), p. 7.

This essay is the culmination of a five-year study to validate empirically three assumptions formulated in 1965. At that time Davis mused that effort-shape analysis possessed great potential. She claimed it:

1. is a replicable technique for describing, measuring, and classifying human movement;
2. describes patterns of movement which are consistent for an individual and distinguish him from others;
3. delineates a behavioral dimension related to neurophysiological and psychological processes.[5]

This essay expands her investigation of these three assumptions. First, Davis concludes that there is an interobserver correspondence of .783 for ratings on all items. Although she compares in this essay similar types of individual movement patterns to similar psychological diagnoses, Davis retains her belief that individual profiles are as personal as fingerprints or dental imprints. Finally, she concludes that schizophrenics have unique movement characteristics in common— features which increase in bizarreness as the client is labeled more and more "sick." These decrease as his condition improves. Subject to multiple interpretations depending on whether bizarre movements are assumed to be primarily symptoms or learned behaviors, her finding implies a significant potential role for movement therapy.

M.N.C.

It has been documented for over a century that certain characteristics of physical movement relate to specific mental illnesses (cf. Rennie, 1941; Wittenborn, 1962). The "waxy flexibility" of the catatonic patient, the grimacing of a hebephrenic, the sluggish, the heavy manner of someone in a psychotic depression are symptoms often noted when the disorders are described. Reich (1949) and Lowen (1967) have presented rich clinical descriptions of individual patterns of muscle "armoring" and physical constriction as they relate to psychopathology. Condon (1968), in detailed film analysis, describes the lack of "self-synchrony" in the movement of schizophrenic patients. The dance therapist in a hospital setting knows perhaps better than anyone how the movement patterns reflect the patient's psychiatric disorder.

The current study has resulted from five years of research in movement patterns of hospitalized psychiatric patients. To study individual

---

5. Irmgard Bartenieff and Martha Davis, *Effort-Shape, Analysis of Movement: The Unity of Expression and Function* (New York: Dance Notation Bureau, 1965), p. 4.

movement patterns and movement behavior in group interaction, Irmgard Bartenieff and the author applied the effort-shape system for analyzing and recording movement style developed first by Rudolf Laban. This method involves systematic description of how one moves in terms of spatial characteristics, "effort"—or dynamic patterns, body part initiation, and so on. The instrument for analyzing patients' movement developed for the current study is in effect a summary of the movement characteristics I have observed over the last five years in many hospitalized patients but rarely in the general population.

It is a preliminary study in systematically analyzing the movement patterns of schizophrenic patients and comparing them with psychiatric evaluations. It focuses solely on the individual, although I will present some observations of how the movement patterns vary in interaction. Further, it focuses on "movement pathology," which of course does not do justice to the richness and complexity of the patient's movement patterns nor to the patient himself. However, the distortions, rigidities, limitations, and so on, in movement of a patient are part of the dance therapist's focus and concern. We need to be able to describe them carefully, to understand their significance, and to find ways of moving with the patient which help him to change them.

The study is based on the following assumptions:

1. That there are movement characteristics which are unique to schizophrenia, and more specifically, that there are movement patterns which correspond to various kinds of behavior-disorganization, stereotyping, regression, and so on—in the illness.
2. That these movement features increase (that is, appear or develop from less pathological characteristics) as the patient becomes seriously ill and decrease as he improves.

Procedure

A rating instrument based on some seventy movement characteristics which in the author's experience were often seen in hospitalized patients and rarely in the general population was developed and pretested.[6] Three movement observers were trained in the use of the

---

6. A few items in the scale such as "lack of successiveness" and "trunk one-unit" were adapted from the choreometric coding sheet, in Irmgard Bartenieff and Forrestine Paulay, "The Choreometric Coding Book" in *Folk Song Style and Culture,* Alan Lomax, ed. (Washington, D.C.: American Association for the Advancement of Science, 1968).

"Movement Diagnostic Scale." All three, Elissa White, Claire Schmais, and Miriam Berger, were dance therapists who had studied Laban's effort-shape analysis of movement from one to three years.

Before observing patients in the study sample, each item in the scale was labeled as either "serious" or "borderline," based on an a priori judgment of which features were most likely to be clear indicators of serious psychopathology and which were likely to occur in patients but were not necessarily unique to schizophrenic illness. That is, it was hypothesized that the borderline features could be seen in a general population and are not necessarily schizophrenic or even borderline, as the term is used clinically. However, when they occur in any number with the "serious" items, they contribute to the pathological picture and in some cases might be early signs of the illness.

Twenty-two patients, thirteen women and nine men, were observed during individual psychotherapy sessions behind a one-way screen. There was no sound and in almost every case the observers had not seen or heard about the patients before the first observation.

The setting for this study was an intensive treatment unit in a state hospital in which first-year psychiatric residents and psychology interns are trained. The unit has a mixed population of psychoneurotic, acute and chronic schizophrenics, and adolescents with behavior problems and/or schizophrenia. While the observers knew the population was mixed diagnostically, they did not know the patients' diagnoses, how many came directly to the unit on admission, how many were first hospitalizations, and so on.

Ten residents and three psychology interns participated in the study and selected which of their patients could be seen. The patients consented to be seen in therapy behind the screen as part of a research project, but they did not know it involved observation of movement patterns. One or two patients of each therapist were seen twice about three weeks apart. There was no rule as to when the patients were first seen but generally it was in the first month of their stay on the unit. The mean age of the group was 25.9, with a range from fourteen to forty-five years old. Fourteen of the twenty-two were single. There was a fairly even mixture of Negro, Jewish, Irish, and Italian backgrounds.

Approximately half of the sessions were observed by two or more movement analysts and almost all of them were seen by the author. During the session the observers made notes of what occurred nonverbally, what movement characteristics were seen, and filled out the scale immediately after the observation. They also summarized their impressions and made predictions as to diagnosis and principle dynamics and conflicts. The main investigator then tallied the results of each scale as to the number of "serious" items and the total number of items checked. She also wrote up movement descriptions and interpretations for each patient based on the scaled items, the notes made during observation, and the final impressions of the observers. (See appendix for a sample of one of these movement summaries.)

After the movement analyses and final reports were finished, information on the patients' background, psychiatric history, hospital treatment, medication, and diagnosis was collected.

Movement Factors
The movement scale is organized according to restrictions and uses of the body, spatial patterns, effort dynamics, and special composites of these. However it could also be organized according to factors such as "fragmentation," "reduced mobility," and so on. For example, there are kinds of fragmentation in body part sequence, in spatial patterns, and several kinds of fragmentation in effort or dynamic patterns. While the idea of such factors was kept in mind throughout the study, they were not isolated and analyzed in depth until after the bulk of the study was finished. On an intuitive basis the scale was divided into eight factors, each composed of different items. The factors, with an example of a typical item within each, are as follows:

Fragmentation:	Movement occurs sporadically in different parts during a phrase with no clear sequence or fluent connections.
Diffusion:	Movement is spatially diffuse and unclear, that is, no clear straight, round, or three-dimensional paths; no clear transitions, difficult to discern spatial phrases.
Exaggeration:	More postural movements than gestures.
Fixed, invariant	Movement in one plane only per phrase.
Bound, active control:	Parts are still for long periods, actively held and restricted.
Flaccid, limp:	Body parts in stillness show flaccidity, complete limpness, and giving into gravity.
Reduced mobility:	Head absolutely still as person talks (serious). No active initiation of movement in lower trunk (border).
Dynamic, vital:	Presence of different effort dynamics which are clearly observable and frequent.

A high score on the last factor is actually considered an indication of health.

Medication
It was impossible to control for medication effects. However, given the medication histories of the patients, some correlations were made between:

1. amount of phenothizine medication at the time of session 1 and severity of movement disturbance.
2. amount of phenothizine medication at time of session 1 and degree of reduced mobility.

The second comparison was made because phenothizines are known to have extrapyramidal effects such as "parkinsonian-like" rigidity and reduction in movement (Kline, 1965). Almost all of the patients were on phenothizines, primarily thorazine, for at least one week before being seen. Each of these patients was rated according to the amount of medication they were receiving at the time of the first session. The rating was on a scale from 0 or no phenothizine medication to 5 or over 1500 mg/day.

Results

Reliability
Observer reliability here is the comparison between the author's ratings and each of the other three observers for half of the sessions. There was a correlation coefficient of .783 for ratings on all items and .877 for the total number of serious items check. Considering that this is generally good agreement and that the author observed all of the patients, her ratings were used in the further analysis of the data. Correlation coefficients between scores on the first session and those in the follow-up were .581 for the total number of items and .679 for the serious items.

Comparison of Movement Pathology with
Diagnosis and Number of Hospitalizations
Presumably the more features checked, the more serious is the illness because the scale is composed of "pathological" movement characteristics. The patients were ranked according to the total number of serious items over both sessions. If the group is divided into those

patients with serious features in both sessions (group 1) and those with no serious features in one or both sessions (group 2), the following characteristics emerge:

1. There are no significant age, sex, or ethnic differences between the two groups, although those in group 1 tend to be unmarried.
2. There is no significant correlation between presence of "serious" features and more than one hospitalization or diagnosis of chronic schizophrenia.

However, within the serious items there are ten which are considered types of fragmentation in movement. Presence of fragmentation in either session correlated significantly with more than two hospitalizations and/or a diagnosis of chronic schizophrenia.

Movement Fragmentation vs. Number of Hospitalizations and/or Chronic Diagnosis

	Movement Fragmentation	None
Three or more hosps. and/or chronic diagnosis	6	1
One or two hosps., not chronic	2	13

$x = 11.31$ (significance at .01 = 6.635)

Medication

There was no significant correlation between a high amount of medication and a high score on movement pathology in general. Neither was there any significant trend between amount of medication and presence of serious vs. borderline features, or between those patients with fragmentation and those without. However, each patient was rated according to amount of medication on a 0-5 scale and these ratings were correlated with their 0-5 point ratings for reduced mobility. The correlation coefficient between amount of medication and degree of reduced mobility in Session 1 is .487. This suggests that extreme forms of rigidity are not the only kinds of extrapyramidal effects, and the relations between phenothizine medication and reduced mobility in its subtle as well as severe forms should be extensively studied.

Further Observations and Nonstatistical Analyses

The following are a posteriori observations of how specific movement factors and profiles compare with the clinical records and diagnoses. That is, the patients who had similar movement factors, and in particular, who had similar composite profiles, were grouped together and then their clinical records were compared. The most compelling comparisons are presented here as leads for further research into the relation between movement patterns and specific diagnoses.

Bound, Active Control

Many people have a predominance of "bound flow" and controlled movement, but the items in this factor are extreme kinds of active restriction, holding and tension. There is some evidence that the bound, active control factor is quite literally related to extreme preoccupations with control of feeling as well as fears of being controlled. Eight out of fourteen patients in the group who had paranoid symptomatology also had this movement feature. In addition, the only catatonic patient and the only patient diagnosed borderline condition with severe obsessive-compulsive defenses had high degrees of bound, active control in their movement.

Dynamic, Vital

A crude comparison between the patients with the lowest vitality in movement during Session 1 and those with the highest is illustrated by notes from the clinical records. Of the patients with the highest dynamic ratings, two were highly delusional and on occasion violent. The third was the only one in the group who was an out-patient at the time of observation, had no psychotic symptoms, and was actively and effectively functioning at home. All three talked animatedly throughout therapy sessions, arguing, laughing, or crying, and so on. In contrast the three patients with the lowest vital rating were described as:

"tired, depressed, speech slow"
"clamp on all affect . . . constantly lies in bed and does nothing."
"she would like to be more vocal on the ward but finds it difficult . . . she is easily ignored" on the ward.

As is suggested here a high rating in dynamic, vital features does not seem directly related to severe psychopathology one way or the other. Several severely psychotic patients were very high in this, some were very low, and so on. What it does appear to be related to is liveliness, ability to express strong affect, and be active in interaction.

Diffusion and Flaccid, Limp Features

Some striking similarities can be seen in the four patients who showed movement features in both the diffusion and flaccid, limp factors. Patient 2 suffered a severe postpartum psychotic depression. Patient 4 was tentatively diagnosed as having an acute schizophrenic reaction, paranoid type. He had an extensive drug history, primarily taking LSD and methedrine. He attempted suicide several months after this hospitalization. Patient 6 was diagnosed as having a depressive reaction in a hysterical character disorder. She also had a history of severe drug abuse, primarily using amphetamines and tranquilizers. This woman committed suicide several months after this hospitalization. Neither she nor the other suicidal patient (4) showed strong suicidal ideation or were considered suicide risks on the basis of psychological tests or clinical interviews during this hospitalization. The fourth patient, 11, was described as having a behavior disorder of adolescence with depression. She had made a serious suicide attempt four years previously.

No other patients in the group of twenty-two had depression as a primary diagnostic feature. Two other patients in the group had made suicide attempts, each described as not serious, and one other patient had suicidal thoughts for a brief period only. Thus three of the four patients with such movement features may be considered the most seriously depressed and three the most seriously suicidal.

Figure 1

Movement Profiles of Patients 4 and 6

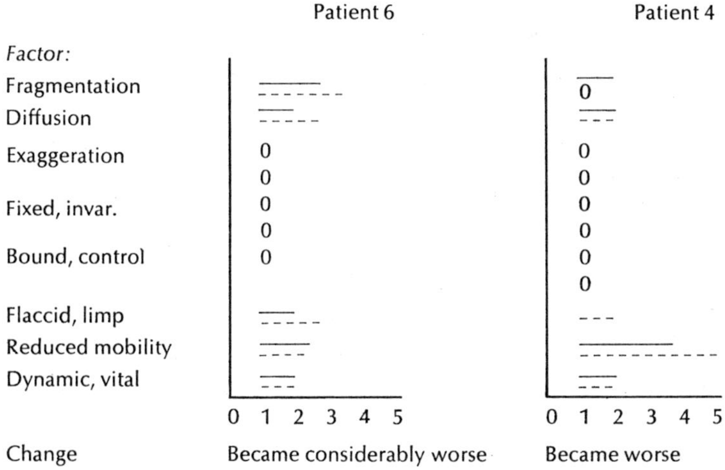

--- = first session   —— = second session

Particularly striking are the similarities between the movement profiles of the two patients who had histories of drug abuse and attempted suicide after hospitalization. We unfortunately had not realized a possible connection between the movement features and potential for suicide until eight months later. These profiles are more similar to each other than to those of other patients who have flaccid, limp features and/or diffusion.

Diffusion appears to occur within two types of profiles: those with limp, flaccid features where it adds to the indefinite, "spaced out" quality of the movement; and those which have many other features where diffusion appears to be another facet of the disorganization.

Figure 2

Movement Profiles of Patients 1, 5 and 10

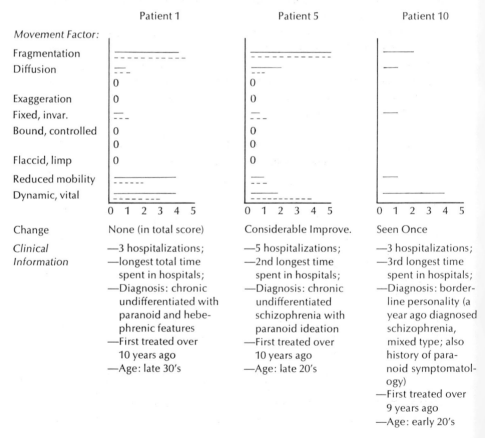

Movement Factor:	Patient 1	Patient 5	Patient 10
Fragmentation			
Diffusion			
Exaggeration	0	0	
Fixed, invar.			
Bound, controlled	0	0	
Flaccid, limp	0	0	
Reduced mobility			
Dynamic, vital			

	Patient 1	Patient 5	Patient 10
Change	None (in total score)	Considerable Improve.	Seen Once
Clinical Information	—3 hospitalizations; —longest total time spent in hospitals; —Diagnosis: chronic undifferentiated with paranoid and hebephrenic features —First treated over 10 years ago —Age: late 30's	—5 hospitalizations; —2nd longest time spent in hospitals; —Diagnosis: chronic undifferentiated schizophrenia with paranoid ideation —First treated over 10 years ago —Age: late 20's	—3 hospitalizations; —3rd longest time spent in hospitals; —Diagnosis: borderline personality (a year ago diagnosed schizophrenia, mixed type; also history of paranoid symptomatology) —First treated over 9 years ago —Age: early 20's

Mixed Profile

The following three patients have remarkably similar profiles and clinical records. They all have at least three out of four of the seriously pathological factors (fragmentation, diffusion, exaggeration, fixed, invariant), some degree of bound control, no flaccid, limp features, and some degree of vitality. Only one other patient was diagnosed chronic undifferentiated schizophrenia, and he was a first admission. No other patients had such long histories of hospitalization and psychiatric treatment as these three patients. Only one other patient had presence of three out of four factors considered seriously pathological (fragmentation, diffusion, exaggeration, fixed, invariant) like the patients described. Significantly this patient, 2 in the group, went from a flaccid, diffuse profile in the first session to a mixed profile in the second. She was diagnosed as having a postpartum psychotic depression, but the psychological diagnosis was acute undifferentiated schizophrenia with strong depressive and paranoid features. That is, the first recording compares with the clinical diagnosis, but the second agrees with the results of the psychological tests. In conclusion, presence of almost all movement factors may be a strong indicator of a chronic undifferentiated schizophrenic process.

The Movement Diagnostic Scale as a Measure of Change

No systematic behavioral measures of clinical evaluations of the patient's progress between session I and II were obtained which could be compared to the movement measures of change. However the scale appears to be useful for fairly fine discriminations in degree and kind of change. The following is an individual case in which a patient not in the study group was seen weekly. Some clinical material on his progress was obtained, thus providing an example of how the movement analysis of change compares with the psychiatric evaluation.

This patient is a young man in his early twenties who has been hospitalized continuously for two and one-half years. At the time of his transfer to the unit where this study was done, he was extremely regressed and withdrawn, beset by delusions and hallucinations. "He was virtually unable to care for himself and paced the ward unkempt" and uncommunicative.

While Robert was on this intensive unit he had a variety of therapies: individual, pharmacologic (400 mg/day of thorazine), milieu, occupational, dance, and family therapy. He was seen behind the one-way screen in brief dance therapy sessions during which he often sat and talked. These sessions averaged about twenty minutes each. His therapist participated with him. The first time he was seen by the movement observer was about two and one-half months after the start of the intensive treatment. He was extremely withdrawn and hallucinating, although he clearly trusted his therapist enough to tentatively participate in the sessions.

The author recorded his movement behavior and filled out a scale each week for seven weeks (one session was missed). The following is a graph of the changes in number of "serious" features and borderline features over the seven weeks.

Figure 3

**Change in Total Number of Serious and Borderline
Movement Features over 7 Weeks for One Patient**

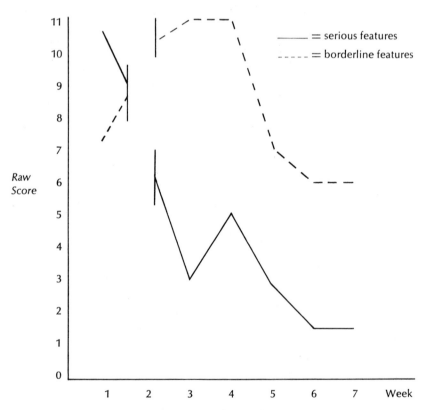

Robert was seen during the middle of his treatment, a turbulent period in which he appeared to be breaking out of his withdrawn, autistic condition. During this period of most dramatic change in movement, between weeks one and three, he was very violent and in a severe panic. He suffered extremely frightening delusions, but was able to relate them to the therapist and to maintain some contact in spite of the stress. After this he appeared more mobile, intense, and less disorganized and bizarre in movement. The number of seriously pathological movement features had decreased from ten to four. (It should be noted that his medication stayed the same throughout treatment.)

After six months of intensive treatment, the therapist wrote, "It is no exaggeration to say he has responded remarkably. . . . He is now able to care for himself to a much greater degree, participates in ward activities . . . and is increasingly able to interact with others. While he continues to have some paranoid delusions, he is less fearful and seems able to function despite these distressing ideas."

Discussion

There are a number of methodological shortcomings to this preliminary study. Further development of it would require larger sample, adequate control groups, more rigorous tests of observer reliability, and better validating data. In addition, the movement diagnostic scale should be tested with brain damaged and retarded individuals and people with motor disorders of a neurophysiological basis to see if in fact schizophrenic patients have distinctly different movement patterns.

However some of the features of this study will be discussed as it is. First, there is an obvious bias here as to what is healthy and what is pathological in movement which has little to do with "coordination" or motor skills per se. Healthy movement is considered integrated, dynamic, and rich in variation. What should be stressed is that "control," "immobility," "fragmentation," and so on, as defined and perceived in this study, are extreme and not simply stiff postures, bland expressions, and the like.

But consider the significance of the observations and results. What, for example, is the significance of movement fragmentation? It does not apparently correlate impressively with thought disorder occurring at the time of observation, although several patients with fragmentation were severely delusional and disorganized at some point in their hospitalization. It appears to be a facet and a reflection of severe personality disorganization. The rhythms of attention and focus, action and repose, speaking and listening appear disrupted and chaotic, which must be extremely distressing to a person. The more severe the fragmentation, the more the patient seemed driven and out of control with parts moving automatically. As one patient said, "It's my body. I can't help it. One part stays fixed and another goes by itself." In some patients the movement fragmentation appeared almost under control. One patient comes to mind who sat arms folded tightly, chest slumped, her movement "neutralized." But at times one realized how desparately she was holding onto herself. When she became distressed or nervous, her movement became a diffuse, disorganized series of small gestures going in different directions. This patient was not diagnosed schizophrenic, but the movement observers felt she was warding off an acute schizophrenic break with tremendous effort.

As mentioned, there are several kinds of fragmentation. Some types seem to emerge from different kinds of prepathological movement patterns and by inference different kinds of psychological conflict. For the patient just mentioned, it seemed that indecision and conflicting impulses had become so extreme and distressful, disorganization was resulting. For Robert, the patient observed for several weeks, the movement had become so controlled and segmented, it became a series of isolated and fragmented moving parts. A third patient, described as manipulative and deceptive, actually had different rhythmic patterns occurring at the same time. One part of her seemed to be tense and anxious, another part slow and "pensive." The movement analysts felt that she herself could not be sure what she felt or wanted, let alone anyone else.

Implied in these observations is a hypothesis that schizophrenic disorganization may develop from a number of different psychological conflicts and personality types. Further, the kind of fragmentation in movement may indicate earlier premorbid personality characteristics.

A relation has been suggested between the presence of bound, active control in movement and paranoid symptomatology, but this is very tentative, and what is more, it seems to relate to a chronic process. Several of the patients who had almost no "pathological" movement features were extremely paranoid and delusional. They looked the most "normal" of any patients in the group, even though they were fraught with delusions and hallucinations during their hospitalization. While some of these patients were hospitalized for the first time and might have been experiencing acute, transient, schizophrenic reactions, most of them had shown signs of disturbance for at least a year.

What may be concluded is that the movement diagnostic scale does not contain movement features which these patients show, although there is some evidence that active, control, and exaggeration factors relate to paranoid symptomatology. It is possible that the aspects of movement focused on in this study are primarily related to affective states: depression, fear, anger, hopelessness, and so on, while a paranoid condition may be considered a "more cognitive" disorder. Affective sides of the illness such as controlled anger, grandiose expansiveness, or exaggeration may be interpreted from movement patterns; but what cannot be discerned in movement, as it is studied here, are mechanisms of projection, delusions, and so on.

It was posited that diffusion and flaccid features may relate to severe depression and even suicidal behavior. Flaccid, limp features alone appear related to strong depression. Of course this is not a prediction that all depressed or suicidal patients will have these movement features. The suicidal patients who had similar movement profiles appeared to have a particular kind of suicidal syndrome. Interpreting the movement this appears to include the following characteristics. There seems to be personality disorganization and psychosis; the patient is extremely depressed and hopeless and fraught with indecision. There also seems to be a diffuse anxiety reflected in a "spaced out," insubstantial quality in their manner. Both patients were quickly becoming worse and seemed to have lost their vitality and their will to struggle and get well. Further study of the relation between depression and movement would seem valuable, especially because judgment of whether someone is depressed appears to be so often inferred from voice quality and movement.

Before linking the movement patterns too irrevocably to traditional psychiatric diagnoses or formulations, it would be better at this stage to evaluate the findings of this study by staying closer to the movement dimension itself. That is, one could propose a model which puts these patterns into some theoretical perspective but which is essentially a movement model. It would seem to be premature to tightly define movement types, trying to approximate traditional psychiatric categories. What movement could uniquely contribute to the understanding of behavior would be distorted or missed.

Condon (1968) speaks of the flow and ebb, the rhythmic patterns of movement which accompany organization and harmony within the individual's actions and synchrony with the movement of others. He found that for a schizophrenic patient disruption of this synchrony and organization may occur. In our research we have also found this lack of "self-synchrony," although apparently different types of it at a grosser level of observation. But as Condon suggests for his observations, the movement patterns seen in this study seem to be a reflection of subtle, complex patterns of interpersonal relationships as well as inner affective states and conflicts. All of the patterns described in the scale, and not only the disorganized ones, might be viewed as "maladaptive rhythms" or styles of reacting which reflect the individual's inner distress as well as the style of his interaction with others. Thus, to be monotonous and repetitive, immobile, persistently exaggerated, extremely controlled or passive, and so forth, is to cope with intolerable feelings of fear, anger, self-hatred, loneliness, and at the same time to avoid or "tune out" contact with others and to "hold one's own" in a particular way, and so on.

While the focus in this study has been on individual style and inner psychodynamics, it is abundantly evident that the patterns of behavior observed are intimately related to interpersonal relationships. An autistic child of six was observed by the author and her movement analyzed using the scale. She had a very high degree of movement pathology, but was also extremely variable. Within one year her score on the scale decreased by half. Even more striking, within one day, depending on the individuals she was with, her movement improved or worsened tremendously. Further research using this method of observation should include a detailed study of when certain patterns of movement occur, in what contexts, and in relation to whom.

APPENDIX 1

Sample of a Movement Summary and Interpretation

The following is a movement analysis of a young patient who had been in therapy for many years but was hospitalized for the first time. His diagnosis was borderline condition in a schizoid personality. He had extreme obsessive-compulsive defenses, was quite withdrawn, and had great difficulty expressing his feelings. The movement analysis was completed before the psychiatric records were studied.

Movement Patterns:

In the first session Martin (patient 12) sat in a parallel position, hands grasping the chair, arms and shoulders held narrow and raised. He talked quite a bit but appeared very controlled in manner. Although he smiled occasionally and at one point began crying, he stayed quite still, the tears rolling down his expressionless face. His movement was actively restricted in many ways: postural shifts and gestures were mainly sagittal, two-phasic, segmented; head and face were often immobile as he spoke; dynamically the movement was very even in flow, with occasional instances of lightness or quickness. He moved several different parts of the body, but his fidgeting stayed very small. However, for all of this restriction Martin was far from inert in his manner. There were glimmers in the foot tapping and hand fidgeting, for example, which were fairly intricate and rhythmic patterns. Also the fact that he looked actively controlled in the postural shifts, gestures, and so on (and not inert or set in a neutral tonus) suggests that he may have more vitality when less anxious.

In the second session Martin was far more mobile and active. He gesticulated as he spoke, got up several times to look at things in the room, spoke directly and with animation throughout the session. The previous restrictions showed primarily in periods of speaking without head or facial movement, moving with an even flow pattern, and moving without much effort variation. Particularly notable was a persistent lack of vigorous or strong gestures or weight shifts.

Interpretation:

Martin improved markedly in movement but still showed pathological features and a great deal of control in the second session. He may be coming out of a schizophrenic episode; however, his illness is probably of fairly long duration.

Martin conveys a feeling of extreme brittleness and fragility. He appears almost delicate in his manner—not so much effeminate as hypersensitive and fragile. His energy seems bound up in control of feelings, particularly anger and depression. It is as if he let down his guard for one second he would be overwhelmed by others, dominated, pushed around, easily hurt. He appears quite cerebral and intellectual, but this does not seem to "successfully" defend him from feeling afraid, hurt, lonely.

While the control is extreme and severely limits his ability to relate to others and his overall functioning, it is still active and not "frozen" or inert. At times the restriction appears actually under his conscious control. That is, there is still much more to him than he is expressing. He is not totally repressed or emotionally debilitated. He particularly seems to be establishing a good relationship with the therapist.

APPENDIX 2

List of Movement Factors Abstracted from the Movement Diagnostic Scale

Fragmentation

1. Impulsive, erratic postural shifts; starting or stopping abruptly or erratic impulses within the phrase.

2. Segmentation (use of one part, a pause or clear separation before movement in another part) which is so severe that in effect the body becomes fragmented into parts.
3. Movement occurs sporadically in different parts during a phrase with no clear sequence or fluent connections.
4. Fingers and/or palm hyperextended; flexion-extension only at the knuckles and/or wrist; with a neutral tonus.
5. Two or more parts simultaneously going in different planes (spatial fragmentation).
6. Erratic fluctuations in the effort-flow pattern.
7. Severe contradictions in the effort-flow characteristics of the body in stillness.
8. Sporadic occurrence of quickness as if "out of nowhere" at (a) the beginning of the phrase; (b) within the phrase; or (c) at the end of the phrase.
9. Different rhythms simultaneously occurring in movement of different parts of the body which appear unrelated.
10. The sequence of weight shifts is disorganized, that is, one part shifts, then another in a different direction, and so on, such that the body does not come to a clear balanced rest.

Diffusion
1. Movement is spatially diffuse and unclear (that is, no clear, straight, round, or three-dimensional paths, no clear transitions, difficult to discern spatial phrases) in either short phrases or long phrases.
2. Continuous diffuse effort patterns; effort-flow and possibly some effort qualities "running on"; difficult to determine distinct phrases and any clear build up or die down in intensity. No clear endings to the movement.
3. An action is not completed before a person starts a new action; no pause or transition but a kind of diffuse overlapping of actions.

Exaggeration
1. Exaggeration, overstressed, too-large postural shifts.
2. More postural movements than gestures.
3. Large, exaggerated, though spatially clear, movements throughout a phrase, that is, no modulation of the size of the movement within a phrase.

Fixed, Invariant
1. Repetitive movement of an isolated part of the body; the dy-

namics are the same throughout; the body part appears unrelated to rest of the body and seems to "go by itself."
2. Movement in the sagittal plane only.
3. Movement in one plane only per phrase.
4. Two-phasic or cyclic movement only.
5. Repetition of one or two effort qualities in an unvarying way; the
   movement may stay intense but with no build up or decrease in
   intensity; the phrase is clear and has a clear beginning and end;
   it is often two-phasic. That is, there is no modulation in the intensity of the movement with only one quality at a time or a combination of two qualities.
6. Frozen gestures: an action apparently related to some expression
   or conventional action but highly repetitive and each time dynamically the same.
7. Ritual: an activity performed in a set order of actions; each time
   done dynamically the same way.

Bound, Active Control
1. The body attitude is rigidly held; there is some bound quality
   and rigid tonus.
2. Parts are still for long periods, actively held, and restricted.
3. Fixed and rigidly held finger constellation or position.
4. The movement is too small or sparse to determine its spatial
   character; has an actively held and restricted quality.
5. The effort-flow is often bound or very bound.
6. The movement is a series of segmented gestures which are spatially clear and controlled because of even bound flow and either
   directness or lightness.

Flaccid, Limp
1. The body attitude is flaccid, inert, limp.
2. Hand goes limp and into "zero" flow at the end of a gesture.
3. Body parts in stillness show flacidity, complete limpness, and giving in to gravity.

Reduced Mobility

Serious features:
1. Body attitude immobile and set, tonus is neutral, not clearly
   bound or free.
2. Virtually no active movement of the trunk; minimal weight shifts
   in standing up, sitting down, or walking; trunk only passively follows limbs in action.

3. Gestural trunk movement only.
4. No movement of head or limbs; person barely walks.
5. Head absolutely still as person talks.
6. Head and shoulders held still, eyes fixed forward as person walks.
7. Little or no movement of face apart from eyes.
8. The movement is too small or sparse to determine its spatial character; it has an inert quality.
9. Fixed shape or position held against gravity for long period; it is not resting on something or holding up an object.
10. In stillness the body parts are neutral or "zero" in flow, neither clearly limp or held.
11. No clear grasp or closing or whole hand.

Borderline features:
1. Trunk is maintained as one unit, no twist.
2. No active, successive spreading of movement through the trunk or part of it (that is, movement is only simultaneous).
3. No active initiation of movement in lower trunk.
4. No active initiation of movement in the upper trunk.
5. "Fleeting" postural movement only.
6. Single phases of postural movement only.
7. Single and double phases of postural movement only.
8. Only distal parts of body move (hands, feet, head, forearms).
9. No successive movement in limbs.

Dynamic, Vital
1. High rate of postural movement.
2. Spatial complexity (that is, shaping, clear directions, curved transitions, diagonal movements, and so on) occur in different body parts and throughout the body.
3. A wide range of effort-flow within a free to very bound range; not even or neutral in character.
4. Effort qualities frequently visible throughout the body.
5. Presence of different effort dynamics which are clearly observable and frequent.
6. Has clear relationship to weight in gestures of head and limbs; either strength or lightness; can give into gravity or make an active impact; varied flow patterns.
7. Has clear placement of or relation to weight in the trunk, can give into gravity or be forceful in trunk shifts, in sitting down, and so on.

Bibliography

Appleby, Lawrence, Jordan M. Scher, and John Cumming. *Chronic Schizophrenia: Explorations in Theory and Treatment* (Glencoe, Ill.: Free Press, 1960).

Bartenieff, Irmgard, and Martha Ann Davis. "Effort-Shape, Analysis of Movement: The Unity of Expression and Function." Unpublished monograph, Albert Einstein College of Medicine, 1965.

————, and Forrestine Paulay. "Choreometric Profiles" and "The Choreometric Coding Book" in *Folk Song Style and Culture*. Alan Lomax, ed. Washington, D.C.: American Association for the Advancement of Science, Publication 88, 1968.

Birdwhistell, Ray L. *Introduction to Kinesics*. Washington, D.C.: Department of State, Foreign Service Institute, 1952.

————. "Kinesics in the Contest of Motor Habits." Paper presented to American Anthropological Association, Dec., 1957.

Coleman, James C. *Abnormal Psychology and Modern Life*. Chicago: Scott, Foresman, 1956.

Condon, W. S. "Linguistic-Kinesic Research and Dance Therapy." American Dance Therapy Association. *Proceedings of Third Annual Conference*, Madison, Wis., 1968.

Davis, Martha Ann. "Methods of Perceiving Patterns of Small-Group Behavior." Unpublished, Yeshiva University, 1966.

Kestenberg, Judith. "The Role of Movement Patterns in Development: Part 2, Flow of Tension." *Psychoanalytic Quarterly* 34 (4) (1965).

Kisker, George W. *The Disorganized Personality*. New York: McGraw-Hill, 1964.

Kline, Nathan S., and Heinz E. Lehmann, eds. *Psychopharmacology*. Boston: Little, Brown, 1965.

Laban, Rudolph, and F. C. Lawrence. *Effort*. London: Macdonald and Evans, 1947.

Lowen, Alexander. *Betrayal of the Body*. New York: Macmillan, 1967.

————. *Love and Orgasm*. New York: Signet Books, 1965.

Malmo, Robert B., Charles Shagass, David Belanger, and A. A. Smith. "Motor Control in Psychiatric Patients under Experimental Stress" in *Studies in Behavior Pathology*. T. R. Sarbin, ed. New York: Holt, Rinehart and Winston, 1961.

————, ————, and A. A. Smith. "Responsiveness in Chronic Schizophrenia" in *Psychopathology: A Sourcebook*. C. F. Freed, I. E. Alexander, and S. S. Tompkins, eds. New York: John Wiley, 1958.

Patients in Mental Institutions, 1943. U.S. Department of Commerce. Washington, D.C.: U.S. Government Printing Office, 1946.

Reich, Wilhelm. *Character-Analysis*. New York: Orgone Institute Press, 1949.

Rennie, Thomas A. "Analysis of One Hundred Cases of Schizophrenia with Recovery." *Archives of Neurology and Psychiatry* 46 (1941).

Scheflen, Albert E. *Stream and Structure of Communicational Behavior.* Philadelphia, Pa.: Eastern Pennsylvania Psychiatric Institute, 1965.

Schmidt, Herman O., and Charles P. Fonda. "The Reliability of Psychiatric Diagnosis: A New Look," in *Research in Psychopathology.* Herbert C. Quay, ed. Princeton: D. Van Nostrand, 1963.

Searles, Harold. *Collected Papers on Schizophrenia and Related Subjects.* New York: International Universities Press, 1965.

Werner, Heinz. *Comparative Psychology of Mental Development.* New York: Science Editions, 1948.

White, Elissa Q. "Child Development Movement Studies, 1." Unpublished, Goddard College, 1969.

Wittenborn, J. R. "The Dimensions of Psychosis." *The Journal of Nervous and Mental Disease* 134 (1962), pp. 117–128.

PART 3

Enhancing Body Awareness

The great object of life is sensation—
to feel that we exist, even though in pain.
It is that "craving void" which drives us
to gaming, to travel, to intemperate but
keenly felt pursuits of any description,
whose principal attraction is the agitation
inseparable from their accomplishment.

Lord Byron
George Gordon

FRANZISKA BOAS

Creative Dance

In 1941 the line of demarcation between dancing lessons and dance therapy was undefined. When Franziska Boas wrote the two articles later consolidated into "Creative Dance," she refers to herself as teacher of creative modern dance but, in describing the lesson content, reveals herself to be as cognizant a movement therapist as our contemporaries.[1]

The unclear distinction between teacher and therapist continues today as a source of confusion. Barbara Mettler, well-known choreographer, complains of the onslaught of student requests for therapy in the studio. The students are guilty of blurring the aesthetic and utilitarian uses of dance, in her opinion.[2] Members of the ADTA registry committee arbitrarily differentiate between the dance teacher and the dance therapist even though both individuals may employ dance for similarly stated purposes in serving the same client groups. How these distinctions are to be applied remains a bone of contention; controversy swirls about several prominent dance therapists who have been denied the gilded "Dance Therapist, Registered" designation.

Boas remains current for other important reasons. She was first to seize upon the significance of dance for effecting therapeutic change in body awareness. Gymnastics, she argues, promotes varied kinesthetic sensations as the body mass shifts weight, direction, and shape. She balances spontaneous play around body image motifs with conscious techniques to bring about changes in self-attitude.

Franziska Boas was greatly influenced by the husband-wife team of Schilder and Bender. Dr. Lauretta Bender coauthored "Creative Dance in Therapy" and wrote *Child Psychiatric Techniques* in which

1. Prepared by Franziska Boas as an enlargement and consolidation of two articles: Lauretta Bender and Franziska Boas, "Creative Dance in Therapy," *American Journal of Orthopsychiatry*, 11 (1941), 235–244; and Franziska Boas, "Psychological Aspects in the Practice and Teaching of Dancing," *Journal of Aesthetics and Art Criticism*, 2 (1941–42), 3–20.

2. Barbara Mettler, "Creative Dance—Art or Therapy?," unpublished essay, January, 1973.

this selection was first published.[3] Dr. Paul Schilder viewed forms of body experimentation as an interface to our continually changing image of ourselves. Constant flux in perceptions of the body image, encouraged by our playful machinations, interweave with social and physical environments as they, too, change.

> Movement affects the body image; the body image affects personality. There is so close an interrelation between the muscular sequence and the psychic attitude that not only does the psychic attitude connect up with the muscular states, but also every sequence of tensions and relaxations provokes a specific attitude. When there is a specific motor sequence it changes the inner situation and attitudes and even provokes a phantasy situation which fits the muscular sequence.[4]

He concludes: "Dance is therefore a method of changing the body image."[5] This revolutionary assertion achieves the force of orthodox dogma for the movement therapist forty years later.   M.N.C.

Dance is the expression of human fantasy and emotion using as its medium the motility of the body passing through space and time. This process of formulation of movement concerns itself not only with the form and action of the joints and muscles, but also with the subjective concept of the body, and with the body as seen and interpreted by an observer.

The dancer's idea of his own body is fantasy based partly on reality and partly on his emotional and intellectual makeup. This can be called the "body image"[6] and must constantly be revised and reestablished. Through experimentation it has to be brought in line with the form or body appearance which is seen by the observer. Since the dancing individual can never see his entire body exactly as it is seen by others, but can see only parts at any one time and never can see certain parts at all without the aid of a mirror, he must become conscious of his own body image and learn to visualize as well as to feel its form. He must also acquaint himself thoroughly with the fundamental structure of the human body, its physical makeup and function, in other words with its anatomy, physiology, and mechanics as

3. Lauretta Bender, *Child Psychiatric Techniques* (Springfield, Ill.: Charles C Thomas, 1952).

4. Paul Schilder, *Image and Appearance of the Human Body: Studies in the Constructive Energies of the Psyche* (New York: Science Editions, John Wiley and Sons, International Universities Press, 1950), p. 208.

5. *Ibid.*

6. Paul Schilder, *Image and Appearance of the Human Body.*

he studies them on his own body during his dance activity. How does he conceive the body image to look? What is its relation to his physical body? What is its relation to the body appearance? Does the concept of his body image change through the influence of different emotional states and fantasies? Does it change when he moves through space at varying speeds? Does it change when he takes different positions in relation to space?

Put the head of an individual in a different position in space and you have changed the world of that individual. The newborn child cannot sit or stand. However it reacts to changes in the position of the head in relation to the body and also in relation to space. One may speak of righting reflexes and postural reflexes which are in connection either with the neck righting reflexes or with the labyrinthine postural and righting reflexes. There are also body righting reflexes acting upon the head. An asymmetrical stimulation of the body surface, for instance, influences the posture of the head. There are also body righting reflexes acting upon the body, and optical righting reflexes. These reflexes are not always obvious in the human individual after infancy, unless there are lesions in the central nervous system.

Everything which disturbs or changes the relation of the individual to the vertical plane (gravitation) affects the motor mechanism of the entire body. The whole system of postures is fundamentally different when an individual is lying on the ground, or when he is standing. Even when one is standing upright the muscle tone is very different according to whether the head is turned forward or to the side. The whole distribution of tone changes with every change in the position of the head, as has been described by Magnus and de Kleijn, Goldstein, Hoff, and Schilder. Voluntarily turning around the longitudinal axis in play or on command stimulates the semicircular canals and causes a great number of changes in postural responses in connection with the vestibular irritation. Such turning may also occur involuntarily under pathological conditions. Turning around the longitudinal axis and rolling on the floor have very different effects, since the tone when lying on the floor is changed by the body righting reflexes. There is a further change in the tone since the head has a different position in space.

Dance routines of the usual type are rhythmical motions which keep the individual in an upright position. In these many of the fundamental physiological activities are neglected, thereby limiting the possible variety of postural experiences. The child is constantly exploring his body and experimenting with its relation to space. It is of the greatest importance to allow him to continue in this without restriction. By observing this activity the instructor gains not only an evaluation of the pupil's physical coordination, but also insight into his thought processes and fantasies. Without such knowledge it is impossible to know what direction should be taken in teaching and what results may be expected.

Walking on all fours is a primitive impulse. The posture itself probably brings with it a great number of primitive attitudes.[7] Jumping also is among the fundamental primitive impulses. It is obvious that important psychological changes take place when physiological mechanisms of this type are brought into play in the dance. Physiological considerations have been particularly stressed, but it should not be forgotten that they will be especially effective when combined with the well-known forces of rhythmical movement, and particularly when all of these factors are integrated purposefully with the fantasy life. Bouncing, rolling, crawling, swaying, and swinging, climbing, jumping, turning, and tumbling are all elemental experiences in the dance. Both the child and the adult must learn to place their bodies in unaccustomed positions and to engage in unaccustomed movements. All types of variations of these movements should be encouraged. This experiment in placing the body in strange positions in relation to space and then resolving those positions into habitual postures establishes assurance of the reality of a fundamental body image. It is by these experiments that the child learns the mechanics of his body and explores space and time. Through motility the individual learns to establish and expand the concepts of his body image, thereby gaining confidence in the reality and control of his body.

Most adults have to be led back to this experience since it forces them to take into account their physical body and reawakens in them the consciousness of their fundamental body image, which may have been repressed. The following is an example of the relation between movement of this type and the concept of the body image. A schizophrenic boy in the children's ward when asked to turn a back somersault obeyed the initial impulse but stopped each time before his back touched the floor and before his legs went over his head, to ask, "What will happen to me? Will I die?" He had to watch someone else a few times before he dared do it at all, and then at first had to be helped. After that he repeated it with all signs of enjoyment and pleasure. The action of turning upside down and putting his legs over his head brought out his insecurity in space and his uneasiness about

7. Compare with Ales Hrdlicka, *Children Who Run on All Fours and Other Animalistic Behavior in the Human Child* (New York: Whittlesey House, McGraw-Hill, 1931).

the reality of his body (unclear body image due to pathological processes) and made him fear that he would lose his body during the activity. The normal individual, through self-observation, knows that distortions and activity, short of injury, do not affect the limbs in their relation to each other or the body in its entirety.

With respect to posture the following points are important: Whether the body is in the horizontal, vertical, or inclined plane; what relation the position of the head has to the posture of the body; whether the body is or is not supported on one surface; and the rotation and speed of rotation of the head on the body.

Fundamental changes in postural motility take place in relation to these four possibilities. It must be borne in mind that with these variations in motility, significant modifications in sensory experiences are also perceived. The orientation of a body is completely altered when various postural and righting reflexes occur. Changes in one's perception of the outside world take place while turning around the longitudinal axis. One also gets a completely different picture of one's own body. The vestibular irritation leads to important changes in the vasovegetative system. The man who is lying down and the man who is standing up are different in their somatic reactions. There are also important changes in mood and in total personality, depending upon the posture.

In applying these data to the modern creative dance in its use with children, it is to be expected that they will have an important influence on the psychological attitudes of the child. During experimentation with activities of this sort, the teacher may play the active role and change the position into a passive one for the pupil by exaggerating it through his intervention. For instance, with the small child who tries to turn a forward somersault but cannot move beyond the point where his head and feet are still on the floor, the teacher may step in and turn him over. Or with an older child who wishes to stand on his own shoulders, the teacher may pick him up by the legs until only his hands still touch the floor. To be passively set in motion, to be carried, swung, turned, and rolled by an adult is important to the child in extending his confidence beyond himself. In the case of the larger child and the adult where these things are not possible without the aid of rings or bars which can bear the person's weight, the pupil must be urged to use his ingenuity with occasional steadying help from the instructor. The degree of proficiency and the number of positions that will be taken depend on the age of the pupil, his muscular coordination, and on his fears and anxieties.

If children at a very early age are allowed to experiment with rhythmic movement without interference, they may outgrow this type of movement as mere self-indulgence and chaotic behavior, and be able later to use the control and body quality gained through such experimentation for the formulation of fantasies. This type of investigation and learning should be allowed to continue to the point of saturation, when the disorganized movements and chaotic themes begin to form themselves into rhythmic repetitions and recognizable fantasies. In other words, the primitive animal-like impulses may furnish material for sublimation into an art expression. During the transition period it will be necessary for the teacher to direct the movement toward a subconscious sublimation. Those children who have been blocked in the process of sublimation will either remain in the infantile type of movement or will develop gestures which are escape patterns:

> David was a very bright 10 year old boy who was entirely unable to control his infantile exhibitionism. His usual reaction to the stimulus of the dance situation was to run wildly through the room, roll on the floor, turn somersaults and crawl in such a manner that he was always in the path of the other children. Then he would lie with his head under a chair and suck his thumb. At home he used the narrow hallway to practice climbing up to the ceiling like an Alpine climber in a crevice. Occasionally in the dance hour he showed excellent coordination and rhythm far beyond that of the other children. These were only flashes of the sublimated form. Here was a case of over-indulgence in chaotic movement. From the point of view of dance the block had occurred during the process of the formulation of motility impulses into sublimated dance material.

The natural dynamic development of the primitive type of motility is the process beginning with the simplest crawling and rolling and continuing through complicated somersaults, headstands, handsprings, backbends, cartwheels, to passive and finally active suspensions in jumps and leaps from various heights. Thereby the pupil investigates all space levels, the ground, middle space, and the air, always with the attraction to depth.

When the attraction to height begins to take shape one is confronted with the problems and rhythms of walking, running, leaping, and their variants; also with the relation of the torso, arms, head, and neck to the lower extremities. Whereas in the first type of movement the body remained comparatively compact, arms and legs serving as supporting points, now there are only the legs as supports. The control of the body begins to fall apart; many movable segments have to be coordinated—ankles, knees, hips, pelvis, chest, shoulders, elbows, wrists, fingers, neck, and head.

In every movement made in the standing position there is the question of balance of these parts on a narrow base which becomes even narrower when one foot is raised from the floor· It is therefore necessary to re-establish the body as an entity, such as it was during the action on the floor.

This can be accomplished if the pupil becomes sufficiently sensitive to feel himself surrounded by a "zone of extension of the body image."[8] The peripheral nerve endings all over the body act as antennae to receive impulses from without when another object approaches. They transmit to the body image the necessity of change in contour or change in its place in space, beyond its zone of extension.

This is a concept similar to that which applies to sculpture. Open spaces are not holes but are substance which is enclosed or surrounded by the solid parts of the sculptured form. The figure holds the space within its form. In sculpture there are single space forms which are made visible, while in dance there is a constant regrouping and re-establishing of space forms which accompany the moving figure.

It is therefore not enough merely to train the muscles and joints in physical coordination and strength. The sensitivity of the entire body and the mind must be trained to register "the body image with its zone of extension." This has to become automatic so that the body will react by itself in movement related to any given situation. The mind must look on and choose that which is more relevant to the idea to be expressed. It is like a dream in which the dreamer actively participates and at the same time watches the action from without. The difference is that the dreamer is a helpless bystander, while the dancer can direct and plan his actions.

The relationship of the single dancer to other dancers in the group must also be considered. There is the problem of the direct contact between two bodies, as for instance, when one is riding on the back of another. The form and duration of contact may determine the difference between frankly sexual and only latently sexual contacts. The contact will in turn be dependent upon factors of aggressiveness and body curiosity.

All these actions take place not only in a specific group but also in a definite space which determines the movement of the single individual. In dancing the relation to space is psychological, not merely

8. Paul Schilder, *Image and Appearance of the Human Body*.

in the ordinary sense. Optic impressions have a definite influence on postural reactions. The situation will be fundamentally altered by the optic experience of the moving bodies of the other dancers which invite imitations and reactions. In addition to the physiological problems there is also the relationship to the leader of the group, as well as the relations of the members of the group to one another. These will depend upon the life history of the individual participants.

Dance is fundamentally a social art. Except for the young child and isolated instances of older persons, the average individual does not dance for or by himself. There is always some other person present either as a participant or onlooker. Dance is basically narcissistic.[9] If there is no outside observer there is always the self as audience. Part of the pleasure of dance is in the self-observation of changes in one's body image and appearance. In group dance each dancer tries to influence others by these changes and is in turn affected by the changes he sees in them.. Aside from the relation of individuals to each other there is also the relation to space and to the objects which divide and fill space. In group dance these space shapes are constantly changing and the speed at which they move varies. If there is a direct meeting of individuals the relation between the two determines whether there is antagonism or cooperation. The character of the individuals determines whether one will change and follow, whether both will change to create new movement, or whether neither will change. If neither changes there may be active conflict, turning away to continue the individual pattern, or spacial coordination, that is, movement through space in the same direction with unrelated tension, rhythm, and gesture because of insistence on separate body movement patterns. The dancer must be extremely sensitive to be able to make use of each new space and body mass, as well as of the speed and rhythm at which they move and change.

The space in which the dancer moves is always three-dimensional. It is circumscribed by the four walls, three real and one imaginary, the floor and the ceiling of the room in which he works. It is divided into three levels, high, middle, and low, which are experienced by the individual as he passes from the floor through the standing position to the tip toes or to the jump. When moving from one place to another the dancer may pass through space from low to high in an inclined plane. When passing through all planes and taking into account all directions, front, diagonal, side, and back, a spiral movement or a turn is created. These direction concepts are projections of the body

9. See Rudolf Arnheim, "Psychology of the Dance," *Dance Magazine* (August, 1946).

direction, ventral, lateral, dorsal, and diagonal, that is, oblique, 45 degrees between middle, ventral or dorsal, and the middle lateral, when the individual is in a standing position facing the imaginary front wall of the room. Such concepts are permanently fixed in space just as the body directions are permanently fixed within the body. However, the relation of the body direction to the space direction is variable. For example, one of our children, Larry, because of unsatisfied curiosity as to what was behind curtains or in corners of the room and as to what the assistant was writing, suddenly began to walk quickly through the dance space from corner to corner, across the back of the room, around the sides, and from wall to wall, always in straight lines, sometimes forwards and sometimes backwards.

Since space has volume it is also divided into smaller cubic forms depending on the distribution of groups of individuals and isolated individuals. These cubic forms shift and change shape as the dancers move. Different densities and tensions are created by these forms causing attraction or repulsion, and passage ways may be created which have a tendency to cause a desire to go from one place to another.

Recognizable rhythmic and dynamic patterns grow out of tension in the individual and tensions in the group or groups, as well as in the space forms that are created. Most of these patterns demand externalization in sound. Some require a rhythmic drum beat, others a mellow gong tone or a sharp cymbal crash. A musical accompaniment of the sounds related to the tension and movement has to be created.[10] The sounds emerging from percussion instruments in themselves have specific qualities which relate to space, time, and tension. The drum bounces its listeners in space and creates a desire for rhythmic action. The cymbal softly played cuts space and spreads out in all directions horizontally. The gong fills space and suspends the hearer in it. Sharp sounds produce strong tension and penetrate space. Soft sounds produce weak tension and fill space. Regularly reproduced sounds produce repetition of movement and activate space. Crescendos produce increase in tension and fill space with activity. Decrescendos decrease tension and quiet the space. Accellerandos increase speed of movement and activate space. Retardandos decrease speed of movement and empty space of action. Sounds fill space with substance. If there is no sound, space has to be filled with the dancer's thoughts, emotions, and fantasies. Without these, space would be empty, a vacuum.

10. See Franziska Boas, "Notes on Percussion Accompaniment for the Dance," *Dance Observer*, 5 (5) (May, 1938), 71.

The sounds which the dancer hears and the space forms and body appearances of the other dancers which he sees and feels, create in him specific reactions which manifest themselves in his movement patterns. A case in point is a modern dance dealing with the concept of forces under water. The accompaniment was gongs, cymbals, and drums. The theme was the activation of two persons, conceived as bodies suspended in water, by the aggressive force of a central figure which disturbed the quiet of the space in which all three were floating. The force and weight of the moving body created currents of motion in the space substance which carried the other bodies out of their original positions. Through repeated attacks and activity at great speed, the two figures were forced into conscious action to preserve their equilibrium. There resulted a transmission of power to the formerly passive forms. In dance human emotions must always be reckoned with. In this case the activity of the central figure created annoyance of unrest which resulted in concerted aggression against the disturbing force, driving it into passivity. From this situation the central figure emerged on an emotional level with the other figures so that the final solution could be a unification of effort.

Any arbitrary group of children moves in a world of everyday life experiences. Accordingly, they have resistances to primitive types of experience, and it is necessary to overcome these inhibitions in order to allow for the breaking through of the deeper lying impulses of rhythmic action and dance. The use of percussion instruments is a decided help in provoking reactions and re-enforcing them when they start to appear. It is advisable to establish a basic metric beat on some instrument or to continue with a repetitious dynamic pattern. Sooner or later the pulse of the rhythm dominates the group and impels the children to rhythmic or dynamic movement. The influence of rhythmic sound very soon has a noticeable effect on the motility of the child since every sensory impression carries with it a command to specific action. It is possible that percussion instruments which seem to be felt all over the body may have a particularly deep psychophysiological influence.

> Helga was a child of high intelligence who had been constantly surrounded by adults. She had been taught extreme orderliness and cleanliness. She was told that she had no right to her own opinion because she was a child. Her fantasied stories had been criticized as falsehoods. At the age of 4 she had a bedtime ritual of carefully folding her clothes and holding a clean handkerchief in her hand. A year later she developed what seemed to be a fear of bed wetting which never actually occurred.

At 8 years she was very excitable and had facial tics. She was blocked in her fantasies. She considered herself unimaginative. She disliked playing with clay because she dirtied her hands or might spot her clothes. She thought that any person who liked her drawings or anything that she made was "crazy." She was easily distracted, asked irrelevant questions during class, had very little originality in movement when dancing with open eyes, but when dancing with closed eyes showed good co-ordination, grace and ease. She was fundamentally musical, imaginative, and rhythmically co-ordinated, but at that time was concerned with externals such as hair, clothes, fingernails. The clay figure which she modeled consisted of a child's head with curls and a hair ribbon; it had no arms and no body, but a dress with long legs was fastened directly to the head. Helga's most outstanding feature was her ability to dance freely when her eyes were closed. The externals which as a rule were her center of attention then became temporarily eliminated. A sensitivity toward her body which she usually disregarded became manifest. A psychological block was overbridged for a time. By using the closed eyes during dancing as one device she could have been guided toward a consciousness of inner values.

Another device used with Helga was persistent repetition of sound. The child responded to the continuous playing of drum rhythms, first with her usual distraction, asking questions, getting a drink, cleaning her hands, looking out of the window—then suddenly with 15 minutes of continuous dancing in the form of crawling, rolling, turning, and arm or hip gestures. In response to continuous repetitious gong melodies, she gradually softened her tone of voice and muscle tension until on two occasions the complete relaxation of her emotional tension was expressed by her lying on the floor and falling asleep.

In 1940–41, the following experiment was undertaken on the children's ward of the psychiatric division of Bellevue Hospital: Groups of six to eight children twelve years old and younger and representing all types of behavior disorders and psychiatric problems were utilized. They included underprivileged children of New York City with a wide range of characteristics determined by race and environment. They were unselected except that boys between six and twelve, or girls of the same age, or mixed groups of boys and girls of six years or under made up the separate groups. On some occasions these groupings were ignored.

Here are brief case histories of six children making up a group, with examples of their dance experiences:

Patsy, a 9 year old boy, could never accept the fact that he was not wanted by his inadequate and alcoholic parents. Although abused in his own home, he was miserable in the Catholic institution to which he was sent after frequent attempts at running away from home. In the Home he developed a severe anxiety state with numerous phobias reactive to his compulsive masturbation, and colored with religious lore.

Carrol, a 9 year old American Negro boy of almost unknown antecedents, lived with an aged couple variously referred to as grandparents or uncle and aunt. He had been exposed to most of the social traumas—gross abuse, neglect, poverty, alcoholism, and sexual attacks. He displayed a distressing hysterical anxiety and believed, both when asleep and awake, that he was being chased by the devil. He could readily be thrown into a state of hysterical terror by the simple suggestion that the devil was behind him. Terror was associated with feelings of guilt for past sexual experiences, many of which were probably fantasied. He was capable of ecstatic as well as terrifying experiences but was apparently equally afraid of both.

Ralph was a 9 year old Puerto Rican Negro boy who was too wild for public schools. While hitching on a car he had fallen off and injured his head, and the question had been raised as to whether a brain injury did not account for his hyperkinesis. However, there were equally serious social factors. The father had deserted the family and the mother had moved from Puerto Rico to New York only two years before. Ralph had none of the supervision and help he needed in adjusting to a new social situation, as his mother worked away from home. His quick responsiveness to the training and socializing influences on the children's ward argued against any serious brain damage.

Fred, a dull 10 year old Italian boy, lived on the lower east side of New York City and was a member of a gang. He was caught stealing with the gang and was sent to the children's court. Because it was evident that he was the dullest, most passive and suggestible member of the gang he was sent to the children's ward for study. He had a vivid but confused fantasy life colored with the lore of the underworld.

Benjamin was a 5 year old boy from a boarding home, where he had been placed by one of the child-placing agencies. He was very bright but had been the source of a great deal of trouble in several boarding homes where he had lived. Abandoned by his mother when a baby, he had never stayed in any home long enough to feel he belonged to anyone, nor did he have the ability to make himself part of any home. For that matter, he did not seem to feel that he belonged to any social situation, either in a home or in a school, or among a group of children. His emotional reactions all seemed of the negative sort. He was always unhappy and at odds and even spoke of suicide or turning on the gas to kill others in the home. At best he was reckless in dangerous situations, such as entering traffic. What the child actually needed was the love and attention which neither his mother nor any substitute had ever given him.

Jerry was a bright 9 year old boy whose home had been made un-happy by a father who deserted, and a mother who could not carry the burden of supporting and caring for a large family. She was both too busy and unhappy to give Jerry anything but a sense of futility. Such children often find satisfaction and human warmth in schools. But in school, Jerry was doomed to failure because he had a severe reading disability in spite of being bright. He spent weeks away from school, living in an empty shack he had located. He was a precocious child, sadly aware of his problems and with an almost adult hopeless-ness in regard to any happy solution of them.

The group was dancing to the even, steady beat of the drum. Two boys sat in the corner weeping because they did not want to dance but wanted to go out of the room. Patsy, who always seemed to take the part of the negativistic group, supported them by beating against the door with his fists and feet and throwing his shoes at it. The two boys joined him and suddenly all three started to march in a circle, chanting: "We want to go home! We want to go home!" Their feet

moved in time with the drum beat. When they were convinced by look-ing through the dance leader's purse that she had no key and could not let them out, Patsy began to work with the group and the other two sat quietly watching the dancing.

Ralph was always active. He was proficient at turning cartwheels and somersaults, and turning around his own axis. He had no fear unless he was being held or carried by someone. On this day, a steady pulse with a repetitive pattern was being beaten on the drum. The children were crawling and rolling on the floor. Ralph rolled over Carrol, grasping him around the neck. Carrol became frightened and, losing control of himself, attacked Ralph. Both became extremely upset and Carrol had to be taken from the room. The steady rhythm of the drum began again. Ralph gave himself up to an orgy of cartwheels and turns. When he fell to the floor, he continued his movement by rolling and turning somersaults without interruption for at least 10 minutes. When the class was dismissed Ralph stayed behind and, taking the drum, began to tell the story of *King Kong* which he had seen in the movies. He punctuated his words with drum beats and occasional explosive sounds and gestures of his whole body. When the next group of children came he participated in the work in a much less spectacular way.

The class was playing "Indians," dancing around in a circle to the steady beat of the drum. Fred decided to be the fire and sat in the center of the circle making hissing sounds and darting movements with his arms and hands. When the class left, Fred was asked to stay. His fire dance was praised and it was suggested that he repeat it and let the fire spread. The drum beat was resumed. He started his fire dance as before, sitting in the middle of the room, twisting his arms and legs and darting them out from his body. Gradually he began twisting and swaying more in his torso and the fire spread through the room with rolls and cartwheels. Fred became dizzy and tried to stop, but he must have felt the movement continuing for he said, "The house is going up." Following this, he rose from the floor, stretching up as far as he could until he was on his toes. Then he started to jump, always reaching up toward the ceiling. He became tired from the jumping, and rested. Suddenly he found a small toy pistol with wooden cartridges that one of the boys had hidden under a radiator and began shooting the doctor and the dance teacher. When they had been killed he danced a dance of triumph and then killed himself. His next game was to throw the cartridges at the wall and pretend he had blown up the building. He acted out very realistically and dramatically the collapsing of the walls and his being buried under the debris. He dug himself out again, only to place the cartridges between his toes and blow up his feet.

A gong was being played with slow, steady beats, producing a swinging tone. The children began to sway back and forth. Patsy who no longer resisted the work, began to swing his arms and legs. As the gong tone became more insistent and faster, Patsy turned slowly first to one side, then to the other, rising on his toes, then dropping his body onto the whole foot with knees bent. The gong beat increased in speed to a steady tremolo. He swung his arms more violently and turned very fast around his own axis, so lightly that his feet seemed to leave the ground.

The following notes on Carrol were taken over a period of about one month. On his first day in class when Ralph grasped him around the neck Carrol became terrified. He lost complete control of himself, screamed and kicked, and tried to get at Ralph. He had to be held by the nurse, who finally took him out of the room. Later he was brought back in a much quieter condition.

The group was playing at being animals. Several children began to ride on the teacher's back. Carrol was very much amused but did not take part. He played at being a buffalo and butted the children and the teacher. Then he tried to make a double animal by putting his arms around the waist of a crawling boy and crawling behind him.

Benjamin was a chicken attacking children. The chicken was killed by a child; it came alive and was killed again. Finally it was really "dead" and should be buried. The children "dug" a grave and "covered" him up. They all wanted to step on the "grave" and then left him. Carroll did not take part until Benjamin was buried. Then he crouched next to him, closed his eyes and performed a kind of sorcerer's dance. He had a slight vibration in his body and passed his hands back and forth over Benjamin's head and body. When the children came back he pushed them away. Finally he slid away of his own accord when the chicken decided to come alive again and attack.

Diary notation: Carrol made another double crawling animal, this time with his head between another boy's legs.

Diary notation: Today Carrol is more active. He tries cartwheels. He started a very good Indian skip. He is very self-conscious and must be coaxed into working. For the first time he really tried some of the stunts. He allowed the teacher to take him by the arms and swing him around parallel to the floor. He was extremely thrilled by the flying sensation when his feet left the ground. He kept urging the other boys to try it. He also jumped up and sat on the teacher's haunches, letting himself down to the ground backward until he could walk on his hands between the teacher's legs. It is characteristic of him that he works for short periods only. He sits quietly in a corner or on a bench between working periods and dreams. He knows he is dreaming but says he does not know what it is about. He has many impulses to start dancing but stops himself.

Diary notation: Carrol alone. An animal that "can walk through walls." He crawled around the room at the very edge, so that his body touched the walls at all times. The third time around he closed his eyes, dropped his head between his arms and felt the ground with his "fore paws" before moving ahead.

Sitting with his legs curled up under him: "Oh! I am sinking in the water, way down! Now I am down on the bottom." This was accompanied by a great many changes of facial expression; then he closed his eyes and lay down.

As a result of the cymbal sound, Carrol was an airplane. He landed in the water and became a hydroplane, moving on his abdomen, legs held quiet, the arms pulling him forward.

He was reminded of his "sorcerer's" dance. He asked for one of the boys to dance with, since he said he could not conceive an imaginary companion. While waiting for the other boy he played with the cymbal and listened to its undertone. He accompanies everything with facial expressions and sounds. Many expressions are like African masks.

Jerry came. The boys played lions; they were sleeping lions, dreaming. Carrol: "I am in a strait-jacket. I am wild." He lay perfectly still, arms at his sides making faces. He crawled around and then lay in the straight-jacket again, sleeping, dreaming. To Jerry: "You'd better watch out when I wake up. I'm wild." He began to talk of being a buffalo, then turned into a rooster. "I'm a rooster laying eggs in my nest. It is a very big nest." He climbed on Jerry's back and stayed there quietly while Jerry tried to crawl, protesting that he was no nest.

Jerry played the cymbal as Carrol lay on his back on the floor. He asked Jerry to hold the cymbal so close to his face that it was practically touching it. He lay still, listening and making faces. Suddenly he said: "Oh! where does that sound come from? I wonder where it is! I must find it." He looked at the teacher and smiled about his joke. Before this he had said the same thing after he had been dancing for some time to the sound of the drum. He is perfectly conscious of the origin of the sound, looks at the teacher to see whether she takes him seriously or knows he is playing.

"I am a monkey. See, I am climbing on you. You are a tree." With that he pretended to climb, holding on to the leader's clothes. He gave up very soon and lay down.

Carrol alternates activity with sitting or lying down with closed eyes, making faces and saying all kinds of things, sometimes snatches of stories, sometimes just sounds. He is full of fantasies, any one of which would be good dance material. He plays good rhythms on the instruments, not for noise, but for quality. His periods of activity are merely short fragments of his prolonged fantasies. The animal crawling through the walls was continued for the longest period.

The atmosphere created by the repetition of sound and the quality of tone provokes movement reactions. It also causes group reactions which seem to force even the more difficult children into participation. The feeling of unreality also seems to be established since an aggressive activity is rarely carried to its realistic conclusion. If the rhythm is discontinued the group begins to fall apart. If one of the children takes the drum and plays, there is a tendency for the dance activity to change into rivalry over the instrument. Only when a child is able to play well and steadily will his accompaniment be tolerated by the other children. Sooner or later, however, they will demand their turns at the instrument. So far, the problem of having the children accompany themselves has not been solved, since playing the instruments is an attraction far greater than dancing.

The intensity of activity may be regulated through the use of the crescendo and accelerando or the diminuendo and retardando. Sometimes especially susceptible children will develop their own dynamics to the accompaniment of a steady quiet bass, or they may create all kinds of dramatic situations. The gong and cymbal may be used to quiet an especially unruly group and hold tensions at a soft or medium level. This is accomplished by playing a steady low tremolo. The crescendo of the cymbal may be used to heighten tensions to an intolerable point of suspense which is broken by a tremendous crash and muting of the cymbal. This leads to jumping or falling, usually accompanied by vocal outbursts. The gong may be used to create a swinging impulse which causes swaying of the entire body and leads to pendulum movements of the torso and arms and legs, finally to a feeling of suspension in which the child allows the body to be carried through space in curved sweeping lines, and to spin and turn.

Creative dance activity in children may also be released by using a circular formation with a rhythmic or dynamic activity such as skipping, leaping, running, and "Indian steps." Another method is to place the children on their backs on the floor and proceed with stunts. From these exercises the usual development is into animal fantasies with their characteristic movements of crawling on all fours, propelling the body across the floor without the use of the hands or feet, rolling over one another, jumping like frogs. Certain children prefer to retain their human character. This leads to dramatic dance games of shooting animals or of animals attacking humans, or horse and rider games.

From the activity on the floor the children begin to climb on one another, first on the backs of crawling children, then riding "piggyback." Finally they attempt to ride on each other's shoulders or climb three high on one another's backs. There seems to be no consciousness of the necessity of a small child's climbing upon a larger one. Often a very large boy tries to ride on the shoulders of a very small boy. When this is frustrated through the interference of the leader or through failure of the experiment, there is usually a reaction of disinterest and a break in the continuity of group work. Soon the climbing activity is taken up again in relation to objects about the room, with the development of all kinds of jumps from various heights with different resulting fantasy activities, such as diving into water and swimming, animals jumping from trees onto people, and so on. Also various jumps from the ground onto and over objects and each other are undertaken. These are soon combined with more complicated rhythms such as cartwheels and somersaults remembered from the work on the floor.

The children soon begin to feel the need of help in these more difficult activities and look to the leader for technical aid. Here, then, is the opening for the leader to place the children in unaccustomed positions in relation to space. They are encouraged to lie on their backs and are lifted by their feet so that they have to put their hands on the floor. They are then told to look between the legs of the leader and walk through on their hands. Their final position is lying flat on the abdomen. Usually the child is so astonished and pleased that this has to be repeated over and over. Or, the child jumps and sits on the haunches of the leader. Then, holding by his feet, he drops over backward and crawls through between the leader's legs. Or, the child lies on his back on the floor with his arms outstretched above his head. In this position he is swung around the leader who holds him by the hands and turns around his own axis. As the momentum increases, the feet leave the floor. This usually results in outbursts of pleasurable excitement and verbal descriptions of the sensations felt while "flying" through the air. Since all of these activities require two persons, often one or two of the stronger, more courageous children imitate the leader, and again the relation of child with child is established.

Usually in early dance training each individual is primarily concerned only with himself. The awareness of others creeps in very gradually. Then the dancer is concerned with preserving his own identity. He must slowly be led to the point where he will dare to have contact, to compete, and to create with others.

The feeling of his own physical strength and the ability to control and direct it is a stage the dancer reaches after having freed himself from anxiety and fear over the dynamic violence of primitive motility and its associated emotions. For the dancer, anxiety and fear of dynamic movement spring from insecurity in the concept of his own body image and from resistance to consecutive changes in himself. Exploration of the dynamic power of movement brings to the fore instincts of self preservation, destructive and constructive drives, and through their mastery brings about an understanding of these elements. In the case of successful sublimation it should lead to a feeling of security through a knowledge of the emotional sources underlying these drives, and therefore to their control. The Hindu and Balinese dance,[11] particularly that of men, is tremendous in the projection of controlled power. The difficulty in teaching this to present-day adults in our civilization is the conventional rejection and fear of the "animal in man."

The ability to manipulate the body on the floor has to be learned. It is partly a technical problem; it is also a purposeful reversal to in-

11. Franziska Boas, ed., *The Function of the Dance in Human Society* (New York: Boas School, 1949).

fantile movement. Often the greater part of this type of movement is resisted by the adult and even by the child because they have been taught at some time that such activity is not proper. In permitting this activity on the dance floor one block, or resistance, is removed and the path is open for acceptance of the psychological content through sublimation in dance form.

If, however, the person is still unable to enjoy this state of reversal, if he has learned technically to perform leaps and falls and rolls without experiencing pleasure, then a further block has been encountered. Such a person will reject this type of movement and will exclude it from his dance, or he will go through the external motions of technically controlled gestures but will avoid clarifying the content. An observer sensitive to movement forms, or a teacher who is aware of the psychological factors, will recognize in such a performance a substitution of form for content. Often a definite block becomes apparent again and again. Of course this may not be constant and the intended sublimation is able to assert itself for moments during an improvisation. However such blocks can be eliminated only by a therapeutic approach.

This therapeutic approach must be handled from many angles. Physical and mental relaxation in movement, combined with the use of rhythm and sound accompaniment, provide one way. The use of drums, gongs, cymbals, and rattles as accompaniment for the dance activity concentrate the pupil's attention on the rhythmic pattern and the quality of the atmosphere so that his attention is diverted from the actions of his physical body. The concentration on sound and the repetition of the same kind of sound activate the body in spite of itself; muscle tone and balance become more homogeneous and the fear of physical injury is lessened. The mind is freed from this particular worry and movement fantasy is set in motion.

This dissociation of mind and body exists to a high degree in some schizophrenic children. It appears to be a suspension, a complete physical balance in an unbalanced emotional state. One such child could, in a standing position, perform a deep backbend with apparently no effort. Another example, in an adult schizophrenic, is a complete wide circular swing of the torso. Dancers can acquire such use of body dynamics, an uninterrupted flow of movement through the entire body, only after extensive training. The mechanism enabling the schizophrenic to do this is still a matter for research, and the reason for spontaneously starting such movements is not as yet clarified. Sometimes the movement can be induced in the schizophrenic; at other times there is no reaction. The particular patterns described resulted not from a verbal demand but came as a reaction to rhythmic sound.

The process of learning to be aware of the body image and its appearance, the anticipation and reaction to the movement of others, and the consciousness of space shape and the changes that occur in the body and in space, are primarily on the sensory level. Each part of the body becomes an entity in itself with its own sensitivity and desires, so that it is possible to speak of the body of an individual as the coordination of many different parts, each with its own personality. Certain parts of the body may be sensitive and alert and react to inner and outer stimuli while other parts may be dull and unconscious of their own existence. These parts may not react because they were neglected when motor impulses were given, or because there was not sufficient sensitivity in the muscles to respond to the message they received; or they may refuse to react because they have been immobilized by a conscious or subconscious inhibitory message due to some physical or psychological block. Such conditions will result in imbalance and poor coordination.

To stimulate the sensitivity to minute movements in the different parts of the body, the dancer sometimes works with closed eyes either in silence, or in the state of suspension created by the soft playing of gong tones. He is then told to move whatever part of the body seems to feel like moving regardless of the gesture which may result, or the relation of one movement to another. Usual beginnings may be scratching the nose, pushing the hair back, shifting of weight, pulling at clothes, twitchings of muscles, and so on—indications of self-consciousness; or stamping of feet, collapse of body, rubbing of hands together, shrugging of shoulders—indications of irritation, despair, disgust. The leader points out these uncontrolled subconscious movements and discusses their significance. The pupil is urged to do exactly what he feels as soon as he feels it. In this way the body is set in motion. Gradually more and more movement is experienced and larger gestures are made. The body begins to respond to the various shifts of weight and begins to travel through different space levels following the laws of inertia, impulse, and momentum. Emotional reactions become manifest and changes in tension begin to create a dynamic and rhythmic flow of movement. During these activities the instructor is constantly encouraging by words and sounds the externalization of gestures and movements which begin to make their appearance. Eventually only the percussion sounds are continued, and the body moves by itself.

There is a logic in the development of one movement into another both in the body and in the use of space. To the trained observer any interjection of an arbitrary movement can immediately be discerned. This is a sign of a break in concentration and usually takes the form of some habit movement pattern which the pupil considers "safe," that is, either it covers up the externalization of a "forbidden" fantasy or sensation, or it prevents exploration into the unknown.

After such experimentation with the dance, the student is sometimes asked to create a figure of himself in clay. These figures invariably show, as was seen in the case of Helga, how much of the body is included in the consciousness of the body image. Sometimes a medium such as clay, paint, wood, charcoal, or chalk is used to resolve a block which is apparent in dance. It has been interesting to see the correlation between the problem in dance and the new medium which is chosen.

For example, one adult enjoyed wallowing on the ground, using the body sensuously. In such a case the presence of physical pleasure observed in the student is to be used as a positive factor. Its translation into an art form can be gradually induced by indirect methods which will change the tone of the muscle tension, increase the amount of passivity or relaxation in the movement. The student must be made conscious of the audience outside herself in order that the movement may be dissociated from self-indulgence and may attain a more direct release from the original tension. This woman was immediately fascinated by clay as a medium of expression. She enjoyed the feel of substance, enjoyed mashing the hard lumps of clay and kneading the clay in preparation for the actual modeling. After a few awkward atttempts at manipulation of the material she quite suddenly was able to mold it and create objects which gave expression in an objective form to her preoccupation with her body and her inner self. It happened that she had been in an accident which had distorted her face. All her figures displayed broad flat noses. The handling of the clay, the tactile element, was an adequate performance during the phase this individual was in. By concentrating the pleasure sensation which had been distributed over her whole body in her hands and fingers, she could free her fantasies and give them form in a medium removed from herself. It seemed that the sensuous feeling enjoyed while working with clay enabled her to formulate what she could not express in her own body. Her dance movement began to change and she was better able to create in both media.

To sum up, the teaching of modern creative dance offers a great many facets for the projection of physical and psychological problems. The process of mastering the elements and techniques of dance parallels closely the processes followed by a patient in psychoanalysis. The mastering of dance techniques and the formulation of emotions and fantasies in dance improvisations may clarify subconscious material and bring it to the surface of consciousness. Careful study of dance movement can become a valuable diagnostic instrument, particularly for children who constantly accompany their dance activity with verbalizations expressing their fantasies.

PHILIP MAY, MILTON WEXLER,
JERI SALKIN, AND TRUDI SCHOOP

Nonverbal Techniques
in the Re-establishment of Body Image
and Self-Identity—A Report

Dr. Philip May, Dr. Milton Wexler, and two movement therapists, Jeri Salkin and Trudi Schoop, explore the dual complexities of body image and movement therapy in this selection. Movement therapists have intuitively grasped the therapeutic effects of dance on the body percept. Rather than assuming the therapy's efficacy, the authors examine specific changes which follow its application.

In this study, thirty-eight clients participate for six months in either dance or music therapy, three times per week. The authors report tangible gains for the clients in movement therapy: "There was a statistically significant difference in improvement between the patients who actually received treatment and the controls, as measured by the number of participants who improved to any extent and as measured by the number who improved the most."[1] If it may be considered established that movement therapy has a measurable impact upon the client's body awareness, then movement researchers may take the next step. By utilizing the standards devised by these authors, various techniques can be checked for efficiency in enhancing body awareness as well as for permanence of their effects.

The authors assign the name of "Body Ego Technique" to the style of teaching employed by Jeri Salkin and Trudi Schoop. In this article they assert that it is an innovative form of therapy, and differs demonstrably from all other forms of dance or movement therapy. Such a claim does not appear to be substantiated. In two later spinoffs from this study, Salkin enumerates the kinds of exercises that she finds

Reprinted with permission of *Psychiatric Research Reports,* Vol. 16, 1963.
1. See the conclusion of this article.

useful, and Schoop, in a separate book, describes some other methods.[2] Judging from literary impressions is often misleading; nevertheless, it appears that these two movement therapists represent the gamut of usual contemporary practice: Salkin stresses skills and Schoop, spontaneity. A movie of the two therapists in action (also entitled "Body-Ego Technique") illustrates how techniques traditionally employed by teachers of creative dance are easily adapted for use with institutionalized adults. As Salkin admits, "The classes in the research project were very much like the classes given to the normal preschool child."[3]

I believe that expressive dance combined with exercises designed to enhance body awareness are not as incompatible as the authors of this report suggest. The combination is part and parcel of the movement therapist's bag of tricks. I use a mixture of these approaches, for example, with Sally, a four-year-old retarded girl. The tumorous left side of her face had been surgically removed. One goal of therapy is to shape her behavior to focus on her misshapen image in a mirror. Sally needs to learn the whereabouts of her facial parts as well as to practice focusing her misaligned eyes on stationary and moving objects. At first she turned away from the sight of herself in the mirror. Today she studies her reflection for longer and longer periods as she and I bounce and swirl our heads to the beat of the music.

Sally, up to this point, refused to sustain any form of gross motor activity with an adult. The first years of her life had been spent with free movement inhibited, particularly after surgery. Well-intentioned adults came to be associated with painful touch. I attempt to sensitize her body to a variety of pleasurable kinesthetic stimuli. I call out names of body parts, emotions, directions, and sensations as we spontaneously dance. Sally's passive behaviors are ignored; her active involvement in the dance is reinforced with her choice of any favorite activity.

The passive child curled in the corner is seen no more. Sally's arrival is heralded from afar by shrieks and giggles and the loud sound of running footsteps toward me.   M.N.C.

---

2. Jeri Salkin, *Body-Ego Technique: An Educational and Therapeutic Approach to Body Image and Self-Identity* (Springfield, Ill.: Charles C Thomas, 1973). Trudi Schoop with Peggy Mitchell, *Won't You Join the Dance?* (Palo Alto, Calif.: National Press Books, 1974).

3. Jeri Salkin, *Body-Ego Technique,* 54.

Introduction[4]

It is possible that disturbances of body image and self-identity are of central importance in the etiology and treatment of schizophrenia, and there is a sound theoretical basis for the use of treatment techniques specifically based on these concepts.

This paper will discuss these concepts and present a new technique based on them—Body Ego Technique—that has important research, diagnostic, and therapeutic implications; it will also present some preliminary results from a therapeutic trial of this technique with chronic regressed psychotic patients.

Theory and Background of Body Ego Technique

The term "body image" refers to the picture of our own body as it is formed in our minds. It is a composite picture, conscious but also largely unconscious, composed of partial impressions but also perceived as a unity, or what Schilder (1950) and Head (1926) refer to as a "body schema." In the realm of neurophysiology, destruction of such "schemata" by a lesion of the cortex renders impossible all recognition of posture or of the localization of a stimulated spot in the affected part of the body. In the realm of psychology, destruction of such mental representations, or their fragmentation, may destroy the relationship to reality or the understanding of what is perceived in the outside world.

Freud (1927) placed great emphasis on the body itself as the basis of the ego. He said that the ego is first and foremost a body ego; it is ultimately derived from bodily sensations, chiefly from those springing from the surface of the body; it may be regarded as the mental projection of the surfaces of the body.

Disturbances of body image produce vast changes in psychic structure, especially in those areas of ego functioning which have to do with reality relationships. Why this is so is simply stated by Kubie (1934). "Since the Child's world begins inevitably with the body, and since the force which instigates the child to expand his knowledge is always the pressure of bodily desires, and since every new fact of experience which enters into psychic life can make its entrance only

4. This investigation was supported in part by a research grant from the California State Department of Mental Hygiene, with the additional support of interested private citizens. We acknowledge with gratitude the support of F. H. Garrett, M.D., Superintendent and Medical Director; Louis R. Nash, M.D., Associate Superintendent; and the nursing staff of Camarillo Hospital, without whose help this study could not have been carried out.

by relating itself to that which is already present, it follows that every new fact apperceived by the child must somehow relate itself to bodily things."

This high valuation of the body image in relation to the development of the ego and psychopathology was elaborated by Paul Schilder in his classic contribution, *The Image and Appearance of the Human Body* (1950), which demonstrated the central importance of body image in connection with a wide variety of pathological pictures, and emphasized the related problems of identity and reality perception.

The importance of body ego and sense of self in the psychopathology of schizophrenia has been discussed by Hoffer (1950); Federn (1952); Scott (1951); Freedman (1954); Greenson (1953); and more recently by Fisher and Cleveland (1958); Freeman, Cameron, and McGhie (1958); Jacobson (1959); and Des Lauriers (1960).

Freeman, Cameron, and McGhie (1958) conclude that "dissolution of ego boundaries is the basic disturbance" in schizophrenia and that "all other manifestations can be viewed as necessary elaborations of it."

A treatment approach could be soundly based on these concepts. Fisher and Cleveland (1958) comment: "These findings . . . would seem to point the way toward special treatment efforts. If one of the major areas of confusion to the schizophrenic involves the limits of his own body, would not any effort directed at attempting to redefine and reidentify these limits prove valuable? Further, if regression has been extreme, would not some definition of body limits necessarily precede other attempts at ego building and strengthening?"

Treatment techniques tend to be verbal or physical-pharmacological. It is, perhaps, impractical to devise a purely nonverbal technique —there are few patients and few therapists who can tolerate totally silent communication. There are, however, as Ruesch and Kees (1956) point out, strong reasons for developing techniques that are heavily weighted in a nonverbal mode for the treatment of psychotic patients who have regressed to relatively nonverbal levels. Moreover, it is mainly in these patients that body image and identity disturbances are most severe.

There have been relatively few attempts to make deliberate use of these concepts as a tactical maneuver in psychotherapy, for example, Reich (1949), Sechehaye (1951), Des Lauriers (1960), Freeman, Cameron, and McGhie (1958), and Rank (1949). Appleby, Proano, and Perry (1960) present a total approach, focusing on psychiatric nursing activities.

Interest in specific treatment sessions concentrating on body image, identity, posture, and movement has been limited. Fisher and Cleveland (1958) in their comprehensive survey mention only unpublished work by Rabinovitch with schizophrenic children at the Children's Memorial Hospital in Montreal.

Apart from individual psychotherapy and play therapy, in those instances where a nonverbal mode of expression is used deliberately as treatment, for example, painting, modeling, occupational therapy, industrial therapy, the goals are usually in terms of diagnostic evaluation, or sublimation and discharge of instinctual energy, or socialization or rehabilitation, rather than in terms of nonverbal contact or a deliberate reintegration of body image and identity. A notable exception is the work of Lauretta Bender and Franziska Boas (1941, 1952), the latter being an exponent of the modern dance movement. They discuss at length theoretical aspects related to body image and their techniques and experience with groups of six to eight patients on the children's ward of the Psychiatric Division of the Bellevue Hospital.

However, in general, dance therapists have tended to concentrate on emotional expression and communication with, at the most, only marginal reference to body awareness, for example, H'Doubler (1940), Zegart (1956), Bainbridge, Duddington, and Collingdon (1953), Genther (1954), and Rosen (1957). Chace (1953, 1961), spoken of by Rosen (1957) as the "first lady" of dance therapy, writes of dance as a means of nonverbal communication of emotion and social reintegration. Her technique does not focus specifically on body image and identity but on emotional expression and awareness of one's emotions. "Basic dance is the externalization of those inner feelings which cannot be expressed in rational speech but can only be shared in rhythmic, symbolic action" (Chace, 1961).

The possibility of change in body image during dance therapy has been recognized, but as a measure of patient change rather than as a therapeutic focus, for example, Marks (1960), Christrup (1958), and Chace (1957).

Body Ego Technique

The technique used in this present study—which we will call "body ego technique"—was developed over the period 1948–60 by two exponents of modern dance (Jeri Salkin and Trudi Schoop), working without any technical assistance from professionals in the psychiatric or psychological field.

The rather clumsy term "body ego technique" is used to make it quite clear that we are not referring to psychodrama or to dance therapy in the sense that these terms are commonly used. The technique is fundamentally different from so-called "dance therapy" and is not the same as the therapeutic dance techniques in use elsewhere: it focuses attention on body posture and movement as they relate to body image; on the patient's sense of time as experienced and expressed in different speeds of movement; on body ego boundaries—the distinction between the person and his surroundings; and on reawakening by bodily movement a range of lost emotional experiences rather than on direct expression of the patient's present emotions.

Comparison with Chace's description of expressive dance therapy (1953) will help to clarify this point. In dance therapy sessions there is an initial warmup period in which there is a free choice of recorded music reflecting the patient's mood, to which they are free to move spontaneously, either alone, with the dance therapist, or in small groups. Chace structures the sessions as *dance*, with the therapist initially leading the group but subsequently transferring leadership to the patients—"after all or nearly all of the group have become involved in this activity, the therapist initiates, to waltz music, a circle. Following the lead of the therapist, the circle of patients goes through simple warm-up movements such as arm and leg swings, gradually moving into body stretches and body swings. By this time, some member has fallen into a peculiarly personal movement pattern, and the therapist relinquishes the leadership to this patient, encouraging the group to move with him. A succession of patients will pick up the role of leadership in movement and thereafter the therapist largely plays the role of a catalyst" (Chace, 1953). At the end of one of Chace's dance therapy sessions, there is "a breakdown into individual or small group movement patterns and a final period of listening to music and conversing. It is during this portion of the session that original dances are improvised. . . . these dances have form and continuity and are organized in response to music rhythms being played. It is possible for the soloist to accept an audience reaction of hand clapping or a dance by the group which is similar to his own, but modified, and still return to the group when his dance is completed" (Chace, 1953).

Body ego technique classes are quite different; I will describe a typical example, although they do not always follow the same pattern; in fact, we would emphasize that in any particular therapeutic situation the therapist must be free to use a flexible approach adapted to the patient's current level of functioning. The procedure may be carried out with individual patients by one therapist[5] working with a pianist assistant, or with a group of patients by one or two therapists. Sessions normally last forty minutes with adults in a group, twenty minutes for an individual session. Most patients respond to rhythm and this seems to be the most acceptable way to start a class; the use of beaters helps them to follow a given rhythm as well as to beat their own rhythm. In working with a group, the patients are drawn into a circle, barefoot and sitting on the floor; they are shown and asked[6] to follow a given rhythm as well as given the opportunity to beat their own rhythm for others to follow, the rhythm being varied in quality, duration, and tempo. Almost all patients will start at this level, but any approach may be used to establish initial contact; treatment is started at whatever level the patient can be reached through movement.

Rhythm is continued in beating actions such as clapping, hitting, and stamping, in other rhythmical movements, and in different tempo and qualities of breathing. Body awareness is stressed by having the patients touch and move different parts of the body separately; carry out coordinated movements of the entire body; carry out extremes of flexion and extension of separate parts and of the entire body. Parts of the body, physical objects and persons, left and right, fast and slow, and so on, are named, seen, or touched simply and clearly as for a child.

Movements that are usually learned in childhood are carried out and varied in tempo and quality—crawling, walking, running, galloping, jumping, hopping, turning, and skipping. Patients recall these childhood movements and often use them in improvisation. Particular attention is paid to direction and use of space—right, left, up, down, circle, square, diagonal, and so forth.

The patients are taught movements and postures that accompany the emotions of childhood—throwing, kicking, stamping, stroking, or caressing. In sharp contrast to dance therapy, in our work it is important that, at first, the patients are not asked to express their own emotions or to express a named emotion, but rather to carry out the movements demonstrated. As with a child learning, the name of the emotion is added to characterize the feeling. Later, as the patient

5. The word "therapist" is used here for lack of a paradigmatic term.

6. It must be understood that most of the communication between patient and therapist is nonverbal.

comes more into contact, he may be asked to associate particular action with a named emotion or person, for example, to chase the therapist as if he were angry; to approach another patient in friendly greeting; or to run away as if in fear. Later, also, he may be asked such things as, "Show me how a child walks. How does an adult walk? How does a sick person walk? How does your mother walk? How do you walk?"

Fans, scarves, and other props are offered to encourage various qualities of movement; in their distribution and collection, the therapist clarifies the acts of giving and taking, accepting, keeping, rejecting, and returning.

From a theoretical and from a practical standpoint, it is necessary to distinguish body ego technique from social dance therapy, dance psychodrama, and expressive dance therapy.

At Camarillo, we do not attempt to get the patient to do modern dancing, or to perform recognized dance steps to an appropriate musical background for recreation and socialization, as in social dance therapy. In expressive dance therapy, the musical accompaniment is structured music suitable for dancing (Chace, 1953); it tends to structure the action, although less rigidly than in social dancing. In our work, the musical accompaniment follows, supports, picks up, accentuates, and sets flexible limits for the changing patterns of the therapeutic interaction—it is improvised rather than readymade, and sensitive, flexible adaptation to the process of patient-therapist interaction is of crucial importance.

In body ego technique, unlike psychodrama and expressive dance therapy, there is a deliberate educational focus. These sessions are "classes" with the patients learning much as a child does through imitation. Patients are guided to experience postures and movements associated with the normal stages of infantile, childhood, and adolescent development. Through movement patterns they are acquainted with the physical experiences that accompany various emotional states, such as anger, love, and fear; and with the postures and movements that accompany a range of attitude patterns from withdrawal to extraversion, control to exuberance. The therapist directs the patient's attention to situations which assist him to make contact with reality, define ego boundaries, alter pathological posture and movement, and recognize the distinction between self and others.

In body ego technique the focus is primarily on the cathexis of ego function in relation to affect discharge—on the process of re-cathexis —reactivating and recalling the lost physical memory traces of emotions, and so of associated lost objects. In dance psychodrama and expressive dance therapy, the focus is primarily on the expression and release of the patient's emotional impulses.

Social interaction and communication may result from body ego technique, but they are the result rather than a central objective, as in expressive dance therapy.

Research Design

In a pilot investigation of the therapeutic use of body ego technique, eighteen female and twenty male chronic, regressed, schizophrenic patients were assigned by a random method to individual treatment, group treatment, and control groups; an attempt was made to get the sickest, most disturbed patients in the hospital, and the group included patients who were assaultive, incontinent, and socially disorganized. No attempt was made to equate experimental and control groups by age, education level, or other variables, but tabulation shows that the treatment and control groups were adequately equated in important variables such as age; sex; marital status; religion; education; social position; occupation; duration of illness; duration of previous hospital care; previous treatment with electro-shock, tranquilizers, or lobotomy; and initial status.

The characteristics of the patients were such that most clinicians would consider them difficult or even hopeless problems for any type of treatment, and especially for verbal therapy.

Age: 22–50, median 35.
Duration of psychotic symptoms: 35–305 months, median 135.
Age at onset of psychotic symptoms: 10–43, median 24.
Duration of previous hospital care: 25–305 months, median 105.
Race: White, 15; Negro, 10; Mexican, 10; Oriental, 3.
Marital status: Never married, 32 (84 percent); married, 2; separated, 1; divorced, 3.
Education: 89 percent high school or less. 42 percent junior high school or less.
Occupational level: Low—none above clerical or sales level.
Social class: None in highest two categories, 68 percent in lowest class.
Previous treatment: EST—range 0–325 treatments, median 60.
Tranquilizers: 85 percent.
Lobotomy: 3 (7.5 percent).
Insulin: 10 (26.3 percent).

All the study patients were transferred to the same mixed-sex ward and lived in the same environment with no discrimination between experimental and control groups except for the experimental treatment given. If a patient was receiving a maintenance dose of tranquilizing drug before the study, this was continued at exactly the same maintenance level during the experimental period, whether the patient was in the experimental or control group. No electrical treatment (EST) was given to any patient.

Treatment group patients received either individual or group experimental treatment, according to the group to which they were assigned, three times a week for six months. Control patients were sent off the ward to a music therapy session for an equal length of time.

All patients assigned to individual treatment attended and cooperated, although some had to be treated on the ward for a few sessions before they would agree to go to the treatment room. One patient assigned to group treatment refused absolutely to attend sessions and could not be persuaded despite intensive effort, including a degree of physical force. Three other patients assigned to group treatment went to the sessions but never participated to any significant extent. One sat on the sidelines for all sessions, refusing to participate because there was a Negro in the group (a trial session showed that he would have cooperated well with individual treatment, but the research design prevented transfer to individual treatment). Another joined in completely only a few times; otherwise, she sat on one side and became aggressive or ran away when attempts were made to get her into the group. The third, a man who kept a shirt over his head all the time, taking only occasional peeks at the world, never joined in completely. He sometimes floated around the edge of the group, disorganizing proceedings somewhat by his appearance and autistic utterances, but mostly pacing up and down the side of the room. He also could have been contacted by an individual approach.

Evaluation of Change

Evaluation was carried out before and after the experimental period as outlined in Table 1.

Quite obviously, evaluation of change in these very regressed patients is a difficult problem. In all probability the most valid and comprehensive method is "blind" clinical evaluation by an independent person accustomed to working with this type of patient. In this study a psychiatrist, who had no other contact with the patients during the study, examined them only at the beginning and at the end of treat-

Table 1

Assessment of Patient Change

I. *By Psychologist* ("blind")
   Rorschach
   Bender-Gestalt
   D. A. P.
II. *By Nurses and Technicians* (consensus ratings)
   a. M. A. C. C. Rating Scale

Motility	(3 items)
Affect	(3 items)
Cooperation	(4 items)
Communication	(4 items)
Total adjustment	(11 items)

   b. *S. S. Nursing Rating Scale* (71 items, including 14 M. A. C. C. items)

Body movement	(10 items)
Emotional tone	(17 items)
Socialization	(10 items)
Cooperativeness	(5 items)
Self-concept	(10 items)
General functioning	(19 items)

III. *By Independent Psychiatrist* ("blind")

a. Ann Arbor Mental Status Scale	(9 items)
b. Jenkins Symptom Rating Sheet	(16 items)
c. Camarillo Dynamic Assessment Scale	(9 items)
d. Improvement Rating Scale	(5 point)
e. Clinical description	

IV. *By Therapist* (treatment group only)

a. Clinical description	
b. Improvement Rating Scale	(8 point)*
c. Patient-Therapist Contact Rating Scale	(9 point)*

* These two ratings were obtained by consensus of a psychologist and a psychiatrist, using therapist's clinical description.

ment. The examination was "blind" to the extent that he was not told what treatment the patient received and had instructions to try not to find out. He completed two behavioral rating scales—the Ann Arbor Mental Status Scale and the Jenkins Symptom Rating Scale—and the Camarillo Dynamic Assessment Scale. This latter scale was devised in another study to assess factors of possible psychodynamic importance in schizophrenic patients; it includes ratings of affective contact, anxiety level, ego strength, the extent to which the environment suffers as a result of the patient's illness, insight, motivation, object relations, sense of personal identity, and sexual adjustment. The psychiatrist also gave a clinical description of the patients, and, at the end of treatment, a rating of improvement on a 5-point scale.

We place greatest reliance on the clinician, but to rely solely on his assessment would be to ignore his very real difficulties. His evaluation is based on a "one shot" sample in an interview situation, and no matter how hard he may try not to find out what treatment the patient is getting, if the interview is of adequate length and rapport, some psychotic patients are bound to tell him directly or indirectly.

The second line of approach was rating scales completed by nurses and technicians. Seventy-one items were used, including the affect, cooperation, communication, and total adjustment scales of the M.A.C.C. and some items from the Lorr Scale, covering the areas of body movement, emotional tone, socialization, cooperativeness, self-concept, and general functioning. These scales have definite limitations. They may detect gross changes in general patient behavior, but there just do not exist, at present, reliable, valid, quantified scales to assess adequately changes in body image, self-concept, and identity. This assessment is less skilled than the clinician's and has the merits and demerits of continuing contact with the patient. There is more danger of bias in that the assessment was not blind; our impression from regular meetings with the ward staff is that, in this instance, tension and competition between therapists and nursing staff might lead to bias *against* the treatment method.

The third method of evaluation is by the therapist. It has not been possible so far to devise satisfactory rating scales to reflect their particular frame of reference, and their recorded evaluations were confined to clinical description, from which rating scales of improvement and patient-therapist contact were completed by a psychologist and psychiatrist team.

Finally, psychological testing was used. This is potentially the most valuable and the most revealing of all methods, yet for regressed patients it is also potentially the weakest, dependent as it is on the degree of cooperation of the patient. The Rorschach test was given to twelve experimental and twelve control patients, selected at random. Of these, six refused to take the test either at the beginning or the end, and the remainder gave an average of less than one response per card; such responses as were obtained were not suitable for scoring by Fisher and Cleveland's Barrier score method, nor were they of value for demonstrating change in any other way. It is an unfortunate fact that psychological tests cannot be used satisfactorily with regressed patients because many of these patients either refuse completely to take tests or else give responses that are defensively random or so autistic and erratic as to be useless for evaluation of change. This applies to even relatively simple tests: of the thirty-eight patients, only thirty-three completed the Draw-a-Person test before and after, and only twenty-nine cooperated with the Bender-Gestalt.

Results

It is not our intention to present this as a final, finished piece of research; there were practical limitations of funds and resources, the numbers are small, there are gaps and deficiencies in the design, the analysis of all the possible criteria of change has not yet been done, and research is still continuing. However, the preliminary results are encouraging and suggest that work in this area should be extended to provide more definite answers.

In this study, the most valid objective assessment of patient change is probably the rating of improvement by the independent "blind" clinician, and this is the only criterion that has been analyzed so far. Analysis of other criteria is in process but the results are not available at this time. Table 2 analyzes the clinician's ratings and also illustrates some of the difficulties of design and analysis.

Table 2
Independent Psychiatrists' Ratings

Experimental Category	Psychiatrist's Rating				
	Moderately Improved	Slightly Improved	No Change	Worse	Total
Controls	0	4	11	3	18
Individual treatment					
Assigned	3	2	1	0	6
Attended	3	2	1	0	6
Participated	3	2	1	0	6
Group treatment					
Assigned	3	3	6	2	14
Attended	3	3	5	2	13
Participated	3	3	3	1	10
Both treatments					
Assigned	6	5	7	2	20
Attended	6	5	6	2	19
Participated	6	5	4	1	16

In assessing a treatment method such as this, which cannot be forced on a patient, uncooperative patients pose a problem in analysis of results when patients are assigned randomly to control and treatment groups, since, if a patient refuses to even attend the treatment sessions, any method of analysis must present a biased picture. If the patient is dropped from the study, the treatment group is biased, possibly but not necessarily, in favor of the treatment; if he is included, the treatment group is not a treatment group at all but includes a patient who never received the treatment. It must also be remembered that failure to enlist cooperation is a relevant factor to be evaluated as one of the criteria of the applicability of any treatment method. In this particular study of the most regressed patients in the hospital, it is a measure of the relevance of the approach that there were so few who failed to cooperate with treatment.

Not unexpectedly, there were no "cures" or marked improvements. Six months is not an adequate trial of treatment in chronic regressed patients who have failed to respond previously to all other treatment, but one has to operate within the practical limits of available funds, recognizing that a negative result in this type of patient may mean that assessment methods and design are inadequate rather than that the treatment method is of no value. Nevertheless, both group and individual treatment showed a higher percentage of improvement than the controls. Individual treatment seems to produce better results than group treatment in terms of degree of cooperation and also in terms of improvement.

Of the eighteen controls, four improved slightly, eleven showed no change, and three became worse.

By comparison, of the six patients assigned to individual treatment, three showed moderate improvement, two slight, and one no change; of the fourteen assigned to group treatment (including the nonparticipators), three showed moderate improvement, three slight, six no change, and two worse. Of the four who were assigned to group treatment but would not participate, three showed no change and one became worse. Thus, if one considers only the ten who actually participated in group treatment, the picture is more positive—three showed moderate improvement, three slight, three no change, and one worse.

Table 3 shows χ^2 tests of statistical significance between major groups. There was a statistically significant difference in improvement between the patients who actually received treatment and the controls, as measured by the number of patients who improved to any extent and as measured by the number who improved the most.

Even if one includes in the treatment group those patients who were assigned but never actually received any treatment, the difference is still significant for the number who improved to any extent

Table 3

Statistical Significance

	Assigned to Treatment		Assigned and Participated	
	Experiment	Control	Experiment	Control
Improved #	11	4	11	4
Not improved #	9	14	5	14
	$\chi^2 = 4.2601$	Signif. $>$ 0.05	$\chi^2 = 7.4379$	Signif. $>$ 0.01
Worse #	2	3	1	3
Not worse #	18	15	15	15
	$\chi^2 = 0.0997$	Not signif.	$\chi^2 = 0.8854$	Not signif.
Moderately improved #	6	0	6	0
Less than moderately improved #	14	18	10	18
	$\chi^2 = 6.4125*$	Signif. $>$ 0.02	$\chi^2 = 8.1964$	Signif. $>$ 0.01
	Corrected* $\chi^2 = 4.3547$	Signif. $>$ 0.05	$\chi^2 = 5.8191$	Signif. $>$ 0.02

* Applying Yates and Fisher's correction for expected cell frequencies less than 5 (as described in Edwards, A. L., *Experimental Design in Psychological Research.* New York: Rinehart & Co., Inc., 1950, p. 83.)

and for the number who improved the most, the probability levels being 1 in 20, and 1 in 50, respectively.

The differences between the groups in respect of the number who became worse was not statistically significant, but it does follow the trend established by the other criteria.

Perhaps the most important defect of our study is that the design precludes adequate study of the value of body ego technique in making a patient more accessible to other forms of treatment; or study of patient-therapist relationship and therapeutic process. One of the main values of a nonverbal approach might well be to make the patient ultimately more accessible to verbal methods of treatment, such as psychotherapy or socialization techniques, group treatment, and so on, rather than producing other types of change. It is also possible that body ego technique might well produce patient change and progress during sessions, but such change might not be transferred to the extratherapeutic situation. In either case there would be the danger of bias in interpretation of results, in that the therapist's entirely valid reports of contact and patient change might be condemned as biased, subjective, and invalid, merely because they conflicted with the reports of the ward observers who are, in fact, reporting on different aspects of the patient's performance in a different test situation. Informal clinical observation of treatment sessions, and of individual patients by nonparticipant observers, is unanimously of the opinion that in some patients improvement occurred that was also manifested in ward behavior, while in other patients there was therapeutic progress in treatment sessions that was not transferred to the ward situation. For example, the therapist made excellent contact with a woman who was hostile, uncooperative, and withdrawn from the staff and repeatedly assaultive toward other patients. Her behavior during sessions changed dramatically. She was able to openly show tenderness and love in sessions and spontaneously mentioned some of her emotional problems; on the ward there was no change and in particular she continued to make almost daily assaults on other patients. It was also clear from clinical observation that some patients, previously mute or uncooperative, reached a point where they were ready and even eager to talk and where verbal psychotherapy could have been started—but was not because the experimental design forbade such contamination.

Conclusion

This study has been carried out within necessary practical limitations of funds and resources; it has its limitations, but from the result of only six months of treatment, there is some reason to be optimistic. One can only expect minimal change, if any, in patients of this sort in such a short time, but some improvement has been observed. It is not possible to say whether it is the ego-defining technique that produces the improvement, or the method of making personal contact; or whether other therapists using the same technique could produce the same results; or whether the results will be transient; or whether delayed manifestations of improvement might occur later that are not now visible. These questions cannot be answered until we have adequate support to do more extensive research and to teach the technique to others.

Body ego technique appears to be a potential basic technique for the restoration of ego integrity in the regressed patient, a preliminary step toward opening up the patient for other psychotherapeutic or sociotherapeutic approaches. It works toward re-establishment of ego identity and body image at a primitive level. This is an important step, but it is not the total therapeutic task; for complete reconstitution, the patient still has to progress to re-establishment of identifications and the revival of memory traces of lost objects. In saying that body image is the nucleus of the ego, Freud did not say it was all the ego.

Summary

Body ego technique is a new, nonverbal technique with a sound theoretical background in ego psychology. Results of a preliminary controlled study of its therapeutic use in severely regressed psychotic patients indicate that in these patients it may produce therapeutic change. Clinically it appears to have value in establishing contact, and in opening the way to more verbal therapies, such as psychotherapy and the social therapies.

This report is confined to a study of its therapeutic value. The technique also has important diagnostic and research implications which are the subject of separate research studies.

Bibliography

Appleby, L., A. Proano, and R. Perry. *Theoretical vs. Empirical Treatment Methods: An Exploratory Investigation in Chronic Schizophrenia.* L. Appleby, J. M. Scher, and J. Cumming, eds. Glencoe, Ill.: Free Press, 1960.

Bainbridge, G., A. E. Duddington, M. Collingdon, and C. E. Gardner. "Dance Mime—A Contribution to Treatment in Psychiatry." *J. of Mental Science* 99 (1953), 308–314.

Bender, L., and F. Boas. "Creative Dance in Therapy." *Am. J. Orthopsychiatry* 11 (1941), 235–244.

Boas, F. "Creative Dance" in *Child Psychiatric Techniques.* L. Bender, ed. Springfield, Ill.: Charles C Thomas, 1952.

Chace, M. "Dance as an Adjunctive Therapy with Hospitalized Mental Patients." *Bull. Menninger Clinic* 17 (1953), 219–225.

———, and W. R. Johnson. "Our Real Lives Are Lived in Movement." *J. of Health, Physical Ed. and Recreation* 32 (1961), 30–56.

Christup, Helen J. "An Exploratory Study of the Effect of Dance Therapy on the Concept of Body Image, as Measured by Projective Drawings in a Group of Chronic Schizophrenics." Ph.D. dissertation, George Washington University, Washington, D.C., 1958.

Des Lauriers, A. "The Psychological Experience of Reality" in *Chronic Schizophrenia.* L. Appleby, J. M. Scher, and J. Cumming, eds. Glencoe, Ill.: Free Press, 1960.

Federn, P. *Ego Psychology and the Psychoses.* New York: Basic Books, 1952.

Fisher, S., and S. E. Cleveland. *Body Image and Personality.* New Jersey: D. Van Nostrand, 1958.

Freedman, A. M. "Maturation and Its Relation to the Dynamics of Childhood Schizophrenia." *Am. J. Orthopsychiatry* 24 (1954), 487–491.

Freeman, T., J. L. Cameron, and A. McGhie. *Chronic Schizophrenia.* New York: International Universities Press, 1958.

Freud, S. *The Ego and the Id.* London: Hogarth Press, 1927.

Genther, S. "A Place to Begin." *Impulse,* 1954.

Greenson, R. R. "The Struggle against Identification." *J. of the Am. Psychoanalytic Assoc.* 1 (1953), 538–549.

H'Doubler, M. *A Creative Art Experience.* New York: Appleton Century-Crofts, 1940.

Head, H. *Aphasia and Kindred Disorders of Speech.* London: Cambridge University Press, 1926.

Hoffer, W. "Oral Aggressions and Ego Development." *Int. J. Psychoanalysis* 31 (1950), 156–160.

———. "Development of the Body Ego." *Psychoanalytic Study of the Child* 5 (1950), 18–23.

Jacobson, E. "Depersonalization." *J. of the Am. Psychoanalytic Assoc.* 7 (1959), 581–610.

Kubie, L. "Body Symbolization and the Development of Language." *Psychoanalytic Quarterly* 3 (1934), 430–444.

Marks, J. B. Dance Therapy Project. V. A. Hospital, American Lake, Washington. Personal communication, 1960.

Rabinovitch, M. S. Unpublished personal communication to S. Fisher and S. E. Cleveland, 1958.

Rank, B. "Adaptation of the Psychoanalytic Technique for the Treatment of Young Children with Atypical Development." *Am. J. Orthopsychiatry* 19 (1949), 130.

Reich, W. *Character Analysis.* New York: Orgone Institute Press, 1949.

Rosen, E. *Dance in Psychotherapy.* New York: Columbia University, 1957.

Ruesch, J., and W. Kees. *Non-Verbal Communication.* Berkeley: University of California Press, 1956.

Schilder, P. *The Image and Appearance of the Human Body.* New York: International University Press, 1950.

Scott, R. D. "The Psychology of the Body Image." *British J. of Med. Psychology* 24 (1951), 254–266.

Sechehaye, M. A. *Symbolic Realization.* New York: International University Press, 1951.

Zegart, D. "Dance Groups for Psychotic Patients." Master's thesis, Smith College for Social Work, Northampton, Mass., 1956.

HELEN CHRISTRUP

The Effect of Dance Therapy
on the Concept of Body Image

Helen Christrup's study and Marian Chace's rejoinder, "Measurable
and Intangible Aspects of Dance Sessions," are classic examples of
the dialogue ever present in clinician, counselor, or whomever is
asked to justify his role as change agent.[1] Ambivalence toward the
dual roles of artist and scientist is confessed to by Christrup, well-
armed with statistics, and Chace, replete with sensitivity.

In citing an example of the quiet woman who, according to
Christrup's time-sample measurements, participated little, Miss
Chace demands: "How do you rate a smile; how can you rate the
reaching out of hands to a trusted person for a few minutes at a
time?"[2] Christrup concurs.

The difficulties of measuring these empathetic responses are compounded by the ephemeral, fleeting quality of the medium. Oftentimes, Chace confesses that her own attempts to describe movement
therapy's effects shift to verbal areas which are not central to the
basic process. But the clinician's cry is Miss Chace's most telling argument: "Counting it or charting it is no substitute for responding to it."[3]

Nevertheless, Christrup and Chace are emphatic that the profes-

Reprinted with permission of New York State Department of Mental Health,
Psychiatric Quarterly Supplement.

From a thesis submitted to George Washington University in partial satisfaction
of the requirements for the degree of master of arts. The views expressed in this
article are those of the author and—although submitted from Saint Elizabeths Hospital, Washington, D.C.—do not necessarily represent the views of the Department of
Health, Education and Welfare.

1. Marian Chace, "Measurable and Intangible Aspects of Dance Sessions," *Music
Therapy* 7 (1957), pp. 151–156.

2. Although neither author acknowledges the other's essay, internal evidence
suggests that they address issues raised by the other. The dates coincide; at points
the language is remarkably similar. The description of the research projects also
tallies.

3. Jarl Dyrud and Marian Chace, "Movement and Personality," American Dance
Therapy Association, *Third Annual Conference Proceedings* (Madison, Wis., 1968),
p. 20.

sion's growth must need be accompanied by reliable measurements. Christrup's facts and figures are an important contribution. She establishes body-image awareness as primary to the process of movement therapy. Impressed with Miss Chace's skills in leading the group, she wonders if "the dance had been of longer duration, attendance more regular, and larger groups employed, a truly remarkable effect of Dance Therapy might have been the result."[4]

Since one of the therapist's ultimate goals is behavioral change, we must continue to grope for measurement techniques which are in line with the techniques used to bring about specific changes. Intuition is not enough. Without systematically derived details to back up insight, movement therapists may go the way of astrological birth-control faddists.   M.N.C.

Problem

Basic assumptions concerning the therapeutic value of the dance have been clinically validated, on an observational level, by observers in differing disciplines, settings, and locales (Bainbridge,[5] Bender,[6] Chace,[7] Genther,[8] Greenwood,[9] Krause,[10] Laban,[11] Martin and Beaver,[12] May,[13] Rosen,[14] and Sharpe[15]). Valuable as these observa-

4. This quotation is taken from Helen Christrup's thesis upon which her essay is based. "An Exploratory Study of the Effect of Dance Therapy on the Concept of Body Image, as Measured by Projective Drawings, in a Group of Chronic Schizophrenics." Unpublished M.A. dissertation, George Washington University, Washington, D.C., 1958, p. 31.

5. Grace W. Bainbridge, et al. "Dance Mime: A Contribution to Treatment in Psychiatry," *J. Ment. Sci.*, 99 (1953), 308–314.

6. Lauretta Bender and Franziska Boas, "Creative Dance in Therapy," *Am. J. Orthopsychiat.* (1941), 235–244.

7. Marian Chace, "Opening Doors through Dance." *J. Am. Assn. Hlth., Phys Ed. and Recreat.*, 23 (1952), 10–11, 34–39; "Personal Gratification: Physiological Aspects," *Music Ther.* (1952), 63–67; "Dance as an Adjunctive Therapy with Hospitalized Mental Patients," *Bull. Menninger Clin.*, 17 (1953), 219–225; "Dancing Helps Patients Make Initial Contacts," in *Ment. Hosp.*, 5 (1954), 2, 4–6.

8. Shirley Genther, "A Place to Begin," *Impulse*, 19 (1954), 22.

9. E. D. Greenwood, "Dancing," *Bull. Menninger Clin.*, 6 (1942), 78–79.

10. R. Krause, "Reality through the Dance," *Recreation* (1952), 326.

11. R. Laban, "The Educational and Therapeutic Value of the Dance," in *The Dance Has Many Faces*, Walter Sorell, ed. (New York: World, 1951), pp. 145–159.

12. D. W. Martin and Nohmie Beaver, "A Preliminary Report on the Use of the Dance as an Adjunct in Therapy of Schizophrenics," *Psychiat. Quart. Suppl.*, 25 (1951), 176–190.

13. Rowena May, "Modern Dancing as Therapy for the Mentally Ill," *Occup. Ther. and Rehabil.*, 20 (1941), 101–106.

tions are, however, they remain only subjective observations and descriptions, and no real experimentation has been conducted to test them. The increasing emphasis on the benefits of the dance as therapy augments the need for experimental studies.

Dance therapy began at Saint Elizabeths Hospital, Washington, D.C., on a volunteer basis, as early as 1942. So impressive were some of the results achieved that it was incorporated into the psychotherapy branch of the hospital in 1943. It has continued to function since its origin under the direction of Marian Chace, who has been rightfully titled by Rosen the "First Lady" of dance therapy. The dance is accepted as so integral a part of this hospital's therapeutic program, that Saint Elizabeths would appear to be the logical setting for the first experimental study in this area. The dance therapy sessions as ordinarily conducted at Saint Elizabeths Hospital do not follow a stereotyped routine, but rather are governed by the responses of the individuals and the group.

The sessions begin with simple arm, leg, and body swings and stretches. These are performed in unison by the patients and leader, while they are in circular formation. As the individuals' muscles become more relaxed, spontaneous movement, which the leader attempts to follow, develops within the group. It is believed that this stimulates the ability of the individuals to become involved in group interaction.

The medium used in dance therapy is the body itself and part of the therapeutic process lies in increasing the individual's awareness of his body and his ability to use it as a means of expression and communication. It would seem, therefore, that projective drawings, which are believed to reflect the individual's concept of his own body image, would be an appropriate criterion by which to measure changes resulting from dance therapy. It was believed that the use and awareness of the body, which dance therapy is believed to modify, would produce a change in body image and might well be reflected in the drawings in such things as attention to detail, proportion, size, movement, sexual differentiation, and social characteristics.

Thus, the present exploratory study was designed in an effort to test the effectiveness of dance therapy through the use of systematic

---

14. Elizabeth Rosen, "Dance as a Therapy for the Mentally Ill," *Teach. Coll. Rec.*, 55 (1954), 215–222; "Dance in Psychotherapy." Columbia University, Teachers College, Bureau of Publications, New York, 1957.

15. Ella Sharpe, "Certain Aspects of Sublimation and Delusion," *Int. J. Psycho-An.*, 11 (1930), 12–23.

observations made during the sessions as means of measurement, and through the use of projective drawings as a criterion. The method used was to administer projective drawing tests to experimental and control groups of hospitalized schizophrenics, following which the experimental groups were placed in dance therapy. At the conclusion of a prescribed course of treatment, the drawings were re-administered, and changes were observed.

Method

The subjects, selected from a hospitalized chronic schizophrenic population, were between the ages of twenty and fifty, with no other known involvement such as organicity, or physical impairment. No subjects were used who were already on other therapies, other than drugs, or engaged in hospital activities off the ward. All subjects were asked to produce two drawings according to a standardized procedure. Two raters scored the drawings on the Goodenough Scale[16] and the Swensen Sexual Differentiation Scale.[17] The reliability coefficient between the two raters was .96 for the Goodenough Scale and .82 for the Swensen Scale. Two groups of twelve women each and two groups of fifteen men each were then matched individually as closely as possible for Goodenough Scale score, length of hospitalization, and age. The ranges and means for the groups on these variables are given in Tables 1 and 2. No differences approaching significance were found between the experimental and control groups. Following this, one group of twelve women and one group of fifteen men were placed in dance therapy for a period of thirteen weeks (twenty-one sessions). The remaining two groups served as controls. The dance

Table 1

Group Differences in Males with Respect to Goodenough Scale Score, Years of Hospitalization, and Age

	Range		Mean	
	Experimental	Control	Experimental	Control
Goodenough Scale Score	0–39	0–42	15.9	16.2
Years of Hospitalization	4–23	3–27	12.6	13.2
Age	31–49	33–48	40.8	39.6

16. Florence L. Goodenough, *Measurement of Intelligence by Drawings* (Yonkers, N.Y.: World, 1926).

17. C. W. Swensen "Sexual Differentiation in the Draw-a-Person Test," *J. Clin. Psychol.*, 11 (1955), 37–41.

Table 2

Group Differences in Females with Respect to Goodenough Scale Score,
Years of Hospitalization, and Age

	Range		Mean	
	Experimental	Control	Experimental	Control
Goodenough Scale Score	5–33	0–34	18.6	19.8
Years of Hospitalization	1–16	1–15	8.0	7.5
Age	22–40	30–40	33.0	35.5

sessions were conducted in the usual manner. During each session, standardized observations were made.

1. Time sampling observations were made by two recorders at five-minute intervals. If the subject were moving in time to the music at the time the recorder observed him, he received a check. The mean of the number of checks by the two recorders became the subject's "activity rating" for that session. The reliability coefficients for the two recorders on the cumulative ratings were .90 for the male group and .99 for the female group.

2. A subjective rating on a five-point scale devised by the dance therapist (Christrup,[18]) was noted by her at the conclusion of each session. This attempted an evaluation of the subject's participation in the group and involvement in the activity. This was the subject's "participation rating."

3. Beginning with the ninth session, each subject was rated by the two recorders on a nine-point scale, devised by the experimenter and the therapist. This scale was designed to measure the freedom of movement. The mean of the scores between the two raters became the subject's "freedom rating." The reliability coefficients for the two recorders on the cumulative ratings were .95 for the male group and .97 for the female group.

At the conclusion of the experimental period, the drawings were re-administered to the four groups and rated on the Goodenough and Swensen scales. The reliability coefficients for the two raters were .95 for the Goodenough Scale and .86 for the Swensen Scale. The following statistical treatment of the data was then undertaken.

The Goodenough and Swensen scores were each subjected to a *t* test for uncorrelated data in order to determine the significance of the difference between the raw scores of the first and second sets of

18. Helen J. Christrup, "An Exploratory Study of the Effect of Dance Therapy on the Concept of Body Image, as Measured by Projective Drawings, in a Group of Chronic Schizophrenics."

drawings for the experimental and control groups. The *difference* scores for the Goodenough and Swensen Scales were then obtained. These scores were obtained by ascertaining the algebraic difference between the raw scores for the first and second drawings for each of the subjects in the matched experimental and control pairs. The *difference* scores were then subjected to the *t* test for uncorrelated data. Finally, the two experimental groups and the two control groups were combined. High-scoring and low-scoring groups were formed from the combined experimental group by ranking the subjects on the basis of the cumulative scores on each of the three measures employed during the session, that is, the "activity ratings," "freedom ratings" and "participation ratings." These high-scoring and low-scoring groups and the control group (no scoring) for each of the three measures were then subjected to an analysis of variance by using the Goodenough *difference* scores as raw scores. The same groups were subjected to three more analyses of variance by using the Swensen *difference* scores as raw scores.

Results

By scanning Tables 3 through 6, one observes that the changes which occurred at the .05 level of confidence were between the following groups:

1. Between the female experimental and control groups when Goodenough *difference* scores were employed as the raw scores.

2. Between the combined experimental groups and the combined control groups when divided into three groups based on high activity ratings, low activity ratings, and no activity ratings (control group). These changes occurred for both the Goodenough and Swensen scales when *difference* scores were employed as the raw scores.

It may be noted that, though results significant at the .05 level of

Table 3

Levels of Significance between the Raw Scores of the First and Second Set of Drawings on the Goodenough Scale

		Male		Female	
		Experimental	Control	Experimental	Control
Standard	First Set	11.85	12.20	9.35	9.75
Deviation	Second Set	11.55	13.79	9.33	11.04
t Value		1.80	—.04	1.94	—.63
P		.1	>.9	.09	.5

Table 4

Levels of Significance between the Raw Scores of the First and Second Set of Drawings on the Swensen Scale

		Male		Female	
		Experimental	Control	Experimental	Control
Standard	First Set	2.02	2.37	1.65	2.05
Deviation	Second Set	1.97	2.46	2.26	2.20
t Value		1.77	1.70	.41	.47
P		.1	.1	.7	.7

Table 5

Level of Significance between the Goodenough and Swensen Difference Scores for the Experimental and Control Groups

		Goodenough		Swensen	
		Male	Female	Male	Female
Standard	Experimental	3.46	7.27	1.69	2.00
Deviation	Control	4.88	6.08	1.02	1.48
t Value		.60	2.24	.84	.52
P		.6	.05	.4	.6

Table 6

Level of Significance of Variance for the Three Ratings of the Three Groups (Based on Goodenough and Swensen difference scores)

	Goodenough *Difference* Scores		Swensen *Difference* Scores	
	F	P	F	P
Activity ratings	3.55	.05	4.55	.05
Freedom ratings	2.16	NS	2.34	NS
Participation ratings	2.53	NS	1.97	NS

confidence were not obtained on the Goodenough scores between the first and second sets of drawings, both experimental groups approached significance, whereas the control groups did not.

One may therefore conclude that significant positive changes did occur among the female subjects and that these changes are probably a result of the introduced variable, that is, the dance. One may further conclude, on the basis of the results of the analysis of variance, that those subjects, both male and female, who were most active in the sessions, showed significant improvement.

Discussion

The results are more indicative than the data alone would suggest when the rigidity of the criterion is considered. Projective drawings are considered to reflect certain aspects of personality. To anticipate that a personality change will take place in thirteen weeks, particularly in a group of chronic schizophrenics with a mean length of hospitalization of ten years, is an extremely rigid requirement. The truly surprising finding is that, considering the limited changes which could be expected in thirteen weeks and the rigidity of the criterion, significant changes were observed with some subjects and that all the changes were in the direction of improvement, so that personality changes in the direction of body image concept may be inferred.

One of the most puzzling aspects of the results of the study is that, according to the criterion, the women showed significant changes, whereas the men did not. This would appear to be particularly puzzling as it was the unanimous opinion of the people working with the experimental dance sessions that the men had been much more responsive and had demonstrated more improvement. However, the mean length of hospitalization for the men was four and one-half years longer than that for the women, so that one might expect the men to be more resistant to change. Furthermore, the male experimental group was initially a very passive group and the way in which improvement was most noted clinically was in the members' ability to assert themselves and to express negativism. This ability might well have been reflected in their willingness to produce the requested drawings.

The most notable observation which can be made from the data is that all the results indicated that improvement was taking place and would have been more marked had the duration of the dance therapy been longer. Three months after completion of the study, a brief survey of the experimental subjects showed that nearly half the women and over half the men had either received ground privileges or had been transferred to better wards. The implications of this for further study are that the duration of the experimental period should be longer and that behavioral criteria should be utilized in studying the longer-term effects resulting from dance therapy.

Summary

The present study was designed to test the effectiveness of dance therapy by means of measuring its effect upon the individual body

Helen Christrup

image concept. The method used was to administer projective d
ings tests to experimental and control groups of hospitalized scl
phrenics, following which the experimental groups were placed in
dance therapy.

Systematic observations of individual responses to dancing were
made during the course of the experiment. At the conclusion of a
prescribed course of therapy, the drawings were re-administered and
changes observed. The results of the analysis of the data led to the
conclusion that dance therapy did produce a change in the concept
of body image among some subjects and that change in the direction
of improvement occurred among all subjects who were most active
in the sessions. It was further found that, in this study, the changes in
the drawings were best measured by the Goodenough Scale and that
the most reliable tool for observing changes which occur as a result
of the dance was to record the amount of activity engaged in by the
subjects during the dance sessions.

SEYMOUR FISHER AND SIDNEY CLEVELAND

Personality, Body Perception, and Body Image Boundary

Dr. Seymour Fisher and Dr. Sidney Cleveland's research is so central to current key concepts of body image that it is not possible to speak of this area without discussing their contributions. The authors explore how people perceive the individuality of their bodies: "What we have found is that some people clearly visualize their bodies as possessing a boundary, or border, that separates them from what is out there and is capable of withstanding alien things that might try to intrude upon them. But there are others who have trouble perceiving their bodies as separate or possessed of a defensive border."[1] In investigating the relationships between personal attributes and characteristic body concepts, Fisher and Cleveland devised a reliable body boundary evaluation based on the individual's responses to ink blots.[2]

Noting that schizophrenic adults and severely disturbed children have been helped by body awareness exercises, Fisher proposes that "more systematic use be made of the gymnasium to provide certain kinds of body experiences that will selectively reinforce different dimensions of the body concept."[3] Marcia Leventhal suggests a developmental sequence that incorporates these concepts:

> early movement therapy experiences should be based upon tactile stimulation of body parts and boundaries, articulation of body parts, and visual-kinesthetic awareness development. These are developmentally some of the early sensimotor awareness activities from which the child becomes able to define internally the parts of his body and its boundaries. The next step sequentially is the experiencing of the

Originally appearing in *The Body Percept*, Seymour Wapner and Heinz Werner, eds., New York: Random House, 1965, and reprinted with permission of publisher.

1. Seymour Fisher, *Body Consciousness* (Englewood Cliffs, N.J.: Prentice-Hall, 1973), p. 21.

2. The test is described in this selection.

3. Fisher, *Body Consciousness*, pp. 37–38.

torso from the lower body; then the child is ready to sense gravity, weight and energy flow.[4]

Fisher and Cleveland can offer the movement therapist a valuable handle around which to organize and focus their techniques.

Techniques for body boundary awareness should be tailormade for each client. A fifteen-year-old deaf and blind girl, for example, has never experienced the teenager's pleasure of viewing her growing body in the mirror, standard operating procedure for establishing body image. In movement therapy sessions, a visually handicapped peer outlined Carolyn's entire body on paper. After the shape was cut out in silhouette form, Carolyn was directed to indicate facial features on it. She seized the crayon and eagerly sketched in barrettes, necklace, glasses, and belt. Turning over the life-sized paper doll, Carolyn added buttons down the back of its dress. Since her tights were ripped, she tore a hole in its knee to complete the accuracy of the image. Then our class danced with the dolls, tried each other's on for size, flapped them in the wind, positioned them as a group, and imitated their joined shapes.

That night Carolyn dressed her double in pajamas and they went to bed.   M.N.C.

Early observers (for example, Head, 1926; Schilder, 1959) of the unusual body image distortions which occur in schizophrenic and brain-damaged patients were aware of the influence of individual personality differences upon the specific character of such distortions. It was noted that individual trait patterns and idiosyncrasies could strongly color the content and form of the body image alterations produced by various types of pathology. With increasing study of body image phenomena we have learned that the normal individual's attitudes toward his body may mirror important aspects of his identity. An individual's feeling that his body is big or small, attractive or unattractive, strong or weak may tell us a good deal about his self-concept or his typical manner of relating to other people. There is evidence that the individual has a unique way of perceiving his own body as contrasted to non-self objects. As such, this body image or body concept frequently serves as a screen or target upon which he projects significant personal feelings, anxieties, and values. Two prime factors distinguish the perception of one's own body:

4. Marcia Leventhal, "Movement Therapy with Minimal Brain Dysfunction Children," in *Dance Therapy: Focus on Dance VII*, Kathleen Mason, ed. (Washington, D.C., AAHPHRR, 1974), p. 44.

First, the body as a perceptual object is unique in that it is simultaneously that which is perceived and also a part of the perceiver. Thus, when an individual touches himself, he concurrently has a sensation of touching and being touched. No other perceptual object ever occupies such a dual position or participates so intimately in the perceptual process. Second, an unusually intense level of ego involvement is evoked by one's body as an object of perception. When the individual reacts to his own body, he is stirred and aroused in a manner that rarely occurs when he reacts to the non-self world. This is not simply a theoretical presumption, but has been demonstrated in a variety of studies. For example, it has been shown by Wolff (1943) and Beloff and Beloff (1957) that when individuals unknowingly respond to pictures of their own bodies, they express more affect than they do when reacting to pictures of other people.

We have indications that the individual starts early to organize his body perceptions. He begins to highlight certain areas and to minimize others (Fisher and Cleveland, 1958). Some body areas may be persistently in the forefront of awareness, and others may be denied to the point where they almost do not exist in a perceptual sense. Kagan and Moss (1962) have demonstrated with unusual clarity the continuity and consistency to be found in the development of body attitudes. They have shown that degree of fearfulness about one's body in adulthood is significantly correlated with the level of such fearfulness in early childhood. Furthermore, they found that early body anxiety appears to have the consequence of encouraging certain long-term modes of behavior. For example, boys with high body anxiety were found to avoid athletic activities and to invest an increasing proportion of their time in intellectual tasks.

It has become a challenging task to formulate the major dimensions of the body concept that each individual evolves and to devise methods for measuring these dimensions. Indeed, there has been an efflorescence of efforts in this direction. Studies have appeared of such diverse body image variables as body anxiety (Secord, 1953), body dissatisfaction (Jourard and Secord, 1955), concept of body size (Nash, 1951), plasticity of body scheme (Schneiderman, 1956), position of body in space (Witkin, et al., 1954), preferred body proportions (Jourard and Secord, 1955), differentiation of values assigned to right and left body sides (Fisher, 1960), and gender designations of various body regions (Nash, 1958). In the course of pursuing such problems, a respectable armamentarium of procedures for tapping body attitudes has been devised. Word association, drawings, distorting mirrors, responses to ink blots, aniseikonic lenses, size estimation tasks, tachistoscopically presented pictures of distorted bodies, and many other techniques have been pressed into service. It is still too early to judge which body image dimensions and which measurement procedures will prove to be most pertinent and powerful. However, there are several generalizations that can be offered concerning the current research strategies and results relating to body image that are appearing in the literature. First of all, there has been a trend to conceptualize the individual's perception of his own body as a special case of perception in general. Numerous studies have now appeared in which the experimental task of the subject has been to make perceptual judgments about his own body in a manner analogous to that in which he would evaluate non-self objects. In many instances the judgments regarding the self have involved such classical perceptual variables as size and shape. One may optimistically speculate that by placing body image variables on the same continuum which embraces other perceptual phenomena, a bridge has been provided for integrating body image concepts into a larger context.

The potential importance of such a bridging process is highlighted by the fact that one of the simplest of perceptual parameters, namely, size, has proven to have exciting possibilities as a means of measuring body image attitudes. It has been clearly shown at an experimental level that an individual's perception of his body size may be affected by the nature of his attitude toward himself and his body. Studies indicate that an individual's perception of his bodily size may reflect such variables as his ability to make independent judgments (Epstein, 1957), his degree of disorganization (Cleveland, et al., 1962), his exposure to sensory isolation (Reitman and Cleveland, 1964), and his ingestion of a psychotomimetic drug (Liebert, Werner, and Wapner, 1958). Also, clinical observers have repeatedly noted that florid experiences of body size change are associated with such phenomena as schizophrenic regression, migraine attacks, transference attitudes during psychoanalytic therapy, and brain dysfunction. Apparently, there is a basic tendency for body feelings to be translated into body size terms. The individual seems to register the many alterations in his body feelings as shifts up and down a scale of smallness-bigness.

Another noteworthy trend in the literature is a sharpened realization that body attitudes are often the result and reflection of interpersonal relationships. One finds fewer instances in which studies tacitly accept that body attitudes pertain simply to the literal physical characteristics of the body. The interpersonal basis of the body scheme has been dramatized by such findings as the fact that body attitudes seem to change during psychotherapy (Cleveland, 1960), by the demonstration that body evaluations are differentially affected by previous success or failure experiences (Popper, 1957), and by the observation that body feelings are correlated with various personality indexes. The decision to view body attitudes as evolving from the same socialization experiences that shape other values and attitudes which have concerned behavioral researchers has an important implication. It leads logically to the idea that the characteristics of an individual's body concept may in paralleling other of his personal attributes provide an indirect means for evaluating them.

Finally, it should be noted that in the body image literature a steadily mounting number of references to the concept of the body image boundary have appeared. In many different contexts there are references to the basic idea that the individual must learn to demarcate his body from his environs and that the clearness of this demarcation may have significant behavioral implications. Since the work of Schilder (1959), the concept of the body boundary has been useful. More recently, the Werner-Wapner group has appealed to a boundary model to explain changes in size perception of the head when stimuli (for example, touch) are applied to it. The psychoanalytic group (Fenichel, 1945) has portrayed body boundary formation as basic to the development of a sense of identity and adequate ego functioning. Kaufman and Heims (1958) refer to boundary disturbance in delinquents. Weckowicz and Sommer (1960) and Cleveland, et al. (1962) have pointed to the possibility of interpreting certain unusual body size experiences in schizophrenics in terms of dissolution of body image boundaries.

Body Image Boundary

The existence and importance of the boundary dimension is difficult for most people to grasp because in the normal course of events most people do not experience any special concern about their body boundaries. They seem to know well enough where they end and the outer world begins. But there are various pathological states in which the individual does grossly lose the ability to identify his body boundaries. In such instances the literal existence and functional value of the body boundary becomes apparent. Brain damaged and also schizophrenic patients have been observed who have marked difficulty in deciding whether certain stimuli come from outside the body boundary or arise from the body itself. Although such gross variations do not occur in a normal population, we do have evidence that even among normal people there are many instances in which individuals experience themselves as not clearly demarcated from what is "out there."

The work we shall describe grew out of the view that it was important to have a means for investigating the correlates and consequences of variations in boundary definiteness. Beginning in 1951 we undertook a series of studies which established that there are distinct individual differences in the definiteness or articulation which one ascribes to the boundary regions of one's body. These studies were built around an index devised to evaluate boundary definiteness. The index, referred to as the barrier score, equals the number of responses elicited by an ink blot series (for example, Rorschach or Holtzman) that are characterized by an emphasis upon the protective, containing, decorative, or covering functions of the periphery. Some examples of barrier responses follow: cave with rocky walls, person covered with a blanket, woman in fancy costume, mummy wrapped up, animal with striped skin, vase. In each of these responses special attributes are assigned to the periphery; in this way the existence of the boundary is highlighted. Boundary definiteness is equated with the number of barrier responses produced.

The barrier index can be scored with high reliability, and adequate test-retest reliability has been shown (Daston and McConnell, 1962). An extended series of studies has proven that the barrier score is related to various behavioral and physiological variables. Thus, it has been found that the more definite an individual's boundaries, the more likely he is to behave autonomously, to manifest high achievement motivation, to be invested in task completion, to be interested in communicating with others, and to serve an active integrative role in small group situations (Fisher and Cleveland, 1958; Cleveland and Morton, 1962; Fisher, 1963). Likewise, at the physiological level, it has been demonstrated in normal subjects and also in patients with psychosomatic symptoms that the greater the barrier score, the greater the tendency to channel physiological response to the skin and muscle in contrast to the body interior, for example, stomach, heart (Fisher, 1963; Armstrong, 1963). Overall a picture has emerged of the individual with definite boundaries as more active, independent, autonomous, communicative, and also more likely to channel excitation to the exterior (effector) layers of the body than the individual with indefinite boundaries.

Despite the profusion of correlates of the boundary scores which have been demonstrated, the nature of the boundary itself has remained somewhat of an abstraction. That is, it has been exemplified by specific kinds of imaginative percepts constructed in response to ink blot stimuli, but the characteristics of this boundary as represented at the level of body sensation and body feeling have been largely undefined. In fact, some (for example, Wylie, 1961) have argued that the barrier score is largely a cognitive style variable describing how one deals with ink blots and having little to do with body sensations or the body schema as such.

It is only recently that experiments have been performed that make it possible to examine the nature of the body image boundary in terms of actual body experiences. These experiments have focused upon the sensory components of the boundary experience.

The first study to be described which helped to clarify the body sensation patterns associated with different degrees of boundary definiteness was carried out by Fisher and Fisher (1964). This study hypothesized that if the barrier score actually does reflect body experience, it should be linked with predictable differences in the degree to which body exterior sensations predominate in the individual's perception of his own body. That is, if the barrier score is anchored in real body phenomena, one would expect to find some body sensation analogue for boundary definiteness. Presumably, the more definite an individual's boundaries, the more perceptually prominent should be the boundary sectors of his body (namely, skin and muscle).

In a wider context, it may be said that this work is also pertinent to the general question whether the relative prominence of various body sensations in an individual's perceptual field can be predicted from a knowledge of his body schema.

As the project was set up, subjects were seen in large groups in a classroom situation where the group Rorschach was first administered. In order to control for response total, twenty-five responses were obtained from each subject. Upon completion of the Rorschach, they were given sheets of paper on which were listed the names of four body sectors or organs in the following order: skin, stomach, muscle, and heart. They were told that when a signal was given, they were to focus their attention upon their bodies. Then, each time a prominent sensation occurred in any of the four body areas listed on the sheet, they were to place a check next to the appropriate designation. The experimenter then said "Start," and after a five-minute interval signaled "Stop." The body sensation reports obtained from each subject were scored by determining the sum of interior perceptions (stomach and heart). This score was considered to represent the relative prominence of sensations in the exterior body layers as compared with nonexterior body regions.

Two samples were studied. They consisted respectively of sixty-four (fourteen male, fifty female) and fifty-one (sixteen male, thirty-five female) college students. In both samples the median difference between the sum of exterior (skin and muscle) sensations and the sum of interior (stomach and heart) sensations was such that the exterior exceeded the interior by four. Analysis of the data indicated that the barrier score was consistently related in the predicted direction to the difference between exterior and interior sensations. In the first sample a rho correlation of .33 was found between the barrier score and the predominance of exterior sensations over interior sensations. This relationship was likewise .33 in the second sample. These coefficients are both significant at the $< .01$ level. Therefore, one could say with confidence that there is a positive, although moderate, relationship between the barrier score and a tendency for exterior body sensations to predominate over interior sensations.

A second study extended the subject's observation of his body into past situations. The question was whether the barrier score would be related in the predicted direction to the difference between the number of interior and exterior sensations reported by the subject in his retrospective appraisal of his body reactions in past circumstances. Again, the subjects were seen in groups. Barrier scores were obtained from their responses to the Rorschach. A measure of exterior versus interior body perception was used which posed for the subject the task of recalling a series of past experiences and indicating his memory of what body sensations each had evoked in him. The instructions were: "Below are listed a number of experiences or feelings. In each instance will you think back to the last time you had such a feeling or experience. Then, try to recall how your body felt at the time. Were the main body sensations at the time in your skin? In your stomach? In your muscles? In your heart? Make your decision and indicate it by placing an X in the proper column to the right of each of the listed experiences. Whenever you are not sure, just guess."

The subject was asked to respond to a list of thirty different situations (for example, When you are angry; When you are very tired; When you are afraid; When you feel successful). An exterior versus interior sensation score was determined by subtracting the sum of stomach and heart responses from the sum of skin and muscle responses.

Two samples were appraised. One consisted of seventy-nine under-graduate college students (twenty-nine male and fifty female). The second was composed of twenty students (seventeen male and three female).

In sample one the median difference between exterior and interior sensations was -4. That is, the median tendency was to designate more interior than exterior sites as foci of body response in the thirty situations described. No sex differences were evident. In sample two the median difference between exterior and interior sensations was -6. In analyzing the data a rho correlation of only .15 was found between the barrier scores and the difference between number of exterior and interior sensations; but a chi-square test indicated a rela-tionship in the predicted direction that was significant at the $< .05$ level (one tail test). In the second sample a rho of .47 was obtained between exterior and interior sensations, a relationship which is sig-nificant at the $< .01$ level. While the results in sample one were equivocal, they do support data from sample two in indicating modest support for the hypothesis.

The overall results demonstrate convincingly that the individual's barrier score is linked with his perception of the relative prominence of exterior versus interior sensations in his body. The higher his barrier score, the more he experiences sensations from the boundary regions of his body (skin and muscle) rather than from its interior (stomach and heart). The barrier score is firmly anchored in body feelings and perceptions.

A puzzling question that arises is why body feelings should find representation in ink blot percepts. Why should there be almost an isomorphic relationship between patterns of exterior-interior body sensations and the properties ascribed to the boundary regions of ink blot images? The possibility that immediately presents itself is that when an individual is asked to react to highly unstructured stimulus materials, the background of sensations represented by his own body in the total perceptual field may intrude with sufficient force to impose some patterning on his reactions. Thus, if his body per-sistently appears to him as an object whose periphery is emphasized and highlighted, he may be stimulated to see similar patterns with highlighted peripheries in perceptual targets that lack form or struc-ture of their own. Actually, this possibility was first implicitly sug-gested by Hermann Rorschach, who speculated that human move-ment responses elicited by ink blots represented projections of an individual's kinesthetic sensations (Rorschach, 1942). It is also very pertinent that the sensory-tonic investigators have discovered that when specific tonus patterns are induced in an individual, they may affect his perception of ambiguous pictures and designs. There is the noteworthy possibility that a significant component of response to ink blots and similar stimuli is contributed by the background matrix of body experiences.

It is interesting that the relationship between the barrier score and exterior-interior sensations could be detected in simple situations. The relationship was apparent even when subjects were merely asked to report prominent sensations experienced in four body regions. This was true even though no efforts were made to create a defined set or to exclude outside stimuli. The exterior-interior differentiation does not need to be isolated under rarefied conditions. Apparently, it can be observed in the circumstance of merely sitting quietly in a room and agreeing to examine one's body sensations for five minutes at the request of a researcher who is a comparative stranger.

The relationship between the barrier score and the patterning of interior-exterior body perception may be regarded as derivative of two factors:

First, there are indications that the person with clear-cut boundaries learns during his socialization to assign great significance in his body scheme to the boundary regions of his body (particularly the musculature) because they take on unusual import for him as a method of coping in an active and "voluntary" manner with the outside world. But the individual with vague boundaries who is less actively oriented ascribes less importance to his body exterior and more to the interior. Presumably, this difference could result in focusing differential attention upon the areas in question. Therefore, the high barrier subject whose boundary region is of relatively special significance to him would scan it with great attentiveness, and relatedly, the low barrier subject would be sensitive to sensations in his body interior.

Second, evidence exists that the high barrier subject exceeds the low barrier subject in level of physiological arousal of exterior body areas (Fisher, 1963). However, the low barrier subject manifests higher arousal of interior regions than the high barrier subject. Probably, this difference in reactivity results in a differential density of sensations at the body sites in question. Therefore, at least partially, the correlation of the barrier score with body sensation patterns would be a function of the contrast in actual arousal levels of the body exterior and interior. Perhaps the sensation differences between exterior and interior which are related to the physiological factors acquire in their persistence over time an influence of their own in reinforcing the psychological dominance of the exterior or interior in the body schema. It is likely that long-term richness of sensation from one body sector could in its own right make that sector a prominent body schema landmark.

Boundary Changes

A second major segment of our work presented here relates to conditions which produce change in the body image boundary. This work may prove to be of unusual significance because it comes closest to the experimentally ideal situation in which an independent variable is manipulated and consequent variations in dependent variables can be observed. Also, by providing information about how the boundary changes under various conditions it presents a more dynamic and real picture of its properties. To observe the boundary in process of change is to take it out of the realm of abstraction and to highlight its adjustment functions. Several studies have now been completed in which boundary attributes have been monitored during the course of intense modifying and altering experiences. All of these studies have recorded boundary alterations which seem reasonable and logically consistent.

It is necessary to digress momentarily to describe another boundary measure used in the studies to be described. This measure, referred to as the penetration score, is based on a count of all ink blot responses in which there is an emphasis on the destruction, evasion, or bypassing of the boundary. Such responses as the following are illustrative of penetration concepts: bullet piercing flesh, x-ray of inside of body, rotting wood, soft material, building burning. The higher the penetration score, the less definite the body image boundary is considered to be. This score typically has low and sometimes negative relations to the barrier score. Its significance is less well established than that of the barrier index, and it has been used in a more exploratory and tentative fashion.

The first study to be described that dealt with boundary change was undertaken by Cleveland (1960). Cleveland measured the alterations in the boundary scores of schizophrenics as they recovered from acute psychotic episodes. Twenty-five male schizophrenics were evaluated with the Lorr Multidimensional Scale for Rating Psychiatric Patients first upon entering the hospital and then again after five and thirteen weeks of treatment with tranquilizers. Another criterion of the patient's response to the drug treatment was whether he ultimately attained sufficient recovery to leave the hospital. Holtzman Ink Blots were administered pre-drug, and five and thirteen weeks after treatment had begun in order to obtain barrier and penetration scores for each of these time points. A significant rho correlation of .60 was found between decrement in penetration scores and decrement in the Lorr morbidity rating during the period from the onset of treatment to the fifth week. The rho correlation for the same relationship from treatment onset to the thirteenth week was .61. There was also a significant trend (.05–.02 level) indicating a decline in penetration scores for patients judged capable of leaving the hospital. This contrasted with the trend for nondischarged patients, who tended to increase their penetration scores. The barrier score proved not to be related to any of the criteria of patient change.

A second phase of this study concerned forty-five schizophrenics who had been administered the Rorschach on admission and again upon leaving the hospital where they had received psychiatric treatment. Each patient was also rated as to clinical condition upon admission and again at time of discharge. It was established that patients rated as improved or markedly improved showed a significant decline in the penetration score (.01 level). For the barrier score the only significant change was an increase from first to second testing in the markedly improved group. Cleveland concluded that his results demonstrated in the recovering schizophrenic a "dramatic firming up and defining of the body image boundary" (1960, pp. 259–260).

Another pertinent study was carried out by McConnell and Daston (1961). They considered the responses of twenty-eight women to the stress occasioned by their own pregnancies. Subjects were seen pre- and post-delivery. Initially, each was given the Rorschach, the Osgood Semantic Differential scales (for example, strong-weak) to be applied to her own body, and a structured interview. The structured interview was primarily designed to determine how favorably or unfavorably each subject had reacted to her own pregnancy. Post-delivery, only the Rorschach and the Osgood Differential were repeated. It was found that the favorableness with which subjects viewed their pregnancies was positively linked with their barrier scores. It was also established that while the barrier score did not shift from the first to the second testing, the penetration score declined significantly during the same interval. The decline in the penetration score was interpreted as indicating that women feel intensified anxiety about the vulnerability of their bodies while they are pregnant, but that such anxiety declines once the delivery has been achieved. The fact that the barrier score did not change was considered by McConnell and Daston to be congruent with past findings that it is relatively independent of actual alterations in the body itself. No correlations were found between the body boundary scores and the ratings that the subjects made of their own bodies on the Osgood scales (evaluative, potency, and activity factors).

The third, and most significant, of the boundary change studies to be cited was carried out by Reitman and Cleveland (1964). It involved an appraisal of boundary alterations in neurotics and schizophrenics consequent upon sensory isolation. Twenty neurotics and twenty schizophrenics were exposed to sensory isolation conditions for a maximum period of four hours. Holtzman Ink Blot tests, measures of tactile sensitivity, and estimates of body size were obtained before and after isolation. A schizophrenic control group also received the pre- and post-battery of tests, but with isolation not intervening. No changes occurred in the scores of this latter group from pre- to post-evaluation. However, there were significant changes in the experimental groups. The neurotics manifested decreased barrier and increased penetration scores following isolation. The schizophrenics, contrastingly, obtained higher barrier and lower penetration scores. It was speculated that sensory isolation by minimizing stimulating input had a disruptive effect upon the nonpsychotics, which decreased boundary definiteness. In the case of the schizophrenics, however, the sensory isolation seemed not to be disruptive. It seemed to provide a nonthreatening pattern of stimuli which fostered more realistic body boundaries. It is important to note that the results from the tactile threshold and body size estimate tasks were similarly reversed for the two experimental groups and in a direction congruent with the concept that isolation produces boundary alterations. Thus, the schizophrenics showed increased tactile sensitivity and a decreased concept of body size following isolation; but the nonpsychotics showed decreased tactile sensitivity and an increased concept of body size. It should be added that neither the neurotics nor the schizophrenics shifted their size judgments from test to retest with regard to nonself objects (for example, baseball). Only judgments with regard to one's own body were sensitive to the sensory isolation effects. As we have already mentioned, previous studies by Wapner and Werner regarding body size experiences suggest that the pattern of changes with regard to the body size estimates in the schizophrenic group was related to increased awareness of the body periphery and the pattern in the nonpsychotic group to lessened awareness of the periphery.

Parenthetically, it should be noted that unpublished research by Fisher and Gaston also indicates that the tendency to underestimate body size is associated with a normal, well-integrated body image. In their study, thirty normal male and thirty normal female students consistently underestimated their own body size when asked to make size judgments of hands, feet, and other body parts. In contrast, Cleveland, et al. (1962), studied 100 schizophrenics and found them to overestimate body size consistently, suggesting that size overestimation is associated with body image pathology.

The findings of Reitman and Cleveland (1964) regarding the differential effects of sensory isolation upon neurotics and schizophrenics are intrinsically exciting not only because they point up a new kind of relationship between degree of psychopathology and response to limitation in sensory input, but also because they lend a literal reality to the body image boundary in a way few other kinds of data can match. Here one sees a literal correlation between changes in the individual's body image boundary concept (as defined by the boundary score) and changes not only in his skin sensitivity but also in his perception of his body size. What is impressive is that skin sensitivity becomes greater in the schizophrenic group at the same time that boundary definiteness increases. But in the neurotic group, where boundary definiteness declines, skin sensitivity decreases. That is, at the same time that the boundary is altered, there is a corresponding and predicted alteration in functioning of the boundary region of the body. Furthermore, the changes in perceived body size which accompany boundary alterations are also congruent with what we know about the effects of boundary definiteness upon perception of one's own body size. As already mentioned, Werner and Wapner have established that when the boundary regions of an individual's body are highlighted by means of touch, heat, or cold stimuli, he judges himself as smaller than when his boundaries are not highlighted in such a fashion. Just so, Reitman and Cleveland (1964) found that with increased boundary definiteness in the schizophrenic group (and with this a presumed highlighting of the boundary regions of the body) there was a decrease in reported size. In the neurotic group there was an increase in the reported body size as boundary definiteness decreased.

The three studies just surveyed indicate that boundary changes accompany really significant life experiences. Phenomena like pregnancy, recovery from psychotic disorganization, or deprivation of basic sensory cues result in alterations in boundary articulation. The possibility of such boundary alterations had previously been conjectured by various clinical observers. However, the results obtained by the use of the boundary scores speak much more explicitly and systematically. They permit one to see that specific types of situations will trigger not only significant alterations in the individual's perception of his boundary but also corresponding alterations in the boundary's sensory properties.

One cannot help but be impressed with the fact that such apparently different phenomena as pregnancy, psychotic disorganization, and loss of sensory experience should all be characterized by boundary changes. One is led to wonder whether the individual's perception of his boundary may not prove to be an unusually sensitive index of modification in his functioning. Of course, the question arises whether boundary fluctuations represent initiating forces in change processes or whether they are subsidiary effects. Available information does not at this point permit a meaningful answer.

It should be indicated that the penetration score rather than the barrier index has been largely linked with change processes. The barrier score has proven to be consistently correlated only with changes initiated by sensory isolation. This is in keeping with results from previous studies demonstrating that the barrier score was largely a measure of persisting attitudes rather than of short-term variations in state. Contrastingly, the penetration score seems to be sensitive to immediate situational conditions. This differentiation, however, can be considered as only tentative and awaits further confirmation.

The material presented points up the rich possibilities of a boundary approach to understanding body experience as well as important personality and psychopathological phenomena.

References

Armstrong, H. E. "The Relationship between a Dimension of Body-Image and Two Dimensions of Conditioning." Ph.D. dissertation, Syracuse University, Syracuse, New York, 1963.

Beloff, J., and H. Beloff. "Perception of Self and Others Using a Stereoscope." *J. abnorm soc. Psychol.* 56 (1957), 87–92.

Cleveland, S. E., S. Fisher, E. E. Reitman, and P. Rothaus. "Perception of Body Size in Schizophrenia." *A.M.A. Arch. gen. Psychiat.* 7 (1962), 277–285.

———. "Body Image Changes Associated with Personality Reorganization." *J. consult. Psychol.* 24 (1960), 256–261.

———, and R. B. Morton. "Group Behavior and Body Image—A Follow-Up Study." *Human Relations* 15 (1962), 77–85.

Daston, P. G., and O. L. McConnell. "Stability of Rorschach Penetration and Barrier Scores over Time." *J. consult. Psychol.* 26 (1962), 104.

Epstein, L. "The Relationship of Certain Aspects of the Body Image to the Perception of the Upright." Ph.D. dissertation, New York University, New York, 1957.

Fenichel, O. The Psychoanalytic Theory of Neurosis. New York: Norton, 1945.

Fisher, S. "A Further Appraisal of the Body Boundary Concept." J. consult. Psychol. 27 (1963), 62–74.

————. "Right-Left Gradients in Body Image, Body Reactivity, and Perception." Genet. Psychol. Monogr. 61 (1960), 197–228.

————, and S. E. Cleveland. Body Image and Personality. Princeton, N.J.: Van Nostrand, 1958.

————, and R. L. Fisher, "Body Boundaries and Patterns of Body Perception." J. abnorm. soc. Psychol. 68 (1964), 255–262.

Head, H. Aphasia and Kindred Disorders of Speech. London: Cambridge, 1926.

Jourard, S. M., and P. F. Secord. "Body-Cathexis and the Ideal Female Figure." J. abnorm. soc. Psychol. 50 (1955), 243–246.

Kagan, J., and H. A. Moss. Birth to Maturity. New York: Wiley, 1962.

Kaufman, I., and L. Heims. "The Body Image of the Juvenile Delinquent." Amer. J. Orthopsychiat. 28 (1958), 146–159.

Liebert, R. S., H. Werner, and S. Wapner. "Studies in the Effect of Lysergic Acid Diethylamide (LSD-25): Self- and Object-Size Perception in Schizophrenic and Normal Adults: A.M.A. Arch. Neurol. Psychiat. 79 (1958), 580–584.

McConnell, O. L., and P. G. Daston. "Body Image Changes in Pregnancy." J. proj. Tech. 25 (1961), 451–456.

Nash, H. "Assignment of Gender to Body Regions." J. genet. Psychol. 92 (1958), 113–115.

————. "The Estimation of Body Size, Personal Ethos, and Developmental Status." Ph.D. dissertation, University of California, Berkeley, 1951.

Popper, J. M. "Motivational and Social Factors in Children's Perception of Height." Ph.D. dissertation, Stanford University, Palo Alto, Calif., 1957.

Reitman, E. E., and S. E. Cleveland. "Changes in Body Image Following Sensory Deprivation in Schizophrenic and Control Groups." J. abnorm. soc. Psychol. 68 (1964), 168–176.

Rorschach, H. Psychodiagnostics. New York: Grune and Stratton, 1942.

Schilder, P. The Image and Appearance of the Human Body. London: Kegan Paul, Trench, Trubner, 1935.

Schneiderman, L. "The Estimation of One's Own Bodily Traits." J. soc. Psychol. 44 (1956), 89–99.

Secord, P. F. "Objectification of Word-Association Procedures by the Use of Homonyms: A Measure of Body Cathexis." J. Pers. 21 (1953), 479–495.

Wapner, S., H. Werner, and P. E. Comalli. "Effect of Enhancement of Head Boundary on Head Size and Shape." Percept. mot. Skills 8 (1958), 319–325.

Weckowicz, T. E., and R. Sommer. "Body Image and Self-Concept in Schizo-phrenia." *J. ment. Sci.* 106 (1960), 17–39.

Witkin, H. A., H. B. Lewis, M. Hertzman, K. Machover, P. B. Meissner, and S. Wapner. *Personality through Perception.* New York: Harper, 1954.

Wolff, W. *The Expression of Personality.* New York: Harper, 1943.

Wylie, R. C. *The Self Concept.* Lincoln: University of Nebraska Press, 1961.

PART 4

The Creative Interface

And what of me?
I work each day in my
leotards at the State School
where the retarded are
locked up with hospital techniques.
Always I walk past the hydro-
cephalic doorman on his stool,
a five-year-old who sits
all day and never speaks,
his head like a twenty-five
cent balloon, three times
the regular size. It's nature
but nature works such crimes.

I go to the large cement
day room where fifty kids
are locked up for what
they strangely call play.
The toys are not around,
not given to my invalids
because possessions might get
broken or in the way.
We can't go out. There are no
snowsuits, sometimes no shoes
so what I do for them is what
I bring for them to use.

The room stinks of urine.
Only the two-headed baby
is antiseptic in her crib.
Now I take the autoharp,
the drum, the triangle,
the tambourine and the keys
for locked doors and locked
sounds, blind and sharp.
We have clapping of hands
and stamping of feet, please.
I play my humming and lullaby
sounds for each disease.

I sing *The Fox Came Out*
On a Chilly Night
and Bobby, my favorite
Mongoloid, sings Fox to me.
I bring out my silk scarfs
for a group of sprites.
Susan wants the blue scarf
and no one is orderly.
I sway with two red scarfs.
I'm in trance,
calling *love me, woo, woo*
and we all passionately dance.

"Eighteen Days without You," *Love Poems*,
Anne Sexton.

Reprinted by permission of Houghton Mifflin Company and The Sterling Lord Agency.
Copyright 1967, 1968, 1969 by Anne Sexton.

NORMA CANNER

". . . and a Time to Dance"

Author, actress, artist—Norma Canner deals with people of all sizes, shapes, varieties, and handicaps. "It is only by degrees that we differ," she proclaims, and then proceeds to prove it. She inspires a jam session from an unlikely combination of plastic wastebaskets, sticks, and a roomful of six-year-olds suffering from a multitude of severe handicaps. She directs a studio jammed with 100 university dance students to create striking group imagery as well as hilarity with sheets of newspaper. In a workshop for elementary school personnel, an overweight, older principal sheds her inhibitions and leads the dance. "Thank you!" she later confesses to the group, "I never felt like a woman before." In this selection you will see an extraordinarily creative person at work—and you will discover that some of the same magic potential exists within yourself.

Norma Canner shares with us sensitive insights into the creative process in . . . and a Time to Dance. Long out-of-print, the book is eagerly sought by dance enthusiasts and classroom teachers.[1] Part of the book's enchantment lies in the photographs which, unfortunately, cannot also be reproduced. M.N.C.

I used to think that only special people had talent and only special people had the need to express their creative feelings. I didn't know that anyone could dance, that people of great differences could communicate through movement, sharing their joys and pleasures, their angers and frustrations. Nor did I know that a large group of people could dance together and feel as one, or that you could dance alone and still be a part of a group.

Many years ago I met Miss Barbara Mettler, teacher of modern

Reprinted by permission of Plays, Inc., Publishers, Boston, Mass., 02116. Copyright 1968 by Norma Canner and Harriet Klebanoff.

1. Originally published by Beacon Press in Boston, 1968; the book has recently been reprinted by Plays, Inc.

dance, who showed me new ways of seeing, thinking, and feeling. She taught me the joy of dancing with others and the exciting potential of improvisation. Most important of all, I learned that each human being has something to say, that it is up to the teacher to provide an atmosphere where people can feel free to express themselves. I found that I was able to work with and teach people who had a variety of physical and mental differences. After all, most of us have a handicap of some sort, and it is only by degrees that we vary or differ. I learned to use and understand the nature of basic dance and was able when confronted with new problems to develop and use creative movement to meet the needs of these new situations.

And so it began to happen with increasing regularity that dance workshops and lecture demonstrations would provoke requests for classes: for children with cerebral palsy, for children who were emotionally disturbed, for the retarded, for mentally ill adults and teenagers, for Headstart children and teachers, for college students of child development and their supervisors. They all seemed to find something of value in this experience with creative movement. Many of these people and groups had special problems so that I had to adapt myself and the material to suit and meet the needs of the people in these different groups. From the first, the successes were greater than the failures. This was an area where everyone could experience some success and satisfaction, both physical and emotional, where they could feel part of a whole. Formerly the pattern of failure had been in many of these lives too familiar, resulting in feelings of frustration and isolation.

For the last six years I have been a teacher-consultant for the Massachusetts Department of Mental Health, in the preschool program for retarded children. These are the children pictured in this book. They have taught me as much as I have them.

For the young child, movement is a way of exploring and discovering his world and himself. As an infant he moves indiscriminately. He soon discovers and then learns to control his body. He uses his body to move about and explore first his immediate environment and then a broader world. At points in his development he discovers his arms, his legs, his eyes and ears, and soon realizes that these are part of him. His self-image is formed in part by these discoveries of and about his moving body. His body is his basic tool for dealing with his world before he learns to verbalize and intellectualize his thoughts and feelings.

As the child matures the pressures of society tend to repress his free body movement. The child must learn to control his need to move when it is time to be still, to control even his joy so that it fits with society's acceptable ways of expressing joy. Because these controls may be necessary in our highly complicated world, it becomes even more important that the child retain some outlets through which he can express what he feels and that he can find a satisfying way to create something unique and know the pleasure of involvement. Art and music have long been recognized as excellent media for the child's self-expression and creativity. In art the child uses images, in music he uses sound, in creative movement he uses his entire body to communicate, to create, and to express. Movement is very much a part of the language of the young child.

What is creative movement? In this instance it is dancing with young children, providing them with an opportunity to explore and discover their bodies, their feelings, and the textures, shapes, and sounds around them, alone or in a group. It is an environment in which the shy child can lose his inhibitions when intrigued by strange, exciting instruments and materials. It is an environment in which the aggressive child is given an outlet for pent-up energies or hostile feelings. It is when every child is offered a time to experience the joy and freedom of using his body and his creative uniqueness . . . a time to dance.

Perhaps the most important reason I believe that creative movement should be part of a child's life is that unlike many other activities in which children participate there is no right or wrong way to express or to discover. There is no failure. All that is required of a child is that he be involved.

While he is learning more about himself, he realizes that he can now use his arms, legs, eyes, and ears to discover a room, the sounds in a room, the child next to him, the textures of materials, the space in which he moves, and the rhythms he can make.

Music as composed by others can regiment or dictate the mood and time pattern. Using the children's own rhythmic feelings and movements increases their sense of acceptance and self-worth. When a child beats a rhythm for others to follow, he is aware that he is the leader, he can decide when the group will dance, and when it will stop, if the sound quality will be loud or soft, or the time fast or slow. When he plays for the teacher alone—it is a duet—between them, a rare and unusual dialogue. They are equal, responding to each other on a level that rarely happens between a child and an adult. For music and sound accompaniments, the children have themselves, their hands and feet, their fingers and toes, their tongues and voices; there are all kinds of instruments—drums, bells, sticks, shakers, the sounds in the room, and the world around them. All this and more can make music for their dances.

Children vary in the advantages and disadvantages with which they are born, but they are all the same because they are children and they all have the same needs. That is why I like to dance with children and their teachers.

It is important that a teacher learn to feel movement, to develop her kinesthetic and visual senses. Her awareness can encourage the children's movement processes. She is the guide and most often the leader. She can expand and give structure to the dance experience. The teacher can reinforce learning by emphasizing the movements with her voice and words. She must be able to see when a child offers original movements, and accept his ideas. Inspiration will come from the children if she will only look.

Since it is up to the teacher to recognize and see with understanding eyes and heart the disposition and needs of her children, it seems only natural that the teacher become involved in movement exploration. Her participation will add another tool for gaining deeper insights into the understanding of children.

The creative movement . . . can provide children with a better awareness of themselves and the various parts of their bodies, with a nonverbal means of communicating, and with an increasing perception of the world around them. As you have seen, it includes body dynamics, dance, and all forms of free spontaneous movement.

The aims of a continuing program of creative movement are: to allow the child sufficient freedom to express himself; to promote the growth of a healthy personality by encouraging awareness of the whole self through body action, by helping the child feel good about himself, by helping him become a member of a group; to foster self-respect and respect for the individuality of others; to help develop social awareness, the ability to make contact with another person and to sustain this relationship; to resolve conflict and hostility by channeling it constructively into body action and dance; to foster and sensitize the child's sensory abilities, stimulating emotional, physical, and intellectual growth; to define and refine concepts.

The teacher's positive attitudes, understanding, and enjoyment of creative movement are essential. The teacher should not attempt to teach the children anything as structured as dancing; rather, she should motivate and stimulate the children to move. Initially, this will be teacher-directed as she helps develop interest in creative movement and as she demonstrates the dynamics of body motion. Ultimately, the sessions should become child-centered and child-directed, with guidance and support from the teacher. This approach will give greater depth to the teacher's awareness and understanding of the needs and nature of her class. She will have another tool to help her interpret the behavior of each child—individually and within the group.

Although the children are in a group, creative movement is initially a personal and individual experience, gradually developing into one-to-one relationships, which culminate in group experiences. Each child has the opportunity to be himself, to explore movement, to be accepted on the basis of participation rather than on a preconceived idea. In this way, each child is encouraged to respect himself and to find his place in the group. When children have the opportunity to explore the space around them, to learn what the separate parts of their bodies are and what they can do, and to feel themselves wholly involved in a creative group activity, their motor and sensory competencies will develop in an atmosphere which can bring success and good feelings.

HELENE LEFCO

The Day They Clobbered
the Dance Therapist

Helene Lefco suggests, "Let's dance it out!," to a hostile and threatening group. She ends clobbered on the cement floor. Ruefully rubbing her wounds, Lefco recommends alternatives for handling such situations. If the reader does not desire to be up-ended on the dance floor beside her, he would do well to consider her advice.

The reader might further ponder if the guilt that overwhelmed the assaulter in this case could be compensated for by any positive cathartic effects. The term "catharsis" entered the world of psychology via a dramatic route. Noting the cathartic effect of the great Greek tragedies upon the audience, Aristotle explored the dynamics of spectators' vicarious participation in the drama through a purgation or healing release of the emotions. Two thousand years later, Freud redefined "catharsis" to signify the complex process of recollecting past emotions and thereby coming to terms with them during psychoanalytic treatment.

Today its meaning twists again. Catharsis is touted as an all-American cure for a host of aggressive ailments. Super-Star Giants lock in competitive contact, individuals smash through a T-group's locked hands barrier, dancers bombard the movement therapist with pillows, children suffocate daddy dolls in play therapy sandboxes—all these are accepted as efficacious substitute targets for the release of anger.

Recently the concept of hostility and aggression catharsis has come under scrutiny. Researchers report no evidence to support the claim that substitute actions do reduce tension; indeed, in some cases, they may actually increase the aggressive level.[1] Dr. Mike Ellis, after a careful review of the literature, concludes that: "The empirical work on hostility catharsis suggests that perhaps the confidence in catharsis

Reprinted from "Dance Therapy—Narrative Case Histories of Therapy with Six Patients," Copyright 1974 by Helene Lefco, by permission of Nelson-Hall, Inc.

1. Mike Ellis, *Play* (Englewood Cliffs, N.J.: Prentice-Hall, 1974), p. 57.

as a mechanism is unfounded."[2] He feels that the ball is in the other court and that the burden now falls to supporters of the catharsis theory to establish evidence of its usefulness.

What does prove therapeutic in this example from Helene Lefco's book is the group's perceptive and gentle handling of the movement therapist after Dr. Jones goads Kevin into his outburst.[3] Sharing tender, loving care for the therapist is an important sign of their growing mental health. Helene Lefco, nevertheless, would be the first to acknowledge that suffering a concussion is a most unsatisfactory technique to inspire this growth.   M.N.C.

One day, I appeared for a dance therapy session and found the patients tense and surly.

"Here comes the goddamn she-bitch," Don said, as I walked into the room.

"You really think I'm a bitch, Don?" I asked.

"Yeah," Don said, hitching up his pants, his pale skin coloring with anger, "yeah, you really stink. Christ, you were a 'no show' last week."

"Well, I was sick last week—but I'm here now."

Don looked straight at me with a sneer on his face. Then he blinked his eyes nervously and raised his arm as if to strike me. Knowing how indecisive Don is, I was fairly certain that he would not physically attack me. But nonetheless, I was wary as I backed away.

Although a dance therapist cannot work in constant fear of an assault, she must be prepared for a sudden blow, a hard jab, or some other unexpected physical expression of a patient's hostility. Sometimes the therapist's faulty or insensitive technique may precipitate a patient's attack. But more often, an assault can be the result of a successful transference on the part of the patient, so that in many instances the dance therapist becomes the patient's "mother." Sometimes even a healthy child who wants more attention from his mother will make his demands in a negative way. He may use unacceptable language, or even poke an elbow into mommy's eyes as she bends down for a kiss. It is not surprising, therefore, to find a mental patient asking for love in similar devious ways.

As I backed away from Don's threatening arm, I remembered an assault incident that occurred early in my career when I was neither watchful nor knowledgeable. I was conducting my class in a locked

2. *Ibid.*, p. 62.

3. This selection is taken from *Dance Therapy—Narrative Case Histories of Therapy Sessions with Six Patients* (Chicago: Nelson-Hall, 1974).

ward of a state hospital. My twenty top-security patients were remarkably submissive, especially when one considered their turbulent
histories, but daily tranquilizers had most of them yawning and spirit-
less. Dance therapy for this listless bunch was an exercise in sleep-
walking to music.

As a novice, I was dedicated to the theory that an instantaneous
response from my patients would insure my success with them. Since
gentle music seemed to bring on an epidemic of yawning, I had
stocked the record player with some wild, African tribal music. I was
thrilled to see some impulsive stomping movement by several members of the group. However, in a corner, by herself, stood a tremendous woman, at least six feet tall, who was paying little attention to
the group, the music, or me. I had turned my attention to the stomping patients, when suddenly I heard the sound of scuffling behind me.
One of the patients who had been dancing near the corner was
screaming and holding her reddened cheek. Apparently, the tall,
seemingly diffident woman had smacked her in the face for no apparent reason and was now blithely jiggling around to the music,
though her fists were still clenched. I comforted the victim, who was
more surprised than hurt, as I watched her assailant dance by, her
fists swinging ominously.

The record then changed to Miriam Makeba's quieter South African songs. "There's a flea in my hair," sang Miss Makeba, and everyone seemed settled and amused. As I danced around the circle, facing each patient for some individual hand contact, I suddenly felt
someone's presence behind me, followed by a light pressure on my
head. For one brief moment, hypnotized by the music, I wondered
whether in fact someone *was* putting a flea in my hair. Then, remembering where I was, I whirled around aggressively to confront the
six-foot face-smacker, who did indeed have her hand on my head.
However, it was the other hand I should have worried about. Startled
by my sudden move, she aimed a barrelhouse wallop at my nose. I
saw it coming and grabbed on to her swinging fist with both my
hands. In a moment, she had swung me around ninety-degrees, so
that I was now nose to nose with her murderous face. Instead of
calling for an attendant or attempting to free myself, I foolishly continued to be the dedicated young therapist.

"Let's dance it out," I gasped as I spun through the air. In point of
fact, I was already dancing, my buckling knees unwittingly doing a
South African native dance, though somewhat above the floor, as I
continued to cling like a leech to the woman's fist.

The ludicrous situation apparently struck my giant assailant as wildly hilarious. With great whoops of laughter, she began to dance, letting me down abruptly to the floor, and propelling me in what was probably an original in the annals of South African tribal rites.

The rest of the patients stood by awestruck, watching the floor show. When the record ended, the performers—my six-foot dancing partner and I—bowed to unrestrained applause. My tall partner was ready for another number, but in deference to my trembling knees, I announced that the session was now officially over. My patients returned to their quarters chattering enthusiastically about the dance therapy session, while I, in turn, leaned weakly against the wall, soaking wet and exhausted. I knew then that I had learned forever to be alert to the meaning of a dangerously clenched fist, and that a patient's light touch on my head might or might not be pure affection. But more to the point, I had learned not to turn my back on any member of a group for more than a few seconds.

That incident took place several years ago. Today, I take my cues more rapidly. After I had cautiously ducked away from Don, I walked toward the record player and put on a restful Viennese waltz. My patients gathered for the opening circle, Kevin on my left, frowning and unyielding, but holding my hand firmly. On my right was soft, round Laura, giving me a mechanical, bland smile, while she took my hand. She then proceeded to bend my fingers back painfully, all the while smiling at me. At this stage of my development as a dance therapist, I knew enough to distrust the smile and react to the fierce finger-pressure message, but my knowledge did not ease the pain in my hand.

I turned my face toward Laura's. "Let's dance this waltz together, just you and me," I said, breathing easier as Laura's grip on my fingers relaxed.

I looked around the circle to see who was lucid and approachable. "Carol, would you start Kevin and Brian and the others in some loosening-up exercise?"

Carol's eyes looked somewhat glazed, but the position of leadership was one she enjoyed, however briefly. While she was weighing the lure of controlling the group against the counter-lure of her apathy, Kevin dropped my hand and turned from the circle. Not willing to let him go yet, I quickly grabbed his hand and attached it to Brian's. "Stay here with Kevin and Carol," I said in Brian's ear. "I'll be back in a jiffy."

Carol had made her decision. She was standing in the center of the circle, issuing orders.

"OK, you guys, I want you to relax . . . and fast!" Carol led the way by slowly rotating her head on her long, slim neck, as her silky dark hair flipped forward and covered her face.

Now I could safely turn my full attention to Laura. She stood with her feet slightly apart, her short block of a body defying me to move her.

I leaned close to her. "OK, Laura, lead me anywhere you want. Make me do anything you like. You will be the leader, and I will follow you anywhere." I looked into her large green eyes and gently pinched her small freckled nose. "I am in your power," I said, in my best "Count Dracula" voice.

Laura smirked at my performance. She put her hands on my shoulder. "Close your eyes, Mrs. Lefco. Go ahead. I won't hurt you."

At this moment of truth, I *half*-closed my eyes. I trust some of my patients—Laura more than most—but not all of them.

Laura then moved me backward, aggressively, as her feet slid forward in waltz time. She led me in a strong, yet unviolent way, with a sustained movement in a direction clearly defined by her. Laura's pudgy fingers dug into my skin as we danced, until suddenly, she had backed me into a corner. I then pretended to collapse, my head down, my shoulders dispirited.

"Is this where you want me, Laura? In the dunce corner?" I asked.

Laura nodded. "Yeah, 'cause you're a dunce." She watched me closely through narrowed eyes as I stayed plastered to the corner, my body meek and submissive.

"You didn't come last week, did you?" she asked.

"No, Laura, I had a sore throat, and I didn't want to give it to you."

"Were your children home with you?"

"No," I answered carefully, suspecting sibling rivalry. "They were all at school." I raised my head and looked into Laura's suspicious eyes. "Did you miss me?"

Laura nodded gravely.

"I really wanted to come, Laura, but the doctor didn't think it was a good idea."

Laura breathed heavily as she assessed my sincerity. Satisfied, she nodded, and put out her hand.

"OK, you can come out of the corner now." This time her hand-clasp was gentle and warm. Hand in hand we returned to the circle.

Carol was still tossing her hair around with obvious enjoyment, but no one else seemed to be moving. Apparently after her opening salvo, Carol's interest in leading the group had gone steadily downhill, and now her self-absorption had set her charges totally adrift.

The group was standing around lifelessly and with the remoteness of children who feel no one cares.

Penny suddenly burst into the room, ten minutes late. She walked quickly and stiffly past all of us, her head down, her chest concave. I put my hand out to her.

"Take your friggin' hand offa me," she said, as she stormed over to the couch and threw herself upon it. "I feel lousy."

In a second, her soft, small, feline face became a blank mask of indifference.

Noting the unusually withdrawn mood of the group, my usual opening swings and stretches seemed too tame, too unchallenging. I put on Elizabeth Waldo's "Rites of the Pagan," a wildly creative musical exploration into ancient Indo-American civilization. Perhaps this primitive theme, the battle of a serpent with an eagle, and the accompanying sound of drums, recorders, double flutes, and whistles might receive a spontaneous response from the group. Glancing around the room eagerly for a reaction to the music, I found that, unfortunately, I was the only one inspired to move.

I resolved to go another round. There are days like this!

"OK," I said to the group, "I'm going to shout out a word and see how fast you can react to it with your body."

"Oh, God, not that crap, again," Penny said, flouncing off the couch. "I'm going to beat the drums while you play your games, though I'm not so friggin' fond of that either!" she muttered.

Her small, vividly painted mouth set grimly, Penny ran off to get the big drum which she used as counterpoint to the music of the record. I listened intently to the music, and at the same time combed the room with my eyes for any movement that I could expand upon and translate into a word that would ignite my patients' desire to move.

"Anybody got an idea for a word?" I asked, stalling for time. "Could it be 'snake' . . . 'slippery,' " and then added, influenced by the serpentine theme of the music, " 'twisting,' 'evil,' 'predatory'?"

Don lunged forward toward me. "What the hell is this supposed to be? A goddamn spelling bee?"

I lunged back at him, and the word I was seeking flew into my head —"revenge." The patients were furious because I disappointed them last week by being absent, and now they were paying me back for my neglect. They were deliberately avoiding my musical cues. Today, they wanted things done their way.

"The magic word is 'revenge,' " I shouted.

The word hung in the air for seconds. I watched, fascinated, as it drifted like a cloud around the faces of the patients. Laura smiled like a cat licking her chops. Penny's eyes burned with an impish delight. Carol stroked her long hair as if limbering her fingers for action.

"Yah! Yah!" Brian ran with an imaginary sword pointed straight to my throat. Don charged in after Brian, screaming, "Revenge! Revenge is sweet!" Brian and Don were like two warriors now, two musketeers, although Brian's fighting position was somewhat unorthodox. His half-cocked arm was thrust forward, while his other arm reached backward, his fingers outstretched. The main thrust of Brian's ferocity was in his scowling face, but his knees were bent, and he had an unaccustomed look of agility about him. Both men were grunting with effort, their mouths open and free. All around the room patients were acting out personal motifs of revenge. Laura and Carol were grappling, their fingers around each other's necks, their faces flushed with the excitement of battle. Penny was shrieking a war cry in between fevered drum beats.

"Kill 'em! Get 'em! Get your red-hot revenge while it lasts! Squeeze 'em! Whack 'em! Slice 'em! Yahoo—it's a goddamn riot!"

Accompanying this dramatic outburst was the considerably milder sound of tribal rites still coming from the record player.

Unable to contain herself any longer, Penny threw down the drum and came hunting for me. With great gusto she jabbed me with her hip and shoulder. I jabbed back with my shoulder, not as strongly, but with conviction. We played the body-bumping game of my childhood, hopping on one foot, crashing into one another with force.

In the middle of this brouhaha, a quiet little vignette was taking place. Dr. Jones, my assistant, was trying to goad Kevin into moving, or, at the very least, into reacting.

"C'mon, Kevin, don't I look like your brother, Lenny? He was the favorite, wasn't he? Everybody liked Lenny, didn't they, Kevin? C'mon, get mad, Kevin! The girls really went for Lenny, didn't they, Kevin? Kevin, whaddya gonna do about Lenny?"

Kevin usually appeared physically paralyzed, but his mumbling was nonstop. Very rarely did he speak in a direct way, though his coded mumbling was loaded with meaning once one learned to discount two out of three of his sentences. His feet were normally glued to the ground, his knees tense and stiff. Yet as I watched, Kevin's shoulders suddenly shot up and his eyes began to dart about the room. One side of his face was twitching.

Brian was watching with interest as Dr. Jones tried to get the reluctant Kevin to react to his suggestions. For many years, Brian had been in Kevin's immobilized condition. To get Brian moving in those dark days, a battery of psychiatric techniques had been unleashed on him. For Brian, this scene between Dr. Jones and Kevin must have touched a nerve, or perhaps started him projecting. Then, suddenly, with fists clenched, teeth gritted, and arms cocked in fighting position, Brian approached Kevin.

"OK, you lazy bastard. Move. Get on with it. What do you think this is? A goddamn mental institution? Are you God or something? Get on with it, Kevin boy!" and then, as an afterthought, "And tell your voices to bug off!"

Brian's tirade had been made in a low, animal snarl, gutteral and coarse, a far cry from his usual, somewhat high-pitched, effeminate voice. His right arm drew back in preparation for a punch. At this point, Brian checked himself, pulled half-way back, and struck Kevin with a weak, ineffectual blow.

All of Brian's movements reduced him to a treadmill of motion. When he ran, one leg shot forward, the other pushed backward. When his head and torso were forward, his lower half seemed to be pulling in the other direction. When he moved one arm in an Australian crawl stroke, the other arm held him stationary with a backstroke. When he kicked his legs forward, his toes turned up, bent almost backward.

Observing Brian's bizarre movements, I am reminded of the air force's comparison of their novice pilots to the kiwi bird. The air force pilots say that the kiwi bird flies backward because he is not interested in where he is going, but rather, in where he has been. He flies backward in ever decreasing spirals, until he flies up his own rectum and disappears.

Kevin, ignoring the force of Brian's outburst, merely replied with another spate of mumbling. Then his vibrating body jerked him loose from his spot on the floor, and he began to stagger toward the door. Dr. Jones, however, was ready to "talk" him back.

"Oh, so you are just going to walk away from Brian's stuff, are you? You're just going to let him punch you anytime he pleases, is that it? Isn't that what your brother has been doing to you all these years, giving you a good jerking around any time he's in the mood?"

Kevin looked frightened. Raised as a southern gentleman, he generally tried to be mannerly and soft-spoken. But now, he was completely cowed by Dr. Jones and Brian. His eyes teared. His mouth trembled. His lips continued to form incoherent words, as his arms flapped up and down against his sides in impotent despair. Kevin's tall, thin frame, elongated further by his heavy, high-heeled cowboy boots, seemed to be tautly pulled inward at the middle as he slinked away from Brian. His eyes sought me out, as he desperately looked around for help.

"Who are *you?*" he asked. "The football coach? The dancing teacher?" Then his eyes lit on my sweater, and he looked away nervously. "You got your bumps on. Are you my mother? Is it safe? Can I talk?"

Imploringly, Kevin faced Brian. "Are you my girl friend? Am I the girl? Are you the boy? Who am I?"

Brian seemed moved by this. Immediately, he dropped his aggressive stance and put his arms around Kevin. Face to face, he wordlessly embraced Kevin—and Kevin, with a deep sigh, hugged back.

As I watched the scene taking place, it was hard to believe that Kevin's clinging, weaving, uncertain figure had the violence within it to have almost killed a man with a golf club.

Suddenly, from the record player, a blast of full volume rock sound shook the room. Carol was dancing around gleefully, moving her pelvis like a belly dancer. "I thought we could use a little action, man. This place is getting awful heavy." Carol inclined her head in the direction of Dr. Jones and Kevin. "Who needs that stuff? It really freaks me out. What we need are the Stones, man."

The Rolling Stones, a rock group alive with a frank sexuality that it projects at a consistent fevered pitch, completely destroyed the more creative mood that the tribal rites music had engendered. Like mechanical windup dolls programmed to respond to the sound of the peer-group beat, the group came shaking and jerking into the center of the room, close to one another, but maintaining a sense of separateness. Brian had left Kevin's side and was now leaping through the air. Even hefty Dr. Jones had thrown himself in with the group and was moving his hips awkwardly but happily. Suddenly Kevin, too, jumped up into the air like a young Masai warrior, high, stiff, in one piece, with enormous elevation. Fascinated by Kevin's African jumps, I got closer and jumped along with him. One jump, two jumps, and we were together in the air. And then, in one, swift, mystifying moment, I was swooped up, sent spiraling through space, and propelled downward until I hit the cement floor.

My initial awareness as I lay there on the floor was not so much of pain, but rather of complete surprise. Having never played football, basketball, or any contact sport that would regularly have exposed me to a sudden fall, I was amazed by the abrupt sound and feeling of bone and flesh on cement. As I mused on this phenomenon, the patients gathered around me, stunned. Kevin was the closest down on his knees, peering into my face.

"I didn't mean it, Mrs. Lefco, I'm sorry," he cried. "I thought you were big, strong, like a football coach. C'mon, hit me! Hit me! It's your turn. Knock me down. It's OK. You can knock me down." Tears spilled down over his face. "I'm sorry."

Much as my head hurt, I was tremendously impressed by the sincerity, coherency, and lack of mumbling in Kevin's speech. I used one hand to feel the bump on my head, and put my other hand on Kevin's arm.

"I'm OK, Kevin, I'm really OK."

Inexplicably, Don was now sobbing. "He didn't do it. I did it. I didn't want to, but it just came over me. Mama's dead. Look at her! Dead." Don's hands covered his face and he sobbed.

I could no longer rub my head. There were more important things to do with my hands. My arms went around Don as he bent over me, sobbing.

"Everybody wants to take a poke at mama, Don. Don't worry about it. Except that you didn't do it this time," I said.

Brian also peered down at me, his face perplexed. "This is a pickle. I'd really like to know. Who did it? Did I?" And then Brian turned questioningly to Dr. Jones, who was kneeling beside me with the rest of the group. "Did you do it?"

This struck me funny, and as I laughed, the fright left my body. When I thought of all the questioning going on as to who had perpetrated the foul deed, I began to feel like the hero Robin, in "Who Killed Cock Robin?," and this made me laugh even harder. One look at Dr. Jones's serious face made me suspect that he thought I was becoming hysterical. Gently, he began to help me to my feet. "Think you can make it, Helene?"

I rubbed my head, flexed my back, wiggled my body a bit, and then decided that my years of practicing dance falls had not been in vain. Instinctively, I had protected myself by landing on all of the soft spots, except for my head. In my bleary state, I recognized that my injury was no more than a slight concussion.

"Get the derrick and pull me up, Jones," I said as he propped me up to a standing position.

Kevin was now completely hysterical, babbling, crying in a high-pitched, childish voice. Dr. Jones quickly led him out of the room, back to his quarters. Over his shoulder, Kevin's tear-stained face looked back at me.

"Can I ever come back to dancing class?" he called out.

"I hope so, Kevin," I said. And then, pointing to my head, "That is, if I can count on *this* not happening again!"

"It wasn't supposed to happen *this time,* Mrs. Lefco!" Kevin said.

I grinned with pure joy. Kevin had answered with humor, clarity, directness. I shook my throbbing head. It was too bad I couldn't employ this technique more often to elicit a clear response from Kevin.

Don was at my side. "So Kevin did it, did he? I hate him. What a disgusting beast!"

Carol was patting my shoulder. "What a bunch of finks in this place. I really hate everyone's guts!"

Laura walked up to me shyly. "You OK? Does your head hurt bad?" she asked anxiously.

I put my arms around Laura's thick waist. "I'm fine."

Laura put her arm through mine. "It was like you were my sister. Like sometimes, when I was young, I really wanted to floor her. But it really scared me when I saw you lying there."

Brian had been standing thoughtfully by listening to Laura. Now he spoke in a quiet, matter-of-fact voice.

"I guess it's all over now . . . all the dancing. The music will stop, eh?"

I then took my first steps since my fall and was relieved to know that all my parts were still functioning. "Brian, I'm going to put a record on now, and I hope to put on ten thousand more for dance therapy sessions." Smiling at him, I added, "I've got a tough noggin."

Brian sighed and put his arms around me, but at the same time, he managed to wind his body away from me. Perhaps our respective roles in the drama that had just unfolded had been too much for him. As I watched, he left me, mind, spirit, and body. But once again, characteristically, Brian could not consolidate all of himself. Although his legs and torso were moving away from me, his head was still turned in my direction.

"What did you say your name was?" he asked.

I put on John Williams's record of "Two Guitar Concertos," and the sound of pastoral musical poetry filled the room. Soothed and quieted, we all settled down on the carpeted area of the room. My head dropped contemplatively on my chest, but my mind anxiously returned to the question of why Kevin had chosen the moment when I was mirroring his high jumps to forcibly push me away.

Dr. Jones, back in the recreation room after escorting Kevin to his quarters, joined our group. He sprawled comfortably on the red carpet with us to discuss the incident.

"I think Kevin was confused, Helene," he said. "Brian had just caressed him, and he felt himself warmly responding. Right on the heels of this encounter, you arrive, literally jumping up at him with passion. He likes you. You are many women to him. His sister, his mother, his girl friend. Think of it. What a bind for a confused boy like Kevin to have responded to Brian's homosexual advance and to be almost immediately tempted by a heterosexual possibility." Dr. Jones shook his head. "I think it was simply too much for him to handle. Kevin had to push something away," he said frowning, "and unfortunately, it was you. I might have precipitated it," Dr. Jones continued, "by trying to release some of his anger." He laughed, gently rubbing my head, "I hadn't figured that he'd work it out on *you*."

Thinking about what Dr. Jones had said, I settled back in a crossed-leg yoga position, and took some deep breaths. Oh well, it wasn't all bad. I looked around at the patients. Their faces were peaceful. Don and Laura had dealt with "Mom" and "Sis" and knocked both of them down summarily. Carol and Penny had shown tenderness and concern. Even Brian had made it through his miasma of confusion, if only for a few minutes. Kevin had organized and spoke his thoughts precisely. On balance, I think I was glad the incident had happened. As if reading my mind, Carol pointed toward my head.

"Your dance therapy lumps are showing, Mrs. Lefco," Carol said. "I guess even *you* don't know all the answers."

"You can say that again!" I laughed, taking Carol's hand. She in turn brought Brian into our sitting circle, while he stretched out an arm to Don, Laura, and Penny. All of us were together, our arms around one another, our bare toes touching, one head inclined toward the other. As the session closed, we hummed and swayed to the sound of guitars.

ALBERT PESSO

Structures in Psychomotor Training

Life seldom allows a replay of the garbled bon mot or the bungled put-down. When opportunity knocks, there is ordinarily but one chance to punch-'em-in-the-nose. Albert Pesso does better by his clients than reality. In a veritable orgy of fantasies, memories of past scenes are restructured during psychomotor training with variations to fit the client's satisfaction. Any Hollywood ending may prevail, depending upon the participant's directorial talents. There may occur patricidal shoot-'em-ups or tearful family reunions. Sometimes both occur simultaneously.

During a semirelaxed state (the so-called species stance), an individual is asked to focus on a private experience. According to relaxation researcher Dr. Edmund Jacobsen, a true state of relaxation is incompatible with the rush of emotions which accompany these memories.[1] The body is thus ripe for action.

At this point the individual directs the group in improvisational replays of the scene. He appoints four "accommodators." The accommodators are platonic ideals which represent the goody-goody and the woefully inadequate "parents" who are part and parcel of Everyman's psychic baggage.

All this fun and these games have a serious purpose, according to Albert Pesso: "Our aim is articulation, flexibility, spontaneity, and control of the motor expressions of the body with no aspect being overaccentuated."[2] Clients are trained to recognize motor responses to emotions and to develop sensitivity to the physical cues that stimulate emotional responses. In the formalized repetition of these scenes, the client works toward clarification of his emotional reac-

Reprinted by permission of New York University Press from *Movement in Psychotherapy: Psychomotor Techniques and Training*, Albert Pesso. Copyright 1969 by New York University.

1. Edmund Jacobsen, M.D. *Anxiety and Tension Control: A Physiologic Approach* (Philadelphia, Pa.: J. B. Lippincott, 1964), Appendix, p. 12.

2. This essay was originally published in *Movement in Psychotherapy: Psychomotor Technique and Training* (New York: New York University Press, 1969). The quotation is taken from p. 5 of the same book.

tions toward parental and other figures. Pesso claims that insight naturally follows from this experience. In this and other ways he reveals his debt to Moreno, pioneer of psychodrama in the thirties.   M.N.C.

The group is now ready to spend the bulk of its time doing structures. A structure is a motoric recapitulation of past or fantasied events. In psychomotor, the recapitulation polarizes the target figures, permitting expression of what was not expressed in actuality. A real recapitulation of a past event would include the actual remembrance of that event in all its aspects. A structured recapitulation of a past event provides the proper environment and arena for doing whatever direct emotional impulses might have arisen in the original event but were not acted upon because of the negative results they would have produced at the time or because of impotence at the time.

Another aspect of a structure differing from an actual recapitulation is that it provides the individual with an alternative, a highly positive and ideal one, that could have provided the maximum pleasure and security had it occurred instead of the original unpleasantness. In a manner different from his original one, the individual in one stroke gains catharsis, insight, and experience, providing a new model for responding to similar present-day situations.

The first structure, to be worked on as an exercise by the group, is the child-parent structure. This exercise permits the expression of childhood fears with the new addition of an ideal parent-accommodator who would be available to comfort, protect, and care for the frightened child. This exercise permits practice in positive accommodation for the group. The group is instructed to split into two even groups with each group lined up on opposite sides of the room facing one another. The members of one group are instructed to recall a time when they were very young and terribly frightened but had no one to go to for help. They are to concentrate on that feeling in the species stance until the force of the imagery is such as to produce the action concomitant with it; that is, running, hiding, and so on. If an individual cannot recall an actual event when he was terribly frightened, he is to invent or imagine such an event out of a movie, perhaps, or a nightmare. The members of the other group play ideal parents who will be available to the frightened individuals. The parent figures are instructed to hold the child figures tightly, caressingly, and parentally when called upon.

The frightened individual is instructed to consider the positive accommodator as an almost godlike figure who can, indeed, protect

him, regardless of the extent of the fear or the extent of the threat. The
use of the godlike image is not to introduce the notion of religion into
the activity but to draw on the feelings of confidence, belief, security,
safety, and "it's all right" that are potential to the human species
which are tapped and evoked by religious ideas. The parent figure is
instructed not to use words in his positive accommodation unless the
frightened figure specifically requests them by saying, "Don't ever
leave me," and so on, whereupon the positive accommodator is to
say such things as "No, I'll never leave you," and so on. Whatever it is
that the frightened individual must know of the parent figure in terms
of his solidity, dependability, eternal vigilance, and so on, the parent
figure is not expected to say, "Are you solid?," but his needs will imply solidity.

The reader may wonder at the believability of the positive accommodation. Positive accommodation is offered in the same spirit as
negative accommodation. When the situation was so structured that
one's anger always "won" and one's negative accommodator always
lost, it was explained that this was necessary in order to fully express
one's hostility without reservation, and with full feeling of satisfaction. The feedback had to indicate the success of one's efforts. That is,
one had to see the effects of one's blows on the person of the negative accommodator. Simply, the environment in that respect is so
structured that the appropriate response is always available to each
type of emotional expression. This is the purpose of accommodation.
The accommodation shows that each emotional expression includes
an expected response which matches it like a jigsaw puzzle. This is
the communication loop mentioned earlier, and it indicates the successful culmination of that emotional expression.

By extension, this argument implies that all the emotional needs
that are possible to a human can be met by human environments,
even though the words that are used to express those needs are not
taken literally. This understanding of words is illustrated when the
enactor tells his negative accommodator to "die," and the accommodator falls limp to the floor. The response that he needs is the limpness and the stillness that the word "die" connotes, not the real
death of the accommodator. For the emotion can "wish" and "ask"
the accommodator to "die" several different times in a period of
minutes without being contradictory or emotionally false. This implies the suspension of the intellectual understanding of reality,
noted earlier, for the sake of emotional reality. This same suspension
of reality in the handling of words is evident in the negative accommodation just described.

When the term "godlike" is used in positive accommodation, the action element is meant and not the intellectual meaning of the term. The action element implies the stability, the protectiveness, the warmth and security of the term "godlike." When the child figure implores the positive accommodator to stay with him "forever," and the accommodator says, "Yes, I will stay with you forever," this is an emotional truth even though it is an intellectual lie.

When such a child figure is permitted to feel the presence of that positive accommodator as a human parent figure (with the godlike attributes noted above), the child figure might wish to experience that security for eternity. When his wish is granted the eternity feeling is satisfied in approximately ten minutes to a half hour or less. It is the emotions that are being addressed by the accommodation, not the intellect. One's intellect is rightly offended by being offered "eternity" by another human, but one's emotions know exactly what is meant. Every normal, fairly satisfied individual has experienced that eternity in his mother's arms when that specific input was needed. When that emotion is satisfied the organism goes on to something else.

We are foolish to give total credence to the intellectual meaning inherent in emotionally packed words. The words are not real but the emotion is. The positive accommodator is lying in reality, yet providing an emotional truth and permitting the organism satisfactions it needs and knows how to use, allowing it to then go on to something else, whatever it may be. This is the crux of accommodation and structures. Without the use of accommodation and structures, an individual in emotional need of a parent figure can only be offered the reality words that "you are too old to be treated that way; you must forget it and go on to something else." Satisfying those needs in emotional action, knowingly suspending one's reality understanding of one's true age, permits the forgetting and the ability to go on to something else. When we suffocate the cries of the child within us in our efforts to go on with the real world, we deaden the senses to the outside world, and awaken the sensitivity to the inside world in a distorted form so that it appears to be the outside world.

How long does one need to cling to one's childhood, cling to one's godlike parent? There is a weaning process involved in all growth and maturation. The weaning comes partially from the inside and partially from the outside. The idea that one is simply forced to mature from the outside is offensive if one understands the maturing process as an unfolding from the inside. A tree is not forced to grow by admonitions and to produce fruit by threats. Through satisfaction of its organic need for water, sunshine, and chemicals it flourishes, matures, and dies with no intervention from any outside agency. In the case of a tree the forces of nature can be seen as positive accommodators. Is there not the perfect match as in a jigsaw puzzle between the needs of a tree and what is supplied it?

What is the place, you might ask, of the human cultivator in the garden? Does he hinder the growth of the tree? Yes, if he does not supply the tree with its own unspoken needs. The gardener can also take a tree that is suffering because of some environmental breakdown such as insufficiency of soil or water, and by application of those needs nurture back that "sick" tree to a return to its own health and normalcy. The positive accommodator in a structure is such a cultivator, such a gardener. He is supplying what the environment may have been unable to fulfill, in the terms requested and needed by the individual, for only he knows what he lacks.

Is it lying to say to that sick individual, "Take this warmth, take this nurturance and place it where it is lacking," so long as he knows that he is no longer a little tree, no longer a little person? I think not. It is to the satisfaction of those organic, emotional ends that accommodation and structures are applied.

What about the weaning process? An organism as complex as man must pass through several stages of growth where those things meaningful to one stage must be left and things meaningful to the next stage must be picked up. The transitions between stages are crucial in the human and there must be sufficient satisfactions made in the preceding stage before the attention can be raised to the oncoming stage. There also appears in the human the need of outside intervention and particularly assistance in making the transitions. If one were left entirely to himself, he might possibly remain at the lowest level or stage of growth. This would ignore the possibility of an inner drive to bring the organism to the fulfillment of its potential. At best, there seems to be a subtle interaction between inner and outer forces which results in the transition being made successfully. Yet, with any complex organism there is always the possibility of return to a less-complex level of organization (assuming that development through stages implies increased complexity), brought on by difficulties either physical or psychological. The nurturance back to health must include satisfaction of those inner needs once again with assistance in the transition process.

There is a point where discomfort must be faced, where one leaves the parent, where one leaves the point of safety and embarks to points unknown. This point is most easily met when satisfactions are sufficient and where the satisfying agents are prepared to relinquish their relationship with the recipient. Perhaps the outside agency supplies a belief in the individual who is in the process of making that transition by saying in effect, "You can do it. I believe in your ability to take care of yourself, and so on." The transitions can also be seen as a time when the individual finds himself saying, "I would like to take the next step, but I am afraid I cannot make it." The wish is an inner push, and the outside help is in terms of support and belief in the individual's ability to make that transition.

There is an oscillation between receiving from others and needing others, and relying on one's own resources, that characterizes the life and growth of man. The positive accommodator must play two distinct roles: one, as the individual who supplies the internal needs for as long as they are desired or needed; and two, as one who supplies the support and belief in an individual's ability to gain his own ends. While the positive accommodator is in the second stance, he must be prepared to resume the first stance if it should be deemed necessary. Some people cannot make the transition in one complete step and must drop back for a time to stage one in the transition and retrench while supplying themselves with sufficient input to feel able to "go it alone" again. We build up our capacity to be individuals by satisfying relations with others. Once we are individuals we do not remain isolated from others but become suppliers for others and producers or satisfactions to others and ourselves. The roles of accommodators have not been developed by theories such as outlined above, but have developed organically out of an attempt to satisfy expressed needs.

Let us return to the still-frightened individual who by now must have developed a most devastating fear. Some individuals in the group will be able to move directly to their imagery and will run in terror to their parent figures. They may clutch, sobbing, to the positive accommodator, holding on for dear life in an anguish of fear and desire to be protected and hidden. What is the state of the positive accommodator at this point? He may be flooded with a desire to protect and hold that individual in a rush of feeling that is surprising to him. He may find himself being protecting and reassuring in a way he has never felt before. He may be shocked by the individual's need, and possibly may identify with that individual so that he becomes frightened too, and feels like crying also. This would be emotional testimony to the fact that he has much fear-expressing to be done himself, and is not fully prepared to be the protecting individual.

He may find himself indifferent to the feelings of the child figure and simply hold him as he has been instructed. If this is the case, the child figure will feel that fact in the quality of the pressure of the arms and will be unable to completely give in to his feeling of need. For the protecting agent is obviously unable to supply what is necessary. In that event the individual might turn off his crying and become his own parent by internalizing or imagining the parent figure as himself, or else abruptly transition himself to a point where he experiences no need.

Some child figures may fall to the ground in terror and huddle in a ball of fear, unable or unwilling to move toward help. In that event the positive accommodator should rush to the aid of that individual, providing him with as much body contact as possible, holding that individual in an embrace where the enactor's arms are also embracing and his chest is in contact with the positive accommodator's chest. This position seems to be most satisfying in a fear situation.

If there is no solid object to wrap one's arms around and no contact with the front of one's torso, there seems to be a feeling of something lacking or missing and one is not as soothed as one would wish. The individual who falls to the ground is expressing a sense of hopelessness that there is any help for him and is capitulating to his fear. The arrival of the concerned parent in the body of the positive accommodator is felt with relief, although with some doubt and fear that it will not be sufficient. The final acceptance, evinced by the embrace and the torso contact, is indicative of willingness to receive comfort and to have a more optimistic viewpoint regarding the receiving of satisfaction.

Some individuals may be unable to find the capacity to express their fear in an overt manner and can be seen standing frozen and uncomfortable. They have not been able to move either way, toward their positive accommodator in an act of panic, or toward the floor in an act of capitulation. They are also unable to accept positive accommodation. If an individual in that state is approached by his positive accommodator with arms outstretched, the positive accommodator is apt to be waved off with the words, "I'm not ready for that yet. I'm not feeling the fear fully enough yet." Or they may acquiesce and go through the motions of holding and being held, but it is obviously pantomimed and tasteless to both participants as there is little or no feeling involved. One can hardly feel the surge of nurturance, wishes, and programs without the stimulus of a crying or frightened individual. One can hardly act nurturative when one is feeling imposed on to do an externally assigned series of movements that one is not particularly inclined to do.

There are those individuals who may feel nothing in response to the fear imagery and who cannot imagine a fearful situation. They may observe the more active members of the group in a mixed attitude of envy and disdain. They may wonder whether the more active individuals are really feeling what they seem to be feeling, or whether they are simply putting on an act. Others may look down on those whose feelings seem to be out of control, complimenting themselves on their greater sobriety and dignity. There may be some who are shocked by the outburst and who see that behavior as a potential example of their own loss of control.

Those who have burst into tears and are frantically clutching their positive accommodators can perhaps experience some of the same concern even while they are giving vent to their emotions. One part of their awareness is seeing the entire situation within its total perspective. Their decision to give in to their emotions does not place them emotonally out of control, as they realize they can stop themselves any time they wish. Their awareness provides them with the knowledge that this is a structure, with the memory that they have chosen the frightening image themselves, consciously concentrated on it themselves, and consciously selected to give in to the emotional action. The awareness in this case does not inhibit, does not modify; it simply oversees.

This type of overseeing has been one of the aims of the early practice exercises in psychomotor training. It has all been developed during the emotional movement training and here it is put to good use. This awareness is one of the important elements in psychomotor training, and without it one should not go into depth structures. This is the reason depth structures are not attempted with certain hospitalized mental patients. Those who cannot make the distinction between reality and a consciously selected structure should not do emotional structures, because for them there would be a belief in the reality of the structure, just as there is a belief in the reality of their delusions or hallucinations. There would not be a conscious selection to return to a childish emotion, but an unconscious compulsion to literally become a child, mentally and possibly physiologically.

With certain classes of psychotics the situation is entirely out of hand. It is almost as if the need for the undone sensations is so great that it causes a bending of the entire structure of the life toward the past, making the individual a child again. There are ways of relating to those individuals within the framework of their delusional systems; however, it requires great care and sensitivity to always lead that individual toward the realization of what was actually occurring without reinforcing the pathological view of reality.

Psychomotor training has been utilized with withdrawn, inactive patients whose overt expression has always been repressed and who are not in manic states. Other patient groups that have had successful application of psychomotor training have included autistic and regressed patients. In their cases there has been a lessening of emphasis on the emotional expression except in a highly structured and modified manner with a concomitant greater emphasis on voluntary movement and sensory input, particularly tactile. It is not my intention to go into the particulars of working with certain classes of mental patients at this time, since that will be the topic of another book. It should suffice to say that the basic tools outlined in this book are adaptable and applicable to most classes of mental patients, with care taken to utilize only those tools, at the proper time, that would lead toward greater satisfaction and ultimate control of the emotions, taking into consideration the difficulties regarding awareness and the reality orientation outlined above.

By the time of this particular exercise, most of the group should be capable of some sort of action in relation to their emotion. Those who have gone the furthest will perhaps cry for some time. As they are being reassured and held, the crying tends to subside, the rhythms of the breathing begin to change, the tension in the arms and body begins to lessen. Finally a state of relaxation and peace begins to develop. A sense of euphoria may be reported with a feeling of peace and comfort seeming to emanate from the parent figures.

This is a pleasant and unexpected development to those who have been crying, and they comment on how peaceful and content and secure they feel. Some may say that they feel like going right out and "playing in the sandbox," testifying to the desire to go on to something else once they are satisfied, and also testifying to the force of the imagery and its relationship to childish memories.

Those who have gone furthest in the exercise may comment that they had recalled a situation in their past where they were frightened of a dream or of some situation. When they had run to the parent, the parent had refused to comfort them, telling them to return to bed and not to bother them. They may say that they have experienced the same kind of fear many times since and that they often felt the sense of isolation of the original situation. Following the satisfying experience in this exercise they may comment that they just don't feel as frightened as before and they don't believe that that particular fear will have the same power. Numerous occasions with groups have indicated that long-term involvement in a psychomotor training group does reduce anxiety and fear.

The comforted expressions on the faces of those who have expressed their fear most directly and who have accepted the ministrations of the positive accommodators is noteworthy. This shows the inactive group members in a concrete way that something must have happened to those members. They may wonder if perhaps they were missing something and were not so well off for maintaining their dignity and sobriety, giving them a motivation to be freer at the next opportunity.

The positive accommodators who found a rush of emotion directed toward the crying individual may feel something quite gratifying. First, they may express surprise at the force and quality of the emotional desire to be helpful that arose in them. Then they may comment on how helpless they first felt in being able to comfort their child figures. They may comment on how seemingly successful were their largely tactile ministrations. Finally they may comment on how good it felt to be useful and successful in their efforts, reinforcing them in the use of touch as a comforting tool.

Some accommodators at the first time may tend to say to their crying child figures, "There, there, don't cry. Everything will be all right," and that is a mistake. When the child figure is venting the crying the last thing he wishes to hear is to be told, "Don't cry." The positive accommodators should simply permit and accept the crying and make themselves available as a protector and warm, loving, embracing individual. Even without words there are those individuals whose manner of holding and caressing in this situation suggests that the child figure should stop crying. These efforts at positive accommodation should be clarified without bringing embarrassment to those individuals who are doing it.

During the time of positive accommodation the child figure might say, "You're not going to send me away, are you?" and the parent figure of course should respond, "No, I will never send you away." The types of requests that are made of the positive accommodator lead one to learn how to be a positive accommodator and to recognize the common denominator in each type of situation. The individual wants to be certain that help is always there, that he will not be abandoned, that he is loved, that the positive figure is not going to die, that he is not bad, that he is wanted, that he is loved unconditionally. Ultimately one tends to demonstrate in one's own real life the same attitudes as one learns as a positive accommodator, and one becomes a better teacher, parent, or therapist as a result.

After the entire first group has completed the child-parent structure, the group is instructed to change roles with the individuals with whom they were coupled. In that way, those who were playing child figure can now explore the parental role, and those who were playing parent figure can now explore the child role. The switching of roles reduces the possibility of emphasizing only one aspect of one's being and reduces the possibility of focusing on only one individual as the giver and on oneself as only the receiver. The group becomes the therapeutic agent, rather than the group leader. The group leader does not become the focus of all the strong emotional feelings, although he certainly is an important figure in the operation of the group.

The group has now had some experience from the first attempt, and it does not take as long for the second group of child figures to work up their emotions to a point of action. When they do begin to move in terms of their fear, the positive accommodators know more clearly what to do, as they know precisely how they wished to be comforted when they were the child figures. There is less fear of embarrassment and less self-consciousness on the second attempt, as the first attempt ostensibly did not bring about any negative results. The group is a little more willing to plunge into the business of feeling.

The positive accommodation is usually better on the second attempt than on the first. The overall attitude toward the development of structures begins to become apparent. The trust within the group is rising even higher, for once the emotion of fear has been expressed and once tears have been shed and once those feelings have been alleviated, the group is firmly on its way to the careful and regular scrutiny of all those life situations and transitions that were not successfully met and traversed.

As one looks back into one's past, the thread of one's life is punctuated by the knots and tangles surrounding important events and feelings. Some people go over those knots and tangles religiously fingering them like a rosary, secure in the knowledge that they are all in the right place and all the pains are the expected pains. In psychomotor training, however, the intent is to unravel those knots and tangles, and, surprisingly for some, this unraveling is anxiety-producing. These people recognize themselves *as* themselves by the familiar bumps and pains on their psyches and are reluctant to give them up. Psychomotor training produces change, and change produces anxiety. One has to decide that the anxiety of change is preferable to the stultifying experience of restraint, fear, and immaturity. After one chooses change, the changes become the expected thing and one

operates on a higher level, prepared to be more effective and successful in what is attempted.

The experience within the child-parent exercise can lead to the development of the first structure. There is a difference between a
structure and the child-parent exercise that is worth noting. The child-
parent exercise allows the entire group to respond simultaneously,
and removes the center of attention from any one individual. A structure is done with a single individual expressing emotions and feelings.
The group leader should be in a position to know which individual is
most likely to do the first structure successfully without too much
inhibiting self-consciousness.

In actual practice, the individual who is most prepared to do a
structure is clearly evident. He may become aware of the possibilities
inherent in emotional movement, accommodation, and structures,
and may have a situation in his life that he wishes to experience
emotionally. He may have to be helped to polarize the targets of his
emotion in his structure. The group leader should lend himself to this
effort.

If one is to do a structure involving a parent figure, one should
concentrate only on the negative features of that parent, knowing
full well that there is more to the parent than that. One should recall
the action or inaction of the parent that provided the pain and frustration, and one should permit oneself to experience the pain and
anger this fosters and to allow this to become action.

One might ask, "You mean structures permit group members to
kill their parents?" The answer is an obvious "Yes," for the killing
is of the same kind done in the controlled rejection exercise. It is not
the intellectual reality kill, but the emotional reality kill. "But what
about guilt?" can be asked. The guilt is handled by first having the
knowledge that this is not a reality kill but an emotional kill; and
second, by having an ideal parent figure hold and accept one following the expression of anguish and rage fostered by the negative parent
figure.

The positive parent figure is not the real parent, just as the negative
parent figure is not the real parent. Both are polarizations of reality
elements. The ideal parent figure may contain elements of the real
parent figure but should be largely invented containing all that the
emotions wish him to contain: that is, unconditional love and support,
understanding, approval, and belief in oneself. It is reasonable to ask,
"Why must all the angry feelings result in a death? Can't someone
get angry without killing in psychomotor training?" The answer seems
to be "No." Anger on the primitive, global, unmodified level that is

practiced in psychomotor training seems to demand the emotional reality death. If such is the case, it is easy to understand why individuals in real life do not express many of their emotions. How could they express the emotional death wish for the frustrating parent? Dreams do permit this, which brings us to the notion that psychomotor training structures are similar in content to dream material, but done in a less symbolic and censored way than in a dream. Dream analysis shows that most individuals have death wishes for loved ones, so it should not be too surprising when direct emotional expression of rage seeks the death of the negative accommodator.

Let us return to the group member who was prepared for and desirous of doing a structure. He may vividly remember having been frightened by a parental figure who came home drunk and threatened to kill him and his mother. The real situation may have resulted in an evening of terror, running from the threatening parent until the parent finally subsided and fell asleep, drunk. It may be assumed that this was one of many such situations with that parent and that this one situation is reminiscent of all the others. How is this handled in a structure? The standard approach to a structure is to provide negative accommodators for the negative elements in a situation and positive accommodators for the enactment of what could have been in an ideal situation to match the internal needs and expectations of a growing child.

Through practice in spatial awareness, the enactor can tell the negative accommodators the kinds of placements, actions, and gestures that would provide the essential negative stimulus. The enactor might decide to stand on his knees if he was small at the time of the original event. In any event, he would attempt to supply himself with the most powerful stimulus to his emotions relevant to that situation and his feelings. If this group member is fully prepared to do such a structure (and the group leader should see to it that he is before allowing it), the setting should be distinctly provocative. At some point when the negative accommodator was threatening either him (the enactor) or his mother, the enactor will likely rise in a fit of fear and panic and go running perhaps to the negative mother figure. At which point he will still not be safe, for that was probably how it was in reality. The threatening negative father figure would probably still pursue the frightened individual and the mother both, and then finally the enactor might turn on the father in a rage and finding a rising tide of hatred, attack the negative father figure ferociously.

The attack might go on for minutes, with a negative accommodator rolling about the floor, responding to punches, kicks, repeated in a bewildering pattern, just this side of loss of control. When, finally, the anger at the father has been satiated and the father figure is perhaps beaten with the bottles of his own whiskey, the enactor may face his feelings toward the negative mother figure. If in real life she had been brutal and unprotective, he may turn upon her all the frustrations her lack of care engendered. Or he may simply be furious at her for marrying such a horrible father.

He may feel some hesitation in attacking the mother figure, depending on the amount of love and warmth she represented in reality, and considering that it was deficient she would receive her share of angry expression. The moment she would finally be "killed" might be a crucial moment in the feelings of the enactor. He might suddenly be overcome by the feelings of loss and isolation and also be giving vent to all the years of misery and pain and begin to sob helplessly.

This points out the need for the existence of the positive accommodators. For once an individual has finally vented his hatred, does it not destroy the potential givers of nurturance, the potential protectors, one's only parents? No wonder people hold their feelings in check. There is no one to replace the miserable parents they have, as bad as they were.

The positive accommodators come to the side of the crying enactor and embrace him and hold him gently and tenderly until he stops crying. They may be asked, "You wouldn't beat me up, would you?" and they may answer, "No, of course not." This type of dialogue may go on or the entire scene may take place in silence with the enactor experiencing how it might have been with ideal parents. He may wish to see his positive accommodators hug one another as if they really loved one another. He may wish to have them both extend their arms to him and be held tightly by them. Whatever he wishes to experience with them they accommodate accordingly. He may wish to be taken for a ride or to be sitting down at the table for dinner or he may simply wish to be held.

When he is through, the group leader can ask him if he wishes to do anything else. This is a crucial moment, and one that should be understood on a nonverbal level much more than on a verbal level. There is a certain quality to a satisfyingly finished structure that a group leader becomes accustomed to. The clues to it are subtle but recognizable, and shortly the group members know if a structure is truly "over" or not.

Some of the clues are in the obvious appearance of relaxation. The expression is more relaxed and the arms hang easily to the sides. This quality of relaxation can also be apparent in the positive accommodation in the structure. Does the enactor accept the warmth of the positive accommodators peacefully and contentedly? Is he smiling? Sometimes the group leader can actually hear the rumblings in the stomach of the enactor which seems to physiologically indicate the change of emotional tone and correspond to the moment that an individual will report that he is feeling better. After the structure is seemingly finished, does the enactor have a strained look about the eyes? Is he making short and abrupt movements of the hands while saying that he is finished? Are one or both of his hands fisted, one perhaps digging into the other? Is he rubbing his eyes with his hands in a manner that suggests tears? Are his hands involuntarily going to his mouth and is he biting his lip? These are some of the clues a group leader becomes accustomed to seeing.

If there are sufficient clues to convince the group leader that indeed, the structure is not over, and that there is an obvious residue of undone emotions, the group leader can suggest to the enactor that perhaps he still has some feelings that he has not completely expressed yet. And would he like to repeat the situation over again? In the event that he does, the negative accommodators pick themselves off the floor, where they have been lying prone all the while until the structure is actually over, and resume the actions and placements the enactor instructed them to have originally.

From his experience in the throes of the emotion, the enactor might have recalled even more specific events and actions in that same or other incidents that he can now include as a stimulus. Once again the negative accommodators can provoke him and once again he can go through the expression of the feelings. This second time can either be stronger or weaker than the first time, depending on the strength of the residue of feelings after the first time. It is possible that it is stronger and if the bulk of the angry feelings are finally purged, the positive accommodators can be responded to with more peace and comfort than before.

The enactor might then say, "That does feel better. Thanks for letting me do it the second time. I was afraid there wasn't enough time left, and I really did not get everything out." It is also possible that he may still feel some residue of feeling at which time he can go through it a third time. The group leader should be in a position to ascertain whether the enactor has done as much as he is capable of doing without imposing on him or placing pressure on him.

In the event that a third time is not sufficient and it appears that there is much yet to be done regarding these particular circumstances, the group leader can suggest that the group hug that individual and have him be held for some time until he feels a lessening of his tension.

The group leader would not have permitted the very first complete structure to be attempted if it were not conducive to easy structuring, so it is unlikely that the enactor would be in the unhappy position where he was still uncomfortable after three tries. Those deep-rooted and hard-to-resolve situations generally do not arise so early in the process of doing structures. A certain amount of unconscious selectivity goes on that produces the kinds of structures in the right order for an individual to resolve when he is ready to resolve them. It is rare that an individual plunges into deeper water than he is capable of swimming in. If he should do so, the group leader should contain him from diving into such waters until he seems ready.

Typically, the first structure tends to be completed satisfactorily, with the enactor physically and emotionally drained. Frequently, the positive accommodators are instructed to sit with the enactor for some time after the ending of a structure during what is called "gape time." Following a successful structure, the enactor often appears in a state of suspended external awareness during which time feelings regarding the past situation are being experienced in a new way. It is reported that this time is not characterized by conscious thinking but by a relaxed awareness of new perspectives and a sense of the reorganization of thought and action patterns. During this gape time the enactor should be held between the positive accommodators so that he does not feel vulnerable and so that he should continue to feel their comforting presence.

The reason it is called "gape time" is that the enactor appears relaxed, with mouth and face slack, with eyes open but not paying attention to what is being seen; in short, he is agape. I do not mean to imply that he is incapable of normal interactions at this time, but experience shows there is something valuable going on in the internal reorganization which should not be disturbed. This gape period can last from one to ten minutes, during which time the group can go on to other structures.

The group's response to this first structure will undoubtedly be varied. There will be those who will have experienced "echoes" in themselves of similar types of treatment. These people will be feeling very strongly as a result of this and they will not feel the sense of resolution the enactor has because they have not done anything about their own feelings, and vicarious responses can only go so far. There will be those who are shocked at the amount of feeling and action that took place and who might be shaken by it without having it refer to anything particular in their own lives. There will be those who will be unaffected by what they saw, and such individuals are among those who have the most difficulty in expressing their own feelings.

Seeing one of their number in such depth of feelings usually produces a closeness of the group. The enactor's willingness to demonstrate strong and personal emotions is extremely important to many group members. They feel that, here in the session, it is possible to be entirely oneself without covering up or hiding and without being hurt as a result of it. The first structure tends to add another brick in the edifice of trust within the group. The many feelings of hopelessness that people carry about due to the distress of feelings that are unexpressible begins to be changed to a feeling of hope that perhaps one can truly relate and share oneself with others.

The group leader can offer to those who have reacted with the most echoes the opportunity to do a structure next. One of those group members may have a specific event pop into his mind as a result of watching the first structure. He may remember a situation when he had done something wrong as a child and his father had come home and threatened him with his belt and subsequently being beaten with that belt. He may recall that he was angry with his mother for not having stood up for him, and that in his own eyes the offense for which he was being beaten was quite minor. The structuring of this can be essentially the same as for the first structure: two figures to be the negative accommodators and two to be the positive accommodators.

The group leader can play either of the roles, positive or negative, depending on the size of the group, the number of males present, and the ability of group members to effectively produce the required stimulus and input. In any given session, the group leader may be in several structures or none, and he should see to it that he does not overemphasize one aspect or the other in his selection of accommodation roles.

Once again the enactor can instruct the negative accommodators in the appropriate placements, gestures, and actions relevant to himself. Words can be used, but it has been found that they tend to disrupt the polarization process and inject other aspects into the situation than were experienced by the enactor, thus tending to reduce the intensity of the focus on the emotions. If words are to be used, they should be only precisely those requested by the enactor, which in this case might be, "Come over here, boy; I'm going to give you what you deserve," repeated as indicated by the enactor.

Bringing the stimulus to a point of reduplication of reality is an impossibility. What should be attempted is the construction of the crucial elements as *felt*, whether they were the actual conditions or not, because those are what will be reacted to. The examination of the stimulus conditions on a reality base is not the aim of structures, but a reasonable inquiry into other, more verbal forms of therapy and learning. The complete reassembling of the conditions as they actually were and not as they were felt would probably lead to inaction, as did the reality conditions. One would be inclined to say, "I suppose my father was right in trying to discipline me, and I guess I did wrong, so I should not be angry at him." This is intellectual reality and must be lived with. The emotional reality is that one was bombarded with emotional impulses that have never been acted upon. That is the point of doing a structure about it.

The structure makes available an arena where all those impulses can come forth in full force, suspending for a consciously selected time the reality conditions. For the successful expression of direct emotions, polarization of target is necessary, and the negative accommodation supplies just that. Following the successful rendering of such a structure, the enactor might very well say that his father was probably right in trying to discipline him, but now the emotions surrounding that situation and the father have been reduced and one can make a more neutral and relevant appraisal of the entire circumstance.

When the negative accommodators have been instructed and the positive accommodators are standing on the other side of the room in readiness, the enactor can do the species stance and focus on the sensations his memories produce. Then he can open his eyes and direct the negative accommodators to behave as previously instructed. As they do so he may find emotions welling up in him; he may particularly find himself reacting to his father's belt. Many group members have noted how powerfully they have reacted to objects which played a part in emotionally charged circumstances. First, he may feel horror and fear in response to the father and the belt. Then he may feel fury as the belt begins to descend, not upon him, but on the floor beside him, close enough to remind him of the actual stinging sensation of the blows themselves.

The moment of the transition from fear to fury is an important one, though it was not highlighted in the description of the first structure. Some individuals find that they cannot make that transition and remain frozen and helpless in fear. They may say that they cannot possibly fight off the father or whoever is their antagonist. To turn and attack him, even if they know they have a right to be angry, would be untrue to their real feelings. It is clear then that fear cannot turn into fury if one believes that one's efforts will inevitably be useless. Angry feelings are not directly available to weak individuals. Fear is more of their province.

In the event that the present enactor finds that he cannot turn on the father, the available alternative would be to call for an ally. The justification for this is that one could have, or wished to have, someone external see the injustice of the beating and intervene in behalf of the enactor. This kind of intervention is done by the positive accommodator. At the height of that beating when the enactor is in pain and fear, the positive male accommodator may grab the belt from the negative accommodator, and proceed to beat the negative accommodator in the enactor's behalf. This may give the enactor a feeling of hope and security. He may run to the positive female accommodator and say, "You wouldn't let him beat me, would you?" and of course the positive accommodator would say, "Of course not." No words may be exchanged, if the enactor wishes, and he may simply watch in vicarious joy and relief as the once invincible father is beaten down in defeat.

It is possible that the enactor might feel guilt or anger at the positive accommodator for beating his father. In that case, the enactor should instruct the positive accommodator to simply stop the negative father figure and have him sent out of the room without hitting at him. All elements should be carefully watched by the group leader so that the structure does not produce actions and feelings in the enactor contrary to what is intended. One should not simply follow out the basic form of a structure and expect it to be relevant and correct for every individual. One must always use the feelings of the enactor, honestly and directly experienced, as the final guide to the direction the structure will take.

One might ask, following an ally's coming to an enactor's defense, "Does this not make the enactor a passive dependent person?" It would if that was all that occurred, but an interesting thing happens following this championing by the positive accommodator. Either at that time or in following structures the enactor may find that he, too, can turn on the father figure for now he has the license and the example. Let us say that following the first rendition of the structure the enactor goes to the positive accommodators. He there experiences ideal parents who would not utilize beatings as a disciplinary measure, and who would be unconditionally loving to the enactor.

Following the question, "Are you finished, is there anything else you might want to do?," the enactor might indicate that he would like to try it over again.

The second run-through of the structure might reach the same crucial point where the negative accommodator is beating the enactor, but now the internal state of the enactor may be different. The enactor has had the benefit of an ally; he has experienced the security and the relationship of other parent figures who would not condone this type of treatment; he has experienced another frame of reference; he has experienced an alternate form of treatment. The full force of the reaction to the pain and the injustice may descend on him. He may turn on the negative accommodator, grabbing the belt from him, and find that this gives him a surge of power that is surprising and exciting. He may attack the negative accommodator and may find himself spontaneously devising all kinds of tortures to impose on the father with his own belt. He may demolish the father figure and chastise the negative mother figure for not defending him. He may even beat her, depending on how he feels on a direct emotional level, and go to his positive accommodators feeling like a stronger, worthier, more powerful individual. He may realize during his gape time that he had accepted a diminished value of himself relevant to his many beatings and that now that value is being revised upward in his mind and feelings.

Psychomotor training structures change the emotional charge that one has in respect to certain circumstances. They permit the physical action relevant to that charge. They change the kinds of behavior that one anticipates relevant to oneself. They change one's self-image depending on how successful one can let oneself become in a structure and depending on the kind of treatment one experiences from one's positive accommodators.

The examples given above of the first two structures should not be seen as hard and fast formulas. Each structure has its own pattern, its own organization. The group leader can assist in making a structure, but he should use as his guide the feelings of the enactor, as they are verbalized to him, and as they appear in the body of the enactor nonverbally. All structures should be flexible with the enactor's inner sense of his emotional changes highly attentive so that he always moves from that center and not as a "formula" structure form might dictate. He should always act in the direction of his feelings, even if they seem contradictory to what would be expected. He should not act in response to the way he thinks he should act, for that would not be true to his emotions, and emotional truth is what is being sought in psychomotor training. The integrating force of doing what is felt is what is sought.

The intellectual understanding on the reality level follows, not precedes, the doing of a structure. After gape time and at some point following the termination of a structure, an individual will verbalize voluntarily regarding finding a completely new way of looking at an event in his life. Insight seems to follow action, rather than action follow insight. Although there is a suspension of reality in the doing of an emotional structure, the resumption of reality following it is of a higher order and not of a lesser order, as one might fear after seeing so much primitive behavior.

KINDER WOOD, M.D.

A Case of the Dancing Mania

Marian Chace at St. Elizabeth's and the voodoo *shamens* of Haiti—the juxtaposition seems, at first glimpse, absurd. It is an intriguing theme explored by many.[1] The youthfulness of movement therapy is acknowledged as the writers seek roots in primitive communal dance.

"A Case of the Dancing Mania" suggests that movement therapy has ties to the past—but a history more in line with our country's social origins. Kinder Wood, an early nineteenth-century English physician, originated a technique that seems highly compatible with others described in this volume. The case study was first published in the 1844 edition of Hecker's *The Epidemics of the Middle Ages*.

The diagnosis that the young woman suffers from St. Vitus dance may strike the reader as quaint, if not patent, nonsense. He would not be alone in this view. Modern researchers, attempting to update the episode, label it an instance of "conversion hysteria."[2] In defense of Dr. Wood, Backman's scholarly account of *Religious Dances in the Christian Church and in Popular Medicine,* translated by E. Classen, should be examined. He presents a strong case for viewing the medieval dance mania as of partly medical origins rather than purely mental.

A detailed comparison of the various symptoms of the dance epidemics and the symptoms of ergot poisoning and ergotism reveals an extraordinary and exact correspondence. The conclusion is irresistible: the dance epidemics were caused by ergot poisoning of grain and bread. Ergot poisons have the power to develop in human beings, possibly in combi-

---

1. Irmgard Bartenieff, "Dance Therapy: A New Profession or a Rediscovery of an Ancient Role of the Dance?," in *Dance Scope 7* (1) (Fall–Winter, 1972–73). Franziska Boas, "The Origins of Dance," American Dance Therapy Association, *Sixth Annual Conference Proceedings* (Washington, D C., 1971). Claire Schmais and Elissa White, "Introduction to Dance Therapy," *Workshop in Dance Therapy: Its Research Potentials.* The Proceedings of a Joint Conference by Research Department of Postgraduate Center for Mental Health, Committee on Research in Dance, American Dance Therapy Association (New York: Committee on Research in Dance, 1970).

2. Berton Roueche, *Curiosities of Medicine* (Boston: Little, Brown, 1963), p. 237.

nation with severe famine and lack of vitamins, muscular spasms and bodily contortions which in those days were considered as "dance." Herein is the explanation of the belief that the sufferers could without interruption dance day and night, for days and weeks.[3]

The physical symptoms that Dr. Wood's patient shares with other victims of St. Vitus dance include: the disease onset with headache and limb trembling before awakening, cramping, bizarre body contortions, and rapid, high leaping continued over a ten-day period.

However old-fashioned Wood's diagnosis might seem to social learning theorists, the doctor operates in the best Skinnerian manner. He first notes the baseline frequency of her behavioral patterns, then shapes the duration of dancing by manipulating the environment. He pinpoints a stimulus that has the effect of immediately stopping the behavior. In order to check on the accuracy of his procedures, Wood observes how the behavior extinguishes if the cue is properly used or returns if reinforced. M.N.C.

February 26—Slight motions of the limbs came on in bed. She arose at nine o'clock after which they increased, and became unusually severe. She was hurled from side to side of the couch-chair upon which she sat, for a considerable time, without intermission, was sometimes instantaneously and forcibly thrown upon her feet, when she jumped and stamped violently. She had headache, the eyelids were frequently affected, and she had often a sudden propensity to spring or leap upward. The affection ceased about eleven o'clock in the forenoon, the patient being very much fatigued, but it returned about noon, and a third time in the afternoon, when she was impelled into every corner of the room, and began to strike the furniture and doors violently with the hand, as she passed near them, the sound of which afforded her great satisfaction. The fourth attack was at night, was very violent, and ended with sickness and vomiting. She went to bed at half-past eleven. Her nights were invariably good. The last three attacks were more violent than the former ones, but they continued only half an hour each.

February 27—The attack commenced in bed, and was violent, but of short duration. When she arose about ten, she had a second attack, continuing an hour, except an interval of five minutes. She now struck the furniture more violently and more repeatedly. Kneeling

3. E. Louis Backman, *Religious Dances in the Christian Church and in Popular Medicine*, translated by E. Classen (London: George Allen and Unwin, 1952), p. 334.

on one knee, with the hands upon the back, she often sprang up suddenly and struck the top of the room with the palm of the hand. To do this, she rose fifteen inches from the floor, so that the family were under the necessity of withdrawing all the nails and hooks from the ceiling. She frequently danced upon one leg, holding the other with the hand, and occasionally changing the legs. In the evening, the family observed the blows upon the furniture to be more continuous, and to assume the regular time and measure of a musical air. As a strain or series of strokes was concluded, she ended with a more violent stroke or a more violent spring or jump. Several of her friends also at this time noticed the regular measure of the strokes, and the greater regularity the disease was assuming; the motions being evidently affected, or in some measure modified, by the strokes upon the surrounding bodies. She chiefly struck a small slender door, the top of a chest of drawers, the clock, a table, or a wooden screen placed near the door. The affection ceased about nine o'clock when the patient went to bed.

February 28—She arose very well at eight. At half-past nine the motions recommenced; they were now of a more pleasant nature; the involuntary actions, instead of possessing their former irregularity and violence, being changed into a measured step over the room, connected with an air, or series of strokes, and she beat upon the adjacent bodies as she passed them. In the commencement of the attack, the lips moved as if words were articulated, but no sound could be distinguished at this period. It was curious indeed to observe the patient at this time, moving around the room with all the vivacity of the country dance, or the graver step of the minuet, the arms frequently carried, not merely with ease, but with elegance. Occasionally all the steps were so directed as to place the foot constantly where the stone flags joined to form the floor, particularly when she looked downward. When she looked upward, there was an irresistible impulse to spring up to touch little spots or holes in the top of the ceiling. When she looked around, she had a similar propensity to dart the forefinger into little holes in the furniture. One hole in the wooden screen received the point of the forefinger many hundred times, which was suddenly and involuntarily darted into it with an amazing rapidity and precision. There was one particular part of the wall to which she frequently danced, and there placing herself with the back to it, stood two or three minutes. This by the family was called "the measuring place."

In the afternoon the motions returned, and proceeded much as in the morning. At this time a person present, surprised at the manner in which she beat upon the doors and furniture, and thinking he recognized the air, without further ceremony began to sing the tune. The moment this struck her ears, she turned suddenly to the man, and dancing directly up to him, continued to do so till he was out of breath. The man now ceased a short time, when commencing again, he continued until the attack stopped. The night before this, her father had mentioned his wish to procure a drum, associating this dance of his daughter with some ideas of music. The avidity with which she danced to the tune when sung as above stated, confirmed this wish, and accordingly a drum and fife were procured in the evening. After two hours of rest, the motions again reappeared, when the drum and fife began to play the air to which she had danced before, namely, the "Protestant Boys," a favorite popular air in this neighborhood. In whatever part of the room she happened to be, she immediately turned and danced up to the drum, and as close as possible to it, and there she danced until she missed the step, when the involuntary motions instantly ceased. The first time she missed the step in five minutes; but again rose, and danced to the drum two minutes and a half by her father's watch, when, missing the step, the motions instantly ceased once more. She rose a third time, and missing the step in half a minute, the motions immediately ceased. After this, the drum and fife commenced as the involuntary actions were coming on, and before she rose from her seat, and four times they completely checked the progress of the attack, so that she did not rise upon the floor to dance. At this period the affection ceased for the evening.

March 1—She arose very well at half-past seven. Upon my visit this morning, the circumstances of the preceding afternoon being stated, it appeared clear to me that the attacks had been shortened. Slow as I had seen the effects of medicine in the comparatively trifling disease of young females, I was very willing that the family should pursue the experiment, whilst the medical means were continued.

As I wished to see the effect of the instrument over the disease, I was sent for at noon, when I found her dancing to the drum, which she continued to do for half an hour without missing the step, owing to the slowness of the movement. As I sat counting her pulse, which I found to be 120, in the short intervals of an attack, I noticed motions of the lips, previous to the commencement of the dance, and placing my ear near the mouth, I distinguished a tune. After the attack, of which this was the beginning, she informed me, in answer to my inquiry, that there always was a tune dwelling upon her mind, which at times becoming more pressing, irresistibly impelled her to commence the involuntary motions. The motions ceased at four o'clock.

At half-past seven the motions commenced again, when I was sent for. There were two drummers present now, and an unbraced drum was beaten till the other was braced. She danced regularly to the unbraced drum, but the moment the other commenced, she instantly ceased. As the missing time stopped the affections, I wished the measure to be changed during the dance, which stopped the attack. It also ceased upon increasing the rapidity of the beat, till she could no longer keep time. It was truly surprising to see the rapidity and violence of the muscular exertion, in order to keep time with the increasing movement of the instrument. Five times I saw her sit down the same evening, at the instant that she was unable to keep the measure. In consequence of this, I desired the drummers to beat one continued roll, instead of a regular movement. She arose and danced five minutes, when both drums beat a continued roll. The motions instantly stopped, and the patient sat down. In a few minutes, the motions commencing again, she was suffered to dance five minutes, when the drums again began to roll, the effect of which was instantaneous: the motions ceased, and the patient sat down. In a few minutes the same was repeated with the same effect. It appeared certain that the attacks could now be stopped in an instant, and I was desirous of arresting them entirely, and breaking the chain of irregular associations which constituted the disease. As the motions at this period always commenced in the fingers, and propagated themselves along the upper extremities to the trunk, I desired the drummers, when the patient arose to dance, to watch the commencement of the attack, and roll the drums before she arose from the chair. Six times successively the patient was hindered from rising, by attending to the commencement of the affection; and before leaving the house, I desired the family to attend to the commencement of the attacks, and use the drum early.

March 2—She arose at seven o'clock, and the motions commenced at ten. She danced twice before the drummer was prepared, after which she attempted to dance again several times; but one roll of a well-braced drum hindered the patient from leaving her seat, after which the attacks did not recur. She was left weak and fatigued by the disease, but with a good appetite. In the evening of this day an eruption appeared, particularly about the elbows, in diffused patches of a bright red color. It went off, however, on the third day.

TRUDI SCHOOP, WITH PEGGY MITCHELL

The Metamorphosis of a Mannerism:
"Nobody Showed Me How to Be a Man"

Macbeth cynically mutters that "Life's but a walking shadow, a poor player/ That struts and frets his hour upon the stage/ And then is heard no more."[1] Brecht, Beckett, Pirandello, as well as dramatists through the centuries, have toyed with audience perception that illusion exists in the "real world" and reality on the stage. Trudi Schoop, a well-known dramatic dancer from Europe, similarly analogizes the theatrical use of expressive movement to the private rituals of the schizophrenic world:

> Spellbound, I watched the portrayals, the personifications. It seemed to me that these men and women had all the attributes and techniques of the stage at their disposal. Here were the symbolic gestures, the magnified expressions, the intensity of projection, the masks, the make-believe, the fantasy. These people played comedy, slapstick, tragedy. Most compelling of all was the clarity of form with which their characterizations were realized. The whole scene had an illusory quality, detached, and suspended in time. Nightmarish: the loneliness, the isolation of the individual. Astonishing: the choreography; eighty-seven soloists, indiscriminately cast, each performing his own little *divertissement à la bravura,* generously giving encore after encore. A ballet of delusions.[2]

Nightmarish images of the artists in the asylum are also vividly depicted in the classic silent film, "The Cabinet of Dr. Calagari."

In this selection, Schoop and Mitchell trace a client's tortuous path out of the thicket of stereotyped movement patterns. Luke's ritualistic greetings were based upon a private symbolism which the movement therapist was not to discover until she accompanied him on his strange journey. She scandalized the hospital staff when she first

Reprinted from *Won't You Join the Dance,* Trudi Schoop, by permission of Mayfield Publishing Company, formerly National Press Books. Copyright 1974.

1. William Shakespeare, *Macbeth,* Act V (iv) 24–26.

2. This essay is taken from *Won't You Join the Dance?* (Palo Alto, Calif.: National Press Books, 1974). The quotation is on p. 24.

suggested that she mirror his movements. Permission ultimately granted, her first such attempt was greeted by Luke with a smile. A door was opened.

The reaction of the hospital nursing staff related by Schoop and Mitchell was not unique. In most institutions bizarre behaviors are either routinely ignored or interrupted in order to extinguish them.

These gestures cannot be easily dismissed as bizarre manifestations of a motility disturbance. Others see another aspect to the phenomenon. Bruno Bettelheim waxes poetic when he claims that the twiddling motion is the autistic child's "greatest achievement."[3] Since stereotyped gestures are performed in ways unique to each individual, the person presents himself to the world through these motions. He asserts something akin philosophically to Descartes' basis of existential being: "I twiddle, therefore I am." As such, his accomplishment must be respected.

One goal of movement therapy sessions is to teach control for performing the action by expanding bizarre movement into expressive dance. Luke's dancing with Trudi Schoop had the significance of his learning the pleasure of moving in synchrony with another person. With increased self-awareness, a wider range of activities was available to him. Luke gradually unfolded his fantasies and danced freely.   M.N.C.

The Shape of Fear

About a year after I had stopped working at the state hospital, I began, one day, to sort through my accumulated masses of notes. Among them was a well-worn chocolate-brown folder with the name "Luke" on its cover. Luke was a patient I had worked with for over a year on a one-to-one basis. The first page in the folder was a brief progress report that I'd written on his case:

> Patient was severely regressed at beginning of treatment. Deteriorated ego; little relationship to himself or to world around him. Physically weak and tense. Afraid to move. Distorted body image and strong mannerism. No verbalization.
>
> Affect: suspicious, fearful, apologetic. Early contact was made with therapist and continued throughout treatment. Patient became aware of mannerism; began to talk about it, explain its meaning, and finally discontinued it altogether. Eventually, patient was able to express his

---

3. Bruno Bettelheim, *The Empty Fortress: Infantile Autism and the Birth of the Self* (New York: Free Press, 1967), p. 164.

real problems. Verbalized clearly. Showed a desire to draw; interest in sketching continued throughout. Personality developed slowly, but consistently. Changes were manifested in movement, in verbalizations, in drawings.

How bland it all sounded! What a cut-and-dried account of all those hours we'd struggled with each other. I remembered so clearly every detail of that first meeting.

Alone in my studio one morning, I glanced up to see a black man standing in the doorway. I hadn't heard him arrive; when my eyes accidentally touched him I didn't know whether he was coming in or leaving. He just stood there, strangely weightless and ghost-like, wrapped in deep silence. Finally, carefully, he began to move, circling the room slowly, like a trapped animal. He kept very close to the walls, and his feet seemed to touch the floor only slightly, as if the touch would hurt him. I sensed fear with him, all around him— but the feeling of fear itself seemed to have been burnt out of his body. All that remained was the shape of fear, a design of fear.

As I stood, fascinated, and watched Luke edge his way around the room, I became acquainted with his peculiar personal mannerism for the first time. It consisted of three distinct, separate actions, repeated one after the other, always in the same order. To begin, he would suddenly raise both arms in a sweeping arc, which ended with his hands forming precise, devil-like horns on his forehead. Maintaining this devilish, or faunlike, position, he would make a great, deep bow, then return to his standing posture. For the second movement he would flatten his hands, palms turned down and, using them as if they were sharp cutting instruments, make slicing gestures along his neck. In the final movement he would drop his head on his chest and stroke his hair forward with soft, tender strokes. These three meticulous motions, done in a definite rhythm and with a gentle grace, created an atmosphere of pious humility.

His mannerism fascinated me. Could it be an extremely devout greeting? And if so, whom does one have to greet so humbly, so frequently, and so elaborately? My curiosity about Luke was not to be satisfied in a hurry. There was very little I could do with him in the beginning, except to be there in the room and accompany him in his silent circling of the walls, observing his appearance and behavior. Luke's skin was a light café-au-lait color. He had a beautiful oval-shaped face, and limbs that were very long and fine; his hands were small and soft looking. His eyes were always downcast—never focusing straight ahead and only occasionally darting quick glances to one side or the other. He kept his body in an extreme backward slant: chest caved in, back rounded, head forced down. He bounced when he walked, but it wasn't a happy bounce: the "down" was emphasized rather than the "up." His rigidly held torso rocked back and forth, so that his body looked as if it were saying, "Yes, yes, yes," over and over again. And always, always there were the horns, the cuttings, and the head pattings.

Little by little I tried to interrupt his walking and introduce other movements. He would respond to my suggestions by muttering, "Oh. Oh-oh," giving the one word every manner of inflection and connotation, like an actor searching for the best reading of a line.

"Will you jump with me, Luke, like this?"

"Oh. Oh!" And he'd give a sort of hop-hop.

"That's good. Now can you jump with both feet at the same time?"

"Oh? Oh, oh, oh . . . ooh-ooh." And he would revert to his mannerism.

Luke seemed to have no knowledge of his body as a whole, and had trouble locating his body parts. He didn't always know where his head was, and if I asked him to touch his shoulders he would touch his elbows. His concentration span was extremely limited, and any new movement I suggested seemed to trigger his mannerism. He couldn't manage a skip, but he would run a bit, and learned to slide. When I asked him for a throwing motion, his hand would make a fist in the throw, and open up on the return. Luke cut off the air sharply when he inhaled, like a gasp, and could only release air in stingy amounts, keeping most of it stored up in his lungs. A tight tension prevailed over his body; he couldn't relax his muscles. He couldn't relax, period. He didn't know left from right, up from down, slow from fast. He wouldn't sit down or remove his shoes. He avoided being touched. And he wouldn't speak—except for his marvelous variety of "Oh, oh's." All of Luke's nondoings were performed with such a self-effacing charm that it almost seemed a pity to interfere with his behavior.

Luke appeared to be fascinated by his hands. He would stretch them out and look at them in amazement, then contort his face into violent grimaces of loathing. I tried to encourage him to make different movements with his hands, but he'd only fall immediately back into his mannerism. One day, I reached out my hands toward him in a gesture of acceptance and friendship. He stared at my open palms for a long moment, then uttered his first clear statement of fact:

"You are a white woman."

"I Want to Greet This Way!"

I think that some of the notes I made during the months that followed reveal Luke's basic conflicts, as well as the progress he made toward a more realistic version of life.

. . . Luke took off his shoes today for the first time. It was a complicated ceremony. He untied his right shoelace first, then the left. Both laces had to be loosened to a precise degree. With great delicacy, he removed the right shoe, as if he were handling Cinderella's glass slipper. Then the left, in the same way. Before he put them down, he examined each shoe critically and thoroughly—its sole, its heel, its lacing. He then pulled off his socks, wadded them up, and stuffed one into each of the shoes. And then began the placement problem. First, he aligned the shoes side by side with the toes pointing toward the door. Apparently satisfied, he got up from his chair and began an exercise with me. But he kept glancing anxiously back at the shoes, and soon went over to place them with the heels together, toes pointing to the sides à la Chaplin, laces draped artistically over their sides. This procedure went on and on and on, interspersed with outbreaks of his mannerism and only brief and distracted attempts to work. His main concern seemed to be that each of his shoes would look at least once into all four corners of the earth. But at least he took the darn things off. And what's more, he said "Good morning," and made his "horns" bow at me. It was quite a day.

. . . Luke always enters the room like someone who hasn't the right to come in. He *steals* in, as softly as a cat. But I think that his insecurity is tinged with curiosity. Today, there was the same preoccupation with his shoes. Once more, I asked him to sit down on the floor with me, and for the first time he made it. It was a very complicated maneuver, interrupted countless times by his getting up to rearrange the shoes to every point of the compass, and by frequent performances of his mannerism. But I feel that the ice has been broken. Luke speaks now, although very little. He does take off his shoes. He will sit on the floor. His eyes follow me a bit more closely under their downcast lids.

. . . Today the shoe-mannerism and the sitting-down procedures were not quite so involved. When Luke was seated on the floor at last, I quickly brought out the beaters. Before taking them, he went through his whole mannerism several times. Then he examined them silently and carefully. He seems to enjoy rhythms, but can't follow the regular beat that Erica (the pianist) gives. He apparently likes to design in the air with his beaters; at least he smiles when he does it. At the end of the session, he held his beaters to his forehead in the "horns" position and bowed several times. I think I'm going to join Luke in his mannerism and see what happens.

. . . I told the nurses that I intended to enter his movement pattern. They strongly disapproved. He would think I was making fun of him. I might engender a "psychotic episode." He might never work with me again. Why would I jeopardize the contact I'd apparently formed? I went up to see Dr. Keermuschel.

"Go ahead, if you want to. It's an unusual experiment, but certainly worth a try."

When Luke and I were seated opposite each other, and he began his talismatic mannerism, I picked it up the second time around. Carefully and precisely I made the horns, bowed, sliced at my neck, and brushed the top of my head. There was a pause. Luke's eyes were still downcast. He repeated the pattern, and again I followed it. We did it a third time. Luke raised his head. His eyes looked straight into mine. And he smiled. I smiled back.

. . . Luke smiled when he came in this morning. We worked on runs, walks, skips, and turns. There was a slight improvement. Later, I asked him if he would like to dance to the music Erica was playing. He listened to it for a while, then selected two scarves—a pale blue one and a pink one—and fluttered them about for awhile. It seemed to me that the softness of the scarves might be recalling tender feelings, and that his body was reacting to them with staccato movements—like stuttering in motion. He was growing increasingly excited, so I asked him if he wanted to do his "favorite movements." He went through his pattern several times and I again accompanied him. I told him that he could feel free to do them any time he wanted to. He said, "Oh, OH!" in a pleased sort of way. He made farewell horns at me when the session was over.

. . . The same anxious fussing over shoes today, but not quite so many repetitions of the mannerism. As we were getting up from the floor where we'd been working on stretches, my hand accidentally brushed against his arm. At once, his body went into contortions and his face twisted into terrible grimaces of revulsion.

"Oooh, oh! Don't touch me! You'll hurt yourself! Oh, oh, oh . . . be careful! You'll scratch yourself!"

Patients have resisted my touch before, but never to protect *me* from *them!*

. . . Luke balked today, more than he ever has before. He looked and acted confused. He wouldn't respond to my suggestions. At times, it seemed that he would have liked to follow my movements, but couldn't permit himself to do so. His conflict showed in his grimaces, his wiggling around, his cramplike actions. But he didn't do so many of his basic mannerisms. He replaced them with staccato up-and-down gestures with his extended arms, like a bird that's trying to take off from the ground and can't. When I said goodbye, Luke apologized with the words, "I'm sorry . . . I'm sorry."

. . . When I came on the ward this morning, the nurse said that Luke had told her he was sorry for having been so cranky at the last session. He had said that his little finger had been hurting him. He came into the studio in his usual way: greeted me with his horn movement, did the ceremony with his shoes, smiled, and said "Good morning." He showed me his perfectly good little finger.

"The doctor sawed it off here," he explained, indicating the middle joint. "Then he found a new one and put the new one on at the wrong place. That's why it hurts."

Gradually he forgot about his finger and worked very well: learned the differences between a round back and a straight back, lifted his head more often. Did his mannerism frequently, and smiled when I did it too. Couldn't find the difference between a strong walk and a soft walk. When I asked him to show me how a strong man walks, he said:

"I am a girl. Nobody showed me how to be a man!" But when I insisted on some strong movements, he began to hit his chest desperately. After a lot of difficulty, I finally got him to direct the blows outward, away from himself. He seemed to enjoy that. When he left the room, he thanked me and said, "Merry Christmas, Merry Christmas, Merry Christmas!"

. . . Today I decided to try touching again. Luke was in a good mood, and smiling a lot. First we touched our own body parts in time to a rhythm. When he touches his head, or shoulder, or knees, he doesn't give the picture of touching portions of himself; he looks as if he's touching strange objects. We worked with the beaters for a while, using them to touch each other's shoulders, elbows, knees. We stood up and did a few jumps and hops. Then I held out my hands to Luke and asked him to take them so we could dance together. He looked at them for quite a while, then looked away, muttering his "Oh, oh's"; then back went his gaze to my hands again. At last, very, very hesitantly, he reached out and touched my fingers—not really holding my hands, but sort of petting them in short, light tappings. He still made faces and twisted his body and peeked at me, but these reactions were less extreme than they had been the first time. We did a few more exercises. When the time was up, Luke made his usual farewell horns. I told him that in Switzerland, people usually greeted each other or said goodbye with a handshake, and I extended my hand. He took it. I gave his hand a firm clasp and released it. He whispered, "Merry Christmas," and departed.

. . . Luke was more defiant today than I have ever known him to be. He looked as if he were questioning everything I did, and everything he did as well. He stared for a long time at Erica, examined the piano, the couch, the chairs, as if challenging their right to be there. He glanced at me furtively from time to time. He stood at the window for a long while, peering through narrowed eyes. I tried very hard to get his attention. He didn't respond. He was one big "WHY?" He started to gaze at the palms of his hands and make frightful faces. Then suddenly he began his mannerism, only this time he added something new: a highly stylized praying position, arms raised over his head, palms pressed flat together—a really beautiful Gothic attitude of supplication. Then the prayerful hands swept forward and downward, and stopped at the point where they covered his genital area. He hadn't taken off his shoes, and he left without a word.

. . . Luke greeted me with his horns this morning, and took off his shoes. He was far away, but whenever I reminded him he would come back and work a bit. For the first time, I noticed his tendency to "freeze" his movements. He would stop right in the middle of a motion and hold the position for quite a long time. He continues to add the praying and the covering of his genitals to his mannerism. His whole manner is increasingly disturbed. Perhaps I've been going too fast with him. I'd better take it easy for a while.

. . . Luke wasn't in very good shape today. We had begun to work, when he asked:

"Why do people have to *do* something with me all the time? I

don't want to dance. What do you want with me anyway? Why don't
you leave me alone?"

He went through his mannerism frequently, and when he left the
studio, he made just the horns and the bow, and announced angrily:
"That is *my* way to greet! *I want to greet this way!*"

. . . More and more, Luke includes the new additions to his mannerism: the praying and the covering of his genitals (he constantly pulls
his T-shirt down over them). Again, he kept hitting his chest with his
fists in that angry, frustrated way. He also smacked his thighs with
straight arms and flat hands. But somehow, today, his look was more
clear and direct. At times, he seemed quite composed. I managed
to pull him out of his negative mood, and he seemed to enjoy this
session. He said "Thank you, ma'am!" when he left.

. . . Luke was more closed up today than last time, seemed further
away. But he only did his mannerism once! I brought in the big mirror
and let him look at himself for the first time. He seemed fascinated
with his image at first. Then he looked at himself with a jack-o'-lantern
grin. He puffed up his cheeks like a blow fish and frowned mightily.
After a while, however, he seemed to become very agitated, and left
the mirror. From that point on, he couldn't bring his head up, couldn't
look at me, and began again to make his frustrated blows against
himself with his fists. I wasn't able to get him to direct his hitting
away from his chest and into space. At the door, Luke mumbled,
"Goodbye, ma'am," and bounced his most depressed bounce down
the hall.

. . . Today Luke came in very aggressively. There was no ceremony
with the shoes and socks. He yanked them off and threw them angrily
on the bench. He fiddled around with the beaters for a while, then
threw those down, too. I asked him if he'd been outside today.

"I work every day!" he replied furiously. "And I can see everything
—just like you and everybody else!"

He talked for a long time. I couldn't understand all of his tirade,
but I think he wanted to express that he is no different from anyone
else. He suddenly interrupted his flow of speech, and said with forlorn
finality:

"I am ugly."

I took his hand and led him over to look out of the window for
a while. Then I brought out the scarves, but he couldn't choose one.
He couldn't tell which color he liked best!

When he left, he said, "I'm sorry I scratched you again. I'm very sorry."

Luke didn't come to the next session, or to the next. I went to the ward to visit him, but he just sat still with his eyes averted and didn't speak to me at all. Finally, after several days, he reappeared.

. . . Luke looked angry when he came in—no horns, no greeting, no shoe ceremony, no words. I determined to work on that anger. I encouraged him to hit the floor really hard with both beaters; then I gave him a drum to beat. I showed him how to lift his arm higher, so that he would have more strength to make his beating even harder. He seemed to like the idea, and really smashed away at that drum. When I began to teach him angry movements, he made strong fists. But instead of hitting with them, he just shook them. It was a gesture of frustrated anger, which I'm sure demonstrated his feelings exactly. I proceeded very slowly, as I showed him how to make his fist-shaking explode into a punch, and how to get the same explosiveness in a kick or a stamp. Though he couldn't manage it fully, there was an indication that some real anger was being expressed. Luke was tired after this session. He put his shoes and socks on slowly. He made only a halfway attempt at his farewell horns.

. . . For several days I've been working on anger with Luke, and he is gaining considerably in both strength and affect. He has become much more cooperative. His movement has improved. He can now locate his body parts quite well, and can activate them separately. He can jump with both feet, and walk backward a little. He made more fluid movements with the scarves today, and began to improvise with them for the first time. He has been walking straighter, and looking ahead instead of down. He can let his hand stay in mine longer. He looks directly into my eyes. He says my name. I really like this Luke!

. . . Luke seems much more relaxed than he's ever been. He still can't push or pull, but today he skipped and slid very well. At the end of the session, he said:

"I really don't want to say it, but I have to. God bless you! You are sensible. I knew a white man once—a wonderful man. I worked for him and made three dollars. I like to work." He bowed toward Erica and shook hands with me.

The nurse told me that on the way back to the ward, he said, "She is beautiful. I mean, Trudi is a beautiful woman!"

. . . Luke continues to improve. His steps are stronger. He can lift his knees higher. He focuses outward, talks a lot. He told me about the flowers he saw in the hospital garden.

"They are white and yellow and pink. But I think something has happened to them."

Today he danced out into space for the first time. He smiles often, and is much less tense. After the session, Amos, another patient, was sitting between Luke and me, talking in a very depressed way.

"You see, Luke, Amos is worrying," I said.

Luke looked directly at me, and replied, "We can't keep from worrying, because the world we live in is so beautiful."

. . . Luke came in today almost like a man calling for his date. He smiled and looked in my eyes. He said that he wants to settle down in Alaska if it is all right with me. We did tension relaxation exercises. I took hold of his arms and moved them about, trying to get him to feel their weight. He seemed to suffer and enjoy it at the same time. It was as if he were experiencing something new, yet vaguely familiar. He liked showing me what to do with the beaters, and used much more imagination in his patterns and rhythms. I followed him in his mannerism again, and this time, almost as if he were joking, he ended with a fancy flourish. I brought him back to his ward after the session, and he laughed a lot when I teased him about his posture. He showed me his hands, especially his nails. I suggested that he should brush them. He liked the idea.

. . . Not much change today. Luke becomes more open with me, often says, ". . . if it is okay with you." The nurse told me that he is now working in the yard, and doing well at it. He seemed pleased when I said that I'd like to come and see his gardening. Luke keeps telling me that he wants a job.

"They call me Negro," he says. "There's nothing wrong with that, is there?"

. . . I went to the yard to see Luke's work. He was proud. He showed me how smooth he'd made the earth, and ran it through his long fingers. When he came for his session in the afternoon I decided to work on space patterns. He walked diagonals, zigzags, and squares all right, but he couldn't seem to grasp the idea of walking in a circle. He always left the closure point open and trailed off uncertainly. I gave him my pad and pencil and asked him to draw a circle. It was exactly like the one he had walked; the line didn't join. As he continued to try, he began to add little designs of his own. Apparently, Luke likes to sketch.

. . . Another commitment caused me to be absent from the hospital for a few days. When I returned, Luke had grown a fancy mustache. He was in a very good mood. He showed me in gestures the work he used to do. It looked like threshing wheat. Then he told me about the little plants he once grew, and I asked him to show me how he did it. The task was involved and involving—beautiful to watch. Luke set his "seedlings" in a straight line from one end of the studio to the other. Two plants had to be placed quite close, diagonally opposite each other. The space between had to be exactly measured. He dug the holes with his hands, picked up each plant carefully, and described it to me as he settled it into the earth.

"This one has bluish-purple flowers . . . this one is pinkish-beige. This one is yellow, with a sort of green in it." The color differences of each plant were described precisely and in loving detail.

Luke spent a whole hour in the fantasy, planting his rainbow-hued garden. Afterward, he said:

"I have a father and a mother. There are three hundred in the family." Then he corrected himself, "Oh, oh-oh, I mean I have two brothers and two sisters. We are five. I lived in a big town in Africa; Kenya, I think it was called. I also lived in Texas. The camps there are very beautiful."

Luke didn't do his mannerism once today!

When he left, he said, "I am very grateful that I met you. You sure are beautiful."

. . . Today Luke's nice moustache was gone. When I asked him about it, he said in a low voice:

"They didn't have time."

He was very depressed—couldn't follow me, couldn't concentrate, kept his head lowered, and wouldn't look up. I asked what was bothering him.

"Why don't I have a dress on?" he replied very sadly. "Why do I have to come here like this?"

I told him that what he was wearing was called a gym suit.

"Oh. Gym suit . . . I would like to be dressed like a man. What am I, anyway, a woman or a man?"

I assured him that he was a man, and asked him to invite me to dance. Suddenly, he was more sure of himself. It was a *big* change!

He took my hand, smiled, and danced me about wildly in a way that Erica told me later was called a *jitterbug!*

On the way back to his ward, we stopped to see his garden in the yard again. As we stood there, he suddenly became angry.

"I would give my life for the white man. Why are you so nice to me? Why do you mix in with my life? Why do people do things with me? What's the use?" Then he added, "I like you okay."

"I like you too, Luke."

"Goodbye, ma'am."

. . . In the morning, I visited Luke in the yard and showed him some little seedlings I brought for him to plant. He didn't seem too pleased.

"I don't know; I'll have to ask my boss. I can't do anything unless he says so, and he just told me to pull all the plants in the courtyard out."

In the afternoon, Luke seemed worried and depressed. I asked him what he would most like to do today.

"I want to work for the white man."

"How would you begin?" I asked.

"I would greet him," and he made his horns and bowed.

"And then?"

"I would greet him again," Luke replied crossing his arms over his chest and bowing much deeper.

"And then?" I asked again.

"I would greet him again." This time he bowed clear down to the floor, then straightened up, and said, "That's too much. That's going too far!"

"I think so too, Luke." And we both laughed.

Next, he acted out his wheat-threshing again, and showed me how he dug the earth with his hands, and how he pulled out weeds. All the movements were done with a smooth, practiced grace—a pleasure to see. As he was leaving, I offered him the plants again. He took them, thanking me very much. Carefully holding the box they were in in both hands, he bounced happily down the hall.

. . . Luke talked about a home today: "A home is beautiful."

He thinks that I should have a vacation, and invited me to visit his ward: "It's like a sanitarium."

He wanted to talk to Erica, too: "Good morning. It's a beautiful day!"

He talked almost *constantly* today. When he talks, he can't move or dance! I'll have to be more firm, and insist on his moving, because when he's moving, he can't talk! When he did move today, his actions were spasmodic and cramplike. He kept pulling down his T-shirt again.

Once, he said, "I have three colors: vanilla, chocolate-brown, and dark blue."

. . . I still don't believe it! Luke came in very "normally." He said "Good morning" without the help of his horns. He removed his shoes and socks very naturally. He sat down opposite me and immediately went through his basic mannerism several times. Then he looked straight into my eyes, and asked matter-of-factly:

"Would you like to know what that means, Trudi?"

"I would like that very much," I replied.

"This," he said, demonstrating the bow and the horns with the index fingers extended, "is a salute to the white man. This," and he made that same first movement, this time using the pinky fingers as horns, "is the greeting of the Boy Scout, or boy. This," the cutting gesture on the neck, "is wiping away the sweat, because I work so hard. And this," and he made the head stroking movement, "means that it's a hot day."

"Thank you, Luke. Thank you very much."

It seemed that Luke had lifted a barrier that had long stood between us. We smiled at each other in mutual appreciation. I went on with the session, and it was a good one. In the past, Luke had frequently referred to himself as a zebra (black and white again?), so we went about on all fours, being zebras first, and then other animals. Luke enjoyed this play so much that he continued his four-footedness even when I wanted him to stand up with me and walk like people do. But I'm sure he was aware of the difference I was trying to make.

. . . Of course, Luke closed up again for several days. He reverted to his horns, couldn't concentrate, covered his genital area, and was silent and depressed. I've only been working on the simple, familiar exercises that he can do easily. And, today, he began to "come back." He worked well with the drum, beaters, and scarves, but still couldn't move into space. He began to question me again.

"What do you want from me? Why don't you leave me alone?"

"Because I want you to get well. Because I like you."

"I like you, too."

"Do I make you angry?" I asked.

"Angry? Angry? Angry? NO!" he said, very angrily, "You don't!" After a pause, he continued with less frustration and more strength:

"I should have a haircut, but they won't give me one. I should have one!"

He made it sound like a drastic, very basic human need. He looked me straight in the eye, like a man fighting for his right to be respected.

. . . This morning, Luke sat beside me in the hall while we waited for the studio floor to be cleaned. I brought out my pad, and asked him if he would draw a flower for me. He draws as if it were a familiar pastime. Once he begins a line, he continues it until the flower is finished. He uses the same continuous line for trees, which all look alike: a trunk with three cut-off branches.

The session was interesting. Luke enjoyed the new little bongo drums. His rhythm was good, and for the first time he could pick up the same beat in a walk. His attitude was quite different; he seemed more open, even joyful. He began to tell me about fruits he had raised, but he couldn't remember what they were called. He talked on and on about them, becoming increasingly frustrated by not knowing their names, so I suggested that he draw them—or whatever else he wanted to sketch. He first drew an empty-looking house.

"This is a big house, a beautiful clubhouse. Very intelligent people live in there. They speak English."

"Where are they, Luke" I asked.

"I think they're asleep . . . or, or, or . . . on vacation."

"Where are you?"

"I am in school and in the third grade."

Then he began to draw his mother.

"My mother is a schoolteacher. She was a very nice mother. She always wears plain colors. Sundays, she took me and two girls to church. Sundays, I had a dress on. Other days I wore britches."

Luke showed me in movement how he went to church. He bounced and bowed and behaved as if he didn't want to be a disturbance or make any noise—he acted just like Luke. Then he put money in the offering box. He remembered the name of a church song: "Down, Down by the River."

. . . Luke again has a strong reaction. He was very closed in and disturbed today—bent his head far down, froze his movements, didn't want to dance. I had brought him some crayons and drawing pads, but he seemed afraid of them and wouldn't touch them. He did talk about the colors of the crayons, however, making definite distinctions between the different reds, browns, greens. . . . He seemed relieved when I told him that I would put them in the drawer and he could have them whenever he wanted them.

. . . Luke has recovered from the last reaction. He moved well and improvised his own dance very openly, using much more space than usual. The nurse told me that she had let him use the crayons and pad whenever he had asked for them, so I gave them to him to take back to the ward. He seemed delighted, and walked backward down the hall holding them tightly, saying:

"Thank you, thank you, thank you. I sure appreciate it very much. They're beautiful."

. . . "I was in a big society camp," said Luke today. "They used to call me 'white man' or 'king.' It was very nice."

Generally speaking, he worked well, concentrated better than usual. He seemed more pulled-together and serious. But he's so mixed up in differentiating between male and female, boy and girl, dresses and britches. Maybe that's why he says "or-or-or" so much. He just doesn't know what he is. Today, he looked out of the window and said:

"The mountains are very beautiful. You are beautiful, too. I want to settle down, if it is okay with you. You know what I mean . . . ? I can't tell you . . . you know what I mean?"

When he left, I gave him a Milky Way candy bar.

"Thank you and Merry Christmas!," he said.

Luke thinks of the dancing sessions as a job he's been given.

"I am thankful and grateful that I got this job. You know what I mean . . . or, or, or. . . ?"

. . . Another "down" day for Luke.

When I asked him if he'd like to sketch, he said, "I don't know if they want me to sketch."

He smiled when I asked him to dance, but the dance he did was rather fragmented. In departing, he said:

"I want you to be my friend at the very end."

. . . Luke was "up" again today. He had news for me!

"I was a zebra, a lion, a girl before I was a girl and then a boy."

So to close the regular movement session, I asked him to move like a zebra. He just walked around the room. As a lion, he bent his knees more. As a girl, he put his hands on his hips and swayed them snappily from side to side, like a stage vamp. As a boy and a man, his stride was more forceful. He seemed happier, but once said:

"I used to be good-looking. That was before they called me 'Nigger.' "

. . . Another depressed day for Luke. I asked him if he had gone to church on Sunday.

"I don't know a church," he answered.

"Did you go to Sunday school, then?"

"I don't go to school any more. And I don't go to church. They didn't want me because I was brown. I don't see why I am here. I didn't want to come here, to the U.S.A. Why don't they give me a job? Nothing is wrong with me!"

"You are here to get well, Luke."

"There is no use in getting well. Now that I'm sick, I never will get well. I don't want to get well. I have no job. Nothing will change."

Luke couldn't move very much; he was terribly cramped. I tried to loosen him up, but he just couldn't relax. I walked with him for a long time. I asked him if he would accept me as a friend.

"If it's okay with you that I am black." And he smiled.

"Regardless of the fact that I am white and you are black, I like you, Luke, and I am your friend."

"I like having you for a friend. But I am worried that you are the friend of somebody else. . . ."

"I have other friends. But I'm happy that you are my friend, too."

Luke wants a home. He wants work. He said he hoped I would get well. He thanked me for everything. It was sad.

. . . Luke had a story for me.

"I met a beautiful woman on the sidewalk. We walked together. She was beautiful. Then I found out that she was my sister."

I asked him to tell me more about the woman.

"She was a beautiful low-class girl."

"How did you meet her?"

"I didn't. She met me."

"How did you find out that she was your sister?"

"I didn't. She said so."

"Did you love her?"

"Yes, I loved her very much. But she said she had a husband, or a boy friend. . . . I want to go home. I want a job. Thank you for the job you got me."

"This isn't really a job, Luke. I'm a therapist."

Later on, he acted out the sidewalk scene. He played all the parts: himself, the low-class girl (beautifully done), and the sister.

. . . Luke had at last been given a haircut; but, as he said, they didn't finish it. The front of his head is almost shaved, and in the back the hair is still very long. We worked on stretches today, and he seemed to be having a good time.

When I asked him to beat a rhythm, he laughed, and said, "I'm not a musician. I don't know how."

But when I joked with him, "Ah, come on now, Luke, you know how, all right!" he made an especially fancy rhythm. Then suddenly, he became disturbed; he began shaking his head and grimacing.

"What's the matter, Luke?" I asked.

"I have a bunch of bees in my head. I don't know how they got in there. I think they came from a foreign country. . . . You are a beautiful schoolteacher. I wish I was a schoolteacher!"

Luke had been sketching maps of the U.S.A. He's very concerned about north, south, east, and west. It's as if he's trying to orient himself. As he was leaving, I gave him a picture book on Arizona, with a lot of landscapes in it. He always thanks me with such touching charm:

"I'm very grateful. . . . It's beautiful. . . . Thank you, thank you. . . . Merry Christmas!"

. . . "I went to school 'til I was five. I was a girl. Then I had a mom and dad. My dad bought me a beautiful suit when I was eighteen or twenty; it had long trousers. When I went to church on Sunday, I had a dress on. I was a girl. Now I am . . . you know . . . sort of a man, or a boy."

"Could you show me, Luke, or act out for me, what you did and how you moved as a girl?"

"I held my left arm with my right hand. And I walked like this!" And he walked about, flouncing up and down.

"Luke, you are a man now. Show me how you walk today."

And Luke walked a masculine walk better than at any time before! Later, I tried communication movements with him. He did very well for a while, but when I asked him to show me in motions that he wanted me to come over to him, he didn't know what to do. He tried, but finally gave up the struggle, and just opened his hands helplessly. Going to the door, he said:

"The boys all looked at the book, and they think you are a beautiful woman. I think so, too. I sure hope you have a good time and get well. Merry Christmas!"

. . . Luke had seemed to enjoy imitating people and animals, so today I began to pantomime different actions. I asked him to act out pouring some water, then drinking it.

"I get dizzy whenever I drink," he announced. "Even water makes me dizzy. So do all the liquids from trees. I even get dizzy when I eat."

"How do you walk when you're dizzy?"

"I walk just like I walked before!"

He insisted on this quite sternly. Then, after a slight pause, "I'm doing terrific. I mean, I'm doing very good. I'm doing okay. I am sixty now; sixty and forty is one hundred."

"You are forty now, Luke?" I asked.

"I was thirty-nine last year. I never was a baby. I was always alone —I had no father, no mother, no sister, no brother. I was all alone. Wouldn't it be nice to have a family and live in a town . . . you know what I mean?"

We went back to pantomimes. I enacted looking around for something I'd lost, and asked him to guess what I was doing. His interpretation:

"You are looking to see if the janitor did a good job. You are a schoolteacher with a nice floor."

I did another one: I wake up in the morning, stretch, wash my hands, my face, my feet. Luke's interpretation:

"You must have a good time. You met nice people and you greeted them." (!!)

It was Luke's turn. He walked in a circle and made a deep bow. His explanation:

"I paced around on a big stage. It was thrilling."

When I asked him how he would wash his hands, he first plunged his arm downward, as if into deep water, and churned it around.

"I'm looking to see if there are snakes in the water." He washed his hands without rubbing them together. To wash his face, he ducked his head into the water; but he never touched his face. Then he said, as he performed the appropriate actions:

"Now I look up at the sky and see beautiful clouds—very white and hygienic. They come Sunday, then they disappear, then they come again . . . white, blue, pink . . . then they roll away." He made soft, rolling gestures as he crawled slowly around—as if he were moving through water. He looked up again and followed the clouds with his eyes:

"They come from the south, but they can't roll back to the south."

. . . Luke had another version of his fascinating past.

"I was a hyena . . . a milkcow . . . a beige dog—the head of a dog family—and now they say I am a human being. When I was a wolf, I met a sheep at the water. It gave me some water to drink. It was a young, beautiful sheep, about twenty-five years old . . . very friendly and nice. The wolf was exactly the same size I am. It was a big wolf."

"What happened then?"

"I made a rag doll. And then I made a grinding machine; and I ground myself . . . and the liquid became grapefruit juice . . . or, or, or . . . orange juice . . . oh, no, it was tomato juice. When you put the rag doll into the juice, it comes alive. Any rag doll you pour juice over comes alive." There was a pause. "I had a sister. I wore dresses. My left leg is my sister's leg. The right leg is my own . . . chocolate and vanilla."

Luke certainly provides fantastic material. I asked him if he would like to act out the same scene with the wolf and the lamb.

"Oh, yes. I want some water. I have to protect my family."

I became the lamb, and Luke the wolf. I scooped up a handful of water and offered it to him. He knelt down in front of me and drank it blissfully. When his thirst was quenched, we jumped and leapt and ran about like two wolves. His movements and gestures were marvelous to watch. Finally, we lay flat on the floor on our stomachs and lapped water from the "lake." Then we changed parts and repeated the same actions, he as the lamb, and I as the wolf. After I had drunk from his hand, we hopped and skipped about like lambs, and again drank together. At last, we stood up, became erect, and walked together as "ourselves." And Luke's walk was amazingly different. His step was firm and secure. His body had straightened out. It was as if he had clearly grasped the posture difference between an animal and a human.

. . . Luke was very disturbed today. Again, he asked why he had come, why I had sent for him. He almost refused to get ready for dancing, but eventually began with the bongo drums, and started a rhythm. Soon, however, he stopped, and began petting them. I didn't try to continue. We just walked around the room together. Finally, he began to talk.

"You are my child. I have many children—as you have. Where are the children? I know. They are inside us."

He was silent for a while, and then:

"Nothing is wrong with eating people. I like to eat people."

He turned toward me questioningly:

"I don't know who gave birth to me. A woman or a man?"

"Your mother gave birth to you, Luke, and she is a woman."

"Oh . . . my mother."

"You seem upset today, Luke," I said. "Did I do anything to make you angry?"

"You never can make me angry. Never. Not today, not tomorrow. Not ever. I just never get angry with you."

"That's good, Luke."

"That's because I'm a very clever Indian," he continued. "Oh, oh, oh . . . I think I'm Japanese. What nationality am I?"

"Luke, you are an American Negro."

"I eat people," Luke announced quietly, looking directly into my eyes to see how I felt about this new revelation.

At the end of the session, Luke had calmed down and was smiling again. He wanted me to buy him a pad and some pencils, and insisted on paying for them:

"They don't have your kind of money here."

He thanked me, assured me that I was a wonderful woman, and when he left, said:

"I am now in the eighth grade!"

. . . "First I was beige, then chocolate-brown, and now I am very dark," mused Luke this morning. "I was once a white man. And I think I will be white again. . . . They say this is a hospital. I will be white again."

For the first time, I didn't connect his color fixation with his racial conflict. I felt that he was talking about well (white) and having been ill (dark).

The session began as usual. We worked on levels: exercising on the floor, taking sitting and kneeling positions, and finally standing and moving into space. Throughout the session, Luke was quiet, and more involved in what he was doing. As we parted for the day, he looked at me directly and said:

"I think I'm going to grow up now. It took me six months." We smiled at each other. He started out of the door.

Luke and I had been working together *exactly* six months!

Bibliography

Adams, Neil. "Use of Psycho-Drama and Modern Dance as Therapy." Master's thesis, University of Wisconsin, Madison, 1952.

Aleszko, Zofia. "The Role of Choreotherapy in the Psychomotor Rehabilitation of Neurotic Teenagers." *Psychiatria Polska*, 6(3) (May, 1972), 345–348.

American Dance Therapy Association. *Newsletter*. Columbia, Md., Vol. 1, 1967 to date. Quarterly.

American Dance Therapy Association. *Proceedings of Annual Conferences*. Columbia, Md., 1967 to date.

Anderson, Jack. "You Brought the Day Alive." *Dance*, 40(7) (July, 1966), 18–21.

Armstrong, Jocklyn. "Movement and Drama in Therapy by Audrey Wethered." *Dance*, 48(7) (July, 1974), 83.

Austin, Patricia, Rachel Kinnerslay, Ted Welland. "An Experimental Dance Study for Children with Learning Disabilities," Binational Dance Conference. *Dance: Verities, Values, Visions*. Waterloo, Ontario, Canada, June, 1971.

Baillio, Earleen. "Shall We Dance?" *Journal of Music Therapy*, 9(1) (Spring, 1972), 37–39.

Bainbridge, G., A. E. Duddington, M. Collingdon, and C. E. Gardner. "Dance Mime: A Contribution to Treatment in Psychiatry." *Journal of Mental Science*, 99 (1953), 308–314.

Balkus, Mary P. "An Experimental Study of the Relationship between Participation in a Dance Therapy Program and Changes in Selected Aspects of Personality of Female Psychiatric Patients at the Terrell State Hospital in Terrell, Texas." Ph.D. dissertation, Texas Women's University, Denton, Tex., 1968.

Bartenieff, Irmgard. "Dance Therapy: A New Profession or a Rediscovery of an Ancient Role of the Dance?" *Dance Scope*, 7(1) (1972–73), 6–18.

————. *Effort Observation and Effort Assessment in Rehabilitation*. New York: Dance Notation Bureau, 1965.[a]

————. "How Is the Dancing Teacher Equipped to Do Dance Therapy?" *Music Therapy* (1957), 145–150.

————. *Notes from a Course in Correctives*. New York: Dance Notation Bureau, 1970.[a]

———— and Martha Davis. "An Analysis of the Movement Behavior within a Group Psychotherapy Session." Paper presented to Conference of American Group Psychotherapy Association, Chicago, 1968.[a]

———— and ————. "Effort-Shape Analysis of Movement: The Unity of Expression and Function" in *Research Approaches to Movement and Personality.* New York: Arno Press, 1972.

————, ————, and Forrestine Paulay. *Four Adaptations of Effort Theory in Research and Teaching.* New York: Dance Notation Bureau, 1970.[a]

Bellew, Ruth, and Eleanor Vandenbergh. "A Study in the Use of Modern Educational Dance in Conjunction with Psychodrama in Group Psycho-Therapy." Master's thesis, University of Wisconsin, Madison, 1949.

Bender, Lauretta, and Franziska Boas. "Creative Dance in Therapy." *American Journal of Orthopsychiatry,* 11(2) (April, 1941), 235–244.

Benders, H. "Psychiatry and Objectivity: Methods in the Therapeutic Use of Movement, Music and Creativity." *Psychiatria, Neurologia, Neurochirugia,* 72(4) (July, 1969), 337–351.

"Benesh Notation Used in Palsy Study." *Dance,* 42(2) (Feb., 1968), 10.

Benford, Margaret. "Case Studies of Five Maladjusted Girls in Modern Dance Class." Master's thesis, University of Southern California, Los Angeles, 1966.

Berger, Milton. "Nonverbal Communications in Group Psychotherapy." *International Journal of Group Psychotherapy,* 8 (1958), 161–178.

Bernstein, Douglas, and Thomas Borkovac. *Progressive Relaxation Training: A Manual for the Helping Professions.* Champaign, Ill.: Research Press, 1973.

Bernstein, Penny. *Theory and Methods in Dance-Movement Therapy.* Dubuque, Iowa: Kendall/Hunt, 1972.

Bevans, Judith. "The Exceptional Child and ORFF." *Education of the Visually Handicapped,* 1(4) (Dec., 1969), 116–120.

Blankenburg, W. "Tanz in der Therapie Schizophrener." *Psychotherapy and Psychosomatics,* 17 (1962), 5–6, 336–342.

Blaskey, Beth. "Toward a Theoretical Basis for Use of Dance as Therapy." Master's thesis, University of Illinois, Champaign, 1972.

Block, Alice. *Harmonische Schulung des Frauenkorpers.* Stuttgart, 1962.[g]

Boas, Franziska. "Creative Dance" in *Child Psychiatric Techniques.* Lauretta Bender, ed. Springfield, Ill.: Charles C Thomas, 1952. Chap. 16.

————. "Psychological Aspects in the Practice and Teaching of Dancing." *Journal of Aesthetics and Art Criticism,* 2 (1941–42), 3–20.

Bobele, Harvey. "An Exploratory Study of the Use of Body Movements as a Personal Growth Adjunct in Sensitivity Training." Ph.D. dissertation, University of California, Los Angeles, 1971.

Boettiger, Janet Adler. "Effects of Dance Therapy on a Young Non-Verbal Child." Master's thesis, University of Pittsburgh, Pittsburgh, Pa., 1968.

Boom, Alfred. *Studies on the Mentally Handicapped Child.* London: Edward Arnold, 1968.

Boyle, Constance M. "Dalcroze Eurhythmics and the Spastic." *Spastics' Quarterly,* 3 (March, 1954), 5–8.

Brown, Malcolm. "The New Body Psychotherapies." *Psychotherapy: Theory, Research and Practice,* 10(2) (Summer, 1973).

Bruce, V. R. *Movement in Silence and Sound.* New Rochelle, N.Y.: Soccer, 1971.

Bunzel, Gertrude. "Psychokinetics and Dance Therapy." *Journal of Health and Physical Education,* 19(3) (March, 1948), 180–181+.

Calabria, Frank. "Sociometric Group Structure and Improvement of Social Dancing Skills in Recreation Groups." Ph.D. dissertation, New York University, New York, 1956.

Calder, Jean. "Dance for the Mentally Retarded." *Slow Learning Child,* 19(2) (July, 1972), 67–78.

Campbell, Douglas. "Posture: A Gesture towards Life." *Impulse* (1951), 25–30.

———. "Psychology and the Modern Dance." *Dance Observer* (Oct.–Nov., 1934), 73, 76–77.

———. "Your Actions Speak so Loudly." *Impulse* (1954), 27–28.

Canino, Leda. "The World Opens." *Dance,* 38(10) (Oct., 1964), 46–47.

Canner, Norma. *. . . and a Time to Dance.* Boston: Beacon Press, 1968.

Carroccio, Dennis, and Lawrence Quattlebaum. "An Elementary Technique for Manipulation of Participation in Ward Dances at a Neuropsychiatric Hospital." *Journal of Music Therapy,* 6(4) (1969), 108–109.

Case, Maurice. *Recreation for Blind Adults.* Springfield, Ill.: Charles C Thomas, 1966.

Chace, Marian. "Comments on the Arts and Mental Illness." Paper presented at the Interdisciplinary Conference, St. Elizabeth's Hospital, 1959.[b]

———. "Common Principles in Music Therapy." *Music Therapy,* 4 (1954), 87–90.

———. "The Contribution of Dance in the Education of Children: The Need for Communication and Creative Release for the Individual." Unpublished article.[b]

———. "Dance Alone Is Not Enough." *Dance,* 7 (July, 1964), 46–47+.

———. "Dance as an Adjunctive Therapy with Hospitalized Mental Patients." *Bulletin of the Menninger Clinic,* 17 (Nov., 1953), 219–225.

———. "Dance as Communication: Its Use in Growth or Treatment Situations." *Music Therapy,* 8 (1958), 119–122.

———. "Dance in Growth or Treatment Settings." *Music Therapy, 1958,* 1 (Oct., 1959), 149–153.

———. "Dance Therapy at St. Elizabeth's Hospital." *The Psychiatric Aide,* 8(9) (Sept., 1951), 3–4.[b]

———. "Dance Therapy for Adults." Unpublished paper presented at the National Education Association Conference, Atlantic City, undated.[b]

———. "Dance Therapy for the Mentally Ill." *Dance,* 6 (June, 1968), 36–38+.

———. "Dancing Helps Patients Make Initial Contacts." *Mental Hospitals* (Feb., 1954).[b]

———. "Development of Group Interaction through Dance," in *Progress in Psychotherapy-Technique of Psychiatry.* J. H. Masserman and J. L. Moreno, eds. New York: Grune and Stratton, 1958. Vol. 3, 149–153.

————. "Hotel St. Elizabeth: A Unique Experiment in Therapy." *Americas* (May, 1955).[b]

————. "Leadership in Dance Sessions within an Institutional Setting." *Yearbook of Brooklyn College Association for Health and Physical Education,* 2 (Oct., 1961), 20–23, 27–28.[b]

————. *Marian Chace: Her Papers.* Harris Chaiklin, ed. Columbia, Md.: American Dance Therapy Association, 1975.

————. "The Meaning of Movement: As Human Expression and as Artistic Communication." Panel discussion with Jarl Dyrud and Jean Erdman. *Third Conference Proceedings.* American Dance Therapy Association, Madison, Wis., 1968. Pages 1–16.

————. "Measurable and Intangible Aspects of Dance Sessions." *Music Therapy,* 7 (1957), 151–156.

————. "Movement Communication with Children." *Third Conference Proceedings.* American Dance Therapy Association, Madison, Wis., 1968. Pages 60–63.

————. "Music in Dance Therapy." *Music Journal* (Nov., 1967), 25–26+.

————. "A Note on Dance Therapy." *Group Psychotherapy,* 13 (Sept.–Dec., 1960), 205.

————. "Opening Doors through Dance." *National Education Association Magazine* (Feb., 1952).

————. "Personal Gratification—Physiological Aspects." *Music Therapy* (1952), 63–67.

————. "Physiological Aspects." *Music Therapy,* 2 (1952), 243–245.

————. "The Power of Movement with Others." *Dance Magazine,* 38 (June, 1964), 42–45, 68–69.

————. "A Psychological Study as Applied to Dance." Unpublished paper presented at meeting of the American Psychological Association, New York, Sept. 4, 1957.[b]

————. "Report of Group Project, Saint Elizabeth's Hospital." *Music Therapy,* 4 (1954), 187–190.

————. "Rhythm in Movement as Used in St. Elizabeth's Hospital." *Group Psychotherapy, a Symposium.* J. L. Moreno, ed. New York: Beacon House, 1946. Pages 243–245.

————. "Rhythmic Action for Communication." Unpublished presentation to the American Association for Humanistic Psychology, Sept. 1, 1966.[b]

————. "The Role of the Psychiatric Nurse in Dance Sessions." *SNANYS Newsletter,* 8(6) (Oct., 1960), 8–9.

————. "Stimulation of Creative Forms in Patient Production." *Bulletin of the National Association for Music Therapy,* 7 (Sept., 1958), 9–10.

————. "The Structuring of Dance Sessions for Varying Needs of Patients." *Music Therapy,* 12 (1962), 63–68.

———. "Techniques for the Use of Dance as a Group Therapy." *Music Therapy*, III (1954), 62–67.

———. Untitled article on professional history. *Journal of the American Dance Therapy Association, Inc.* Deborah Thomas, ed. 1(1) (Fall, 1968), 2–4.

———. "Use of Dance Action in Group Setting." Unpublished paper presented at the American Psychiatric Association convention, Los Angeles, Calif., May, 1953.[b]

———. "The Use of Dance in Ward Programs."[b]

———. "When Expressive Therapy in the Dance is Contra-Indicated." Unpublished presentation to the American Association for Humanistic Psychology, Sept. 1, 1966.[b]

——— and Judith Bunney. "Some Observations on the Psychodrama Sessions at Chestnut Lodge." Eighth Annual Chestnut Lodge Symposium, Nov. 9, 1961. Pages 19–31.[b]

——— and Jarl Dyrud. "Movement and Personality." *Third Conference Proceedings.* American Dance Therapy Association, Madison, Wis., 1968.

——— and Warren R. Johnson. "Our Real Lives Are Lived in Movement." *J. of Health, Physical Ed. and Recreation,* 32 (1961), 30–56.

Chaiklin, Sharon. "Concepts of Dance Therapy." *Group Psychotherapy,* 20(3–4) (Sept.–Dec., 1967).

Chapman, Ann, and Miriam Cramer. *Dance and the Blind Child.* New York: American Dance Guild, 1973.

Chenney, Gay. "It Is a Gift." *Impulse: Extensions of Dance.* Marian Van Tuyl, ed. San Francisco: Impulse Publications, 1970. Pages 65–68.

Christiansen, Bjorn. *Thus Speaks the Body.* New York: Arno Press, 1963.

Christrup, Helen. "Effect of Dance Therapy on the Concept of Body Image." *Psychiatric Quarterly Supplement,* 36(2) (1961), 296–303.

———. "Exploratory Study of the Effect of Dance Therapy on the Concept of Body Image, as Measured by Projective Drawings, in a Group of Schizophrenics." Master's thesis, George Washington University, Washington, D.C., 1958.

Cohen, Rhoda. "Dancing Class in a Crippled Children's Hospital." *Physical Therapy Review* (Jan., 1951).

Committee on Research in Dance. "Dance Therapy Bibliography." *CORD News,* 4(2) (Dec., 1972).

———. *Workshop in Dance Therapy: Its Research Potentials.* Proceedings of a Joint Conference by Research Department of Postgraduate Center, Committee on Research in Dance, and American Dance Therapy Association, New York City, 1968.

Costonis, Maureen. "Dance Therapy for Mentally Retarded Children." *Expanding Horizons in Therapeutic Recreation II.* Urbana-Champaign, Ill.: University of Illinois Office of Recreation and Park Resources, 1974. Pages 76–86.

———. "Expanding Stereotyped Object Manipulation into Expressive Dance

Movement: Dance Therapy with an Autistic Child." Master's thesis, University of Illinois, Champaign, 1972.

Cowles, Sage. "Movement Therapy." *Washburn Newsletter,* 5(4) (Winter, 1976), 3.

Dalcroze, Emile. "Blind Children and Eurhythmics." *Catholic World,* 130 (1934), 47–54.

Davis, Diana. "Movement Therapy." *Laban Art of Movement Guild Magazine,* 36 (May, 1966).

Davis, Doris. "A Study of the Influence of Structural Integration (Postural Release) upon Selected Measures of Body Image in Nine Subjects." Master's thesis, University of California, Los Angeles, 1969.

Davis, Flora. *Inside Intuition: What We Know about Nonverbal Communication.* New York: McGraw-Hill, 1973.

Davis, Martha. "An Effort-Shape Movement Analysis of a Family Therapy Session." Unpublished paper, Yeshiva University, 1966.[a]

———. "Methods of Perceiving Patterns of Small-Group Behavior." New York: Dance Notation Bureau, 1970.[a]

———. *Understanding Body Movement: An Annotated Bibliography.* New York: Arno Press, 1972.

Dell, Cecily. *A Primer for Movement Description: Using Effort-Shape and Supplementary Concepts.* New York: Dance Notation Bureau, 1970.

Delta Sigma Omicron. *Wheelchair Square Dancing.* Distributed by Rehabilitation Center, University of Illinois, Champaign, undated.

Dewey, Margaret. *Recreation for Autistic and Emotionally Disturbed Children.* Washington, D.C.: U.S. Government Printing Office, 1973.

Dickenson, Mildred. "Music as a Tool in Psychotherapy in Children." *Music Therapy* (1957), 97–104.

Dietz, Betty. "Dance, Inc., Has a 3–Day Clinic for Teachers of Handicapped Children." *Dance,* 40(9) (Sept., 1966), 72.

Dobbs, J. P. *The Slow Learner and Music: A Handbook for Teachers.* New York, N.Y.: Oxford University Press, 1966.

Donelon, Frances, ed. *Monograph 1, 1971; Monograph 2, 1972; Monograph 3, 1974.* Columbia, Md.: American Dance Therapy Association, 1971, 1972, 1974.

Dowling, Katherine. "Dance Therapy for Selected Psychiatric Patients." Master's thesis, Trinity University, San Antonio, Tex., 1955.

Dugger, Margaret. "Dance for the Blind." *Journal of Health, Physical Education and Recreation,* 39 (May, 1968), 28–30.

Dulicai, Dianne. "Movement Therapy on a Closed Ward." *Journal of the Bronx State Hospital,* 1(4) (Fall, 1973).

Dunn, Beryl. *Dance Therapy for Dancers.* London: Neinemann Health Books, 1974.

Durlacher, E. "Square Dancing for the Handicapped." *Recreation,* 44 (Sept., 1950), 190–192.

Ehrlich, Milton. "The Role of Body Experience in Therapy." *Psychoanalytic Review,* 57 (1970), 181–195.

Eichenbaum, Bertha, and Norman Bednarek. "Square Dancing and Social Adjustment." *Mental Retardation,* 2(2) (1964), 105–108.

Eiten, George. "Modern Dance and the Non-Verbal." *Dance Observer,* 18(8) (Oct., 1959), 116–117.

Ellis, Rhoda, and K. Wersen. "Motion and Emotion: Questions and Answers about Dance Therapy for the Mentally Ill." *Dance,* 32 (Aug., 1958), 48–51+.

Espenak, Liljan. "Body Dynamics and Dance as Supportive Techniques in Individual Psychotherapy." Unpublished paper.[c]

———. "Changing the Lifestyle through Psychomotor Therapy: A Case Presentation." Paper presented to the 11th Congress of the International Association of Individual Psychology, New York, 1970.[c]

———. "Movement Diagnosis Tests and the Inherent Laws Governing Their Use in Treatment: An Aid in Detecting the Lifestyle." *Individual Psychologist,* 7(1) (May, 1970), 8–13.

———. "A New, Non-Verbal Approach to Personality Evaluation." Paper presented at American Association on Mental Deficiency, Region 10 Conference, 1970.[c]

Estano, Charles. "Psychiatric Squares." *American Squares* (Sept., 1955), 8–9.

Evan, Blanche. "Therapeutic Aspects of Creative Dance." *Dance Observer* (Nov., 1959), 135–136.

Fait, Hollis. *Special Physical Education: Adapted, Corrective, Developmental.* Philadelphia: W. B. Saunders, 1972.

Feher, Milton. "Dance and the Disabled Veteran." *Dance,* 19(7) (July, 1945), 6, 45.

———. "Dance Therapy for the Disabled." *Crippled Child,* 26(1) (June, 1948), 21–23+.

———. "Dance Therapy for Polio Patients." *Dance,* Part I in 32(6) (June, 1958), 50, 85; Part II in 32(7) (July, 1958), 88–93.

———. "The Dancer's Anatomy: Dance Therapy for Disabled Dancers." *Dance,* 23(5) (May, 1949), 28–29, 32.

Feldenkrais, Moshe. *Awareness through Movement: Health Exercises for Personal Growth.* New York: Harper and Row, 1972.

———. *Body and Mature Behavior.* New York: International Universities Press, 1949.

———. *Twenty-five Lessons.* Notated by Margalit Sonnefeld and Michal Shoshani. Holon, Israel: Movement Notation Society, 1971.

Fine, Reiko, Dennis Daly, and Leon Fine. "Psychodance: An Experiment in Psychotherapy and Training." *Group Psychotherapy,* 15 (1962), 203–223.

Fink, Herschel. "Dance Teachers Find Retarded Challenging." *ICRH* (Information and Research Utilization Center in Physical Education and Recreation for the Handicapped) *Newsletter,* 3(9) (1968), 3–4.

"Folk Dancing for Rehabilitation." *Dance,* 19(7) (July, 1945), 9.

Freeman, Roslyn. *Motion and Music for the Maladjusted.* Brooklyn, N.Y., 1949.[g]

Frimet, Adrienne. "An Application of Montesorri's Principles and Practices in a Special Education Program for the Cerebral Palsied Child." Dance Research Monograph One, 1971–1972. Patricia Rowe and Ernestine Stodelle, eds. New York: CORD, 1973.

Galper, Jeffry. "Nonverbal Communication Exercises in Groups." Social Work, 15(2) (April, 1970), 71–77.

Gardner, Chloe. "My Experience of Teaching Movement to Psychiatric Cases." Laban Art of Movement Guild Magazine, 34 (May, 1965).

Garnet, Eva. "Geriatric-Calisthenics." Retirement Center Management (March–April, 1966).

Gavin, Ann. "An Evaluation of Musical Experiences for the Trainable Mentally Retarded Children at the Langford School in East Hartford." Master's thesis, American University, Washington, D.C., 1973.

Gendzel, Ivan. "Marathon Group Therapy and Nonverbal Methods." American Journal of Psychiatry, 127(3) (Sept., 1970), 286–290.

Genther, Shirley. "A Place to Begin." Impulse (1954), 19–22.

Gerber, Kathleen. "Self-Confrontation in a Motor Development and Creative Movement Program for Handicapped Children." Master's thesis, California State University, Long Beach, 1973.

Gillies, Emily. Creative Dramatics for All Children. Washington, D.C.: Association for Childhood Education International, 1973.

Ginglend, David. The Expressive Arts for the Mentally Retarded. Arlington, Tex.: National Association for Retarded Children, 1967.

———— and Winifred Stiles. Music Activities for Retarded Children: A Handbook for Teachers and Parents. Nashville, Tenn.: Abingdon Press, 1965.

Gittens, John A. G. "The Effects of a Program of Modern Educational Dance on the Perceptual-Motor Skills and Psycholinguistic Attributes of Trainable Mentally Retarded Children," Master's thesis, University of Saskatchewan, Saskatoon, Saskatchewan, undated.

Glass, Henry. Action Time—With Story, Chant, and Rhyme. Volume I. Hayward, Calif.: Alameda County School Dept., 1973.

Goodnow, Catherine. "The Use of Dance in Therapy with Retarded Children." Journal of Music Therapy, 5(4) (1968), 97–102.

Goodwin, Betty. "The Study of the Use of Dance as a Therapeutic Aid, with Special Reference to the Mentally Ill." Master's thesis, University of North Carolina, Chapel Hill, 1954.

Gordijn, Carl, et al. Wat Beweegtons. Baarn: Bosch and Keuning, 1975.

Graham, Richard. "Suggested Procedures for Conducting Rhythm Activities on Wards of Chronic and Regressed Mental Patients." Master's thesis, University of Kansas, Lawrence, 1958.

Grassman, Cyrus. "Modified Folk and Square Dancing for the Mentally Retarded." The Physical Educator, 15(1) (March, 1958), 32–35.

Greenwood, E. D. "Dancing." Bulletin of the Menninger Clinic, 6(3) (May, 1942), 78–79.

Gromska, Jadwiga, Barbara Domoslawska, Jolanta Koczurowska. "Poradina Zdrowia Psychicznego dla Dzieci i Mlodziezy" (Music Therapy in Treatment of Hyperkinetic and Anxiety Neuroses in Children"). *Psychiatria Polska,* 9(6) (1975), 605–612.

Groves, Lilian. "Music, Movement and Mime." *Nursing Times* (London), 64(9) (1968), 295–297.

Gunning, Susan, and Thomas Holmes. "Dance Therapy with Psychotic Children: Definition and Quantitative Evaluation." *Archives of General Psychiatry,* 28(5) (May, 1973), 707–713.

Gunther, Bernard. *Sense Relaxation—Below Your Mind.* New York: Macmillan, 1968.

Hagen, Sandra. "Dance in a Silent World." Master's thesis, Southern Methodist University, Dallas, Tex., 1972.

Haley, Betty. "The Effects of Individualized Movement Programs upon Emotionally Disturbed Children." *Dissertation Abstracts International,* 30 (11–A) (May, 1970), 4811.

Harding, Marlene. "Beginnings of D.A.N.C.E." *Dance,* 35(12) (Dec., 1961), 18–21, 62–63.

Harris, Joanna Gewertz. "Dance for Psychotic Children." *Journal of Physical Education, Health, and Recreation,* 35 (Jan., 1964), 63–64.

———— and Judy Beers. *Bibliography on Dance Therapy, 1974.* Columbia, Md.: American Dance Therapy Association, 1974.

————, Marietta Eng, and Maleta Boatman. "The Occupational Therapy Program." *Inpatient Care for the Psychotic Child.* Palo Alto, Calif.: Science and Behavior Books, 1971. Vol. 5.

Harrold, R. "Dancing with a Difference, or Wheelchair Dancing." *Dance Gazette,* 131 (1972), 2.

Hecox, Bernadette, Ellen Levine, and Diana Scott. "A Report on the Use of Dance in Physical Rehabilitation: Every Body Has a Right to Feel Good." *Rehabilitation Literature,* 36(1) (Jan., 1975), 11–15.

Helm, Jocelyn, and Kathleen Gill. "An Essential Resource for Aging: Dance Therapy." *Dance Research Journal of Committee on Research in Dance,* 7(1) (Fall–Winter, 1974), 1–7.

Hering, Doris. "A Sliver of Hope." *Dance Magazine,* 39(9) (Sept., 1965), 46–48.

Hill, Madeline. "Development of a Program of Dance Therapy for Pre-School Boys and Girls at the Juliette Fowler Home for Children in Dallas, Texas." Master's thesis, Texan Christian Women's University, Denton, 1966.

Hood, Claudia. "Challenge of Dance Therapy." *Journal of Health, Physical Education and Recreation,* 30(2) (Feb., 1959), 17–18.

Horvei, Carol. "Comparison of Normal and Psychotic Adolescents in Their Reactions to Dance Therapy Techniques." Master's thesis, University of Minnesota, Minneapolis, 1965.

Hoseason, Gerald. "Rhythm-Motor Experience in Motivating Chronic Catatonic Patients." Master's thesis, University of California, Los Angeles, 1961.

Hospital, Pierre. *Histoire Medicale de la Musique et de la Danse.* Paris: Clermont-Ferrand, 1897.

Huang, Al Chung-liang. *Embrace Tiger, Return to Mountain—The Essence of T'ai Chi.* Moab, Utah: Real Peoples Press, 1973.

Huberty, C. J., J. P. Quirk, and W. Swan. "Dance Therapy with Psychotic Children." *Archives of General Psychiatry,* 28(5) (May, 1973), 707–713.

Huckenpahler, Victoria. "Body Ego Technique by Jeri Salkin." *Dance,* 48(7) (July, 1974), 23.

———. "The Silent Muse: A Look at the Dance Department of Gallaudet College." *Dance,* 45(3) (March, 1971), 24–26.

Hunt, Valerie. "The Biological Organization of Man to Move." *Impulse* (1968), 51–62.

———. "Movement Behavior: A Model for Action." *Quest: Monograph 2* (April, 1964), 69–91.

———. *Recreation for the Handicapped.* New York: Prentice-Hall, 1955.

Hutchinson, Ann. "Dance for Deaf Children: A Visit to an Institute for the Deaf in Holland." *Dancing Times* (March, 1971), 308.

Information and Research Utilization Center in Physical Education and Recreation for the Handicapped. *Materials on Creative Arts (Arts, Crafts, Dance, Drama and Music) for Persons with Handicapping Conditions.* Washington, D.C.: American Alliance for Health, Physical Education and Recreation, 1975.

Jeayes, Isabel. "Margaret Morris Jubilee: Fifty Years of Achievement." *Dancing Times* (Dec., 1960), 173, 175.

Johnson, Dorothy, et al. *Special Education, Music and Dance. An E.S.E.A., Title III Project Evaluation.* Shoreline School, District 412, Seattle, Wash., 1970.

Jones, Clarice. "Folk Dancing." *The Pointer,* 12(3) (1968), 18.

Judd, Louise. "Dancing for the Deaf." *Dance* 28(4) (April, 1954), 54–55.

Kalish, Beth. "Aaron—A Case Study." Unpublished paper, 1971.[d]

———. "Behavior Rating Instrument for Atypical Children—With Emphasis on a Scale for Assessing Movement Behavior." Paper presented at American Orthopsychiatric Conference, San Francisco, Calif., April, 1974.

———. "Body Movement Scale for Autistic and Other Atypical Children: An Exploratory Study Using a Normal Group and an Atypical Group." Ph.D. dissertation, Bryn Mawr College, Bryn Mawr, Pa., 1976.

———. "Eric." Unpublished paper, 1970.[d]

———. "The Role of Movement Cues in Observing, Assessing, and Therapeutically Engaging an Autistic Child." Paper presented at American Orthopsychiatric Association, San Francisco, Calif., 1970.[d]

Kaslon, Florence. "Dance and Movement Therapy—A Study in Theory and Applicability." Master's thesis, Bryn Mawr School of Social Work, Bryn Mawr, Pa., 1966.

Kaslow, Florence W. "Movement, Music and Art Therapy Techniques Adapted for Special Education," in *Teaching the Mentally Handicapped Child.* R. Hyatt and N. Rolnick, eds. New York: Behavioral Publications, 1974.

Kavaler, Susan. "Dance Therapy with Retarded Children." *International Mental Health Research Newsletter,* 16(1) (Spring, 1974), 9–11.

―――. "Effects of Dance Therapy on Mentally Retarded Children." Ph.D. dissertation, Adelphi University, Garden City, N.Y., 1974.

Keleher, C. "Modern Dance as Mental Therapy." *Dance Observer,* 23(3) (March, 1956), 37–38.

Kestenberg, Judith. *Children and Parents: Psychoanalytic Studies in Development.* New York: Jason Aronsen, Inc., 1975.

―――. "Comments on 'Movement Therapy as a Psychotherapeutic Tool.' " *Journal of the American Psychoanalytic Association,* 21(1) (1973), 347–350.

―――. "Rhythm and Organization in Obsessive-Compulsive Development." *International Journal of Psycho-Analysis,* 47 (1966), 151–159.

―――. "The Role of Movement Patterns in Development: I, Rhythms of Movement." *Psychoanalytic Quarterly,* 34 (1965), 1–36.

―――. "The Role of Movement Patterns in Development: II, Flow of Tension and Effort." *Psychoanalytic Quarterly,* 34 (1965), 517–563.

―――. "The Role of Movement Patterns in Development: III, The Control of Shape." *Psychoanalytic Quarterly,* 36 (1967), 356–409.

―――, Hershey Marcus, Esther Robbins, J. Berlowe, and A. Buelte. "Development of the Young Child, as Expressed through Bodily Movement: I." *Journal of American Psychoanalytic Association,* 19(4) (Oct., 1971), 746–764.

Klafs, Carl. "Rhythmic Activities for Handicapped Children." Ph.D. dissertation, University of Southern California, Los Angeles, 1957.

Koslow, Sally. "New, Exciting Direction in Psychiatry: Dance / Music / Art Therapy." *Mademoiselle* (Jan., 1976).

Kratz, Laura. *Movement without Sight.* Palo Alto, Calif.: Peek Publications, 1973.

Kraus, Richard. "Reality through the Dance." *Recreation,* 46(6) (Nov., 1952), 326–327.

Laban, Rudolf. "The Educational and Therapeutic Value of the Dance." *The Dance Has Many Faces.* Walter Sorell, ed. New York: World, 1951. Pages 145–159.

Lachman, Mildred. "The Use of Movement in Art Therapy." *American Journal of Art Therapy,* 13(1) (Oct., 1973), 22–34.

Lamb, Warren. "Movement Profile Procedure." Unpublished paper.[a]

―――. *Posture and Gesture: An Introduction to the Study of Physical Behavior.* London: Gerald Duckworth, 1965.

―――. "Report into Movement Therapy at St. Bernard's Hospital." Unpublished article, 1954.[a]

Last, Brenda. "Dance! Therapy for Dancers by Beryl Dunn." *Dancing Times* (Dec., 1974), 135.

Lau, Julianna. "The Use of Reinforcement Procedures in Dance Therapy." Binational Dance Conference. *Dance: Verities, Values, Visions.* Waterloo, Ontario, Canada, June, 1971.

Laws, M. "Teaching the Handicapped." (Letter) *Dance Gazette,* 134 (1973), 7.

Lawton, Shailer. "Dance as an Instrument of Healing." *Dance News* (Jan., 1946), 6.

———. "Dance as Therapy." *Dance Encyclopedia.* Anatole Chujoy, ed. New York: A. S. Barnes, 1949.

———. "What You Should Know about Polio." *Dance,* Part I in 31(1) (Jan., 1957), 34–37; Part II in 31(3) (March, 1957), 42–44.

Lefco, Helene. *Dance Therapy: Narrative Case Histories of Therapy Sessions with Six Patients.* Chicago: Nelson-Hall, 1973.

Lehmann, Eugenia M. "A Study of Rhythms and Dancing for the Feeble-Minded, the Blind and the Deaf." Master's thesis, Ohio State University, Columbus, 1936.

Leonard, Anna. "Extra Problems." *Broad Sheet,* 4(3) (March, 1972), 6–9.ᵉ

Lert, Ruth. "Dance: A World of Wonders to Handicapped Children." *Dance,* 43(9) (Sept., 1969), 60–63.

Leventhal, Marcia. "A Dance-Movement Experience as Therapy with Psychotic Children." Master's thesis, University of California, Los Angeles, 1965.

Linford, Anthony, and Claudine Jeanrenaud. *Systematic Instruction for Retarded Children: The Illinois Program. Experimental Edition/Part IV. Motor Performance and Recreation Instruction.* Urbana, Ill.: Office of the Superintendent of Public Instruction, State of Illinois, August, 1972.

Lloyd, Marcia. "An Examination of Research Concerning the Use of Creative Dance as Applied to Therapy for Mentally Ill." Master's thesis, University of Wyoming, Laramie, 1965.

Lofthouse, P. "Educational Dance and Expressive Movement with Mentally Handicapped Children at the Piddington School, Strathmont Centre, Adelaide." *Discover,* 5(4) (1972), 5–10.

Look magazine. April 5, 1966. Article featuring Rhoda Russell.

Lowen, Alexander. *Betrayal of the Body.* New York: Macmillan, 1967.

———. *Physical Dynamics of Character Structure.* New York: Grune and Stratton, 1958.

———. *Pleasure: A Creative Approach to Life.* New York: Coward-McCann, 1970.

Lumb, Virginia. "Dance and the Retarded: A Comparative Study of Ghetto and Suburban Children." Master's thesis, Southern Methodist University, Dallas, Tex., 1972.

Mansfield, Portia. "Help Them Move Young; a Series of Conditioning Exercises for Older People." *Dance,* Part I in 40(9) (Sept., 1966), 82; Part II in 40(10) (Oct., 1966), 76–77; Part III in 40(11) (Nov., 1966), 78.

———. "Let Us Help Them Move Young: An Open Letter." *Dance,* 40(8) (Aug., 1966), 16–17.

Marek, Patricia. "Dance Therapy with Adult Day Hospital Patients." Ph.D. dissertation, University of Tennessee, Knoxville, 1976.

Martin, Donald, and Nohmie Beaver. "A Preliminary Report on the Use of

Dance as an Adjunct in the Therapy of Schizophrenics." *Psychoanalytic Quarterly Supplement*, 25(2) (1951), 176–190.

Mason, Kathleen, ed. *Dance Therapy: Focus on Dance VII.* Washington, D.C.: American Association of Health, Physical Education, and Recreation, 1974.

Matteson, Carol. "Finding the Self in Space." *Music Educators Journal*, 58(8) (April, 1972), 63–65, 135.

May, Philip, Milton Wexler, Jeri Salkin, and Trudi Schoop. "Non-Verbal Techniques in the Re-establishment of Body Image and Self-Identity—A Preliminary Report." *Psychiatric Research Report*, 16 (1963), 68–82.

May, Rowena. "Modern Dancing as a Therapy for the Mentally Ill." *Occupational Therapy and Rehabilitation*, 20(2) (1941), 101–106.

McCarthy, Henry. "Use of the Draw-a-Person Test to Evaluate a Dance Therapy Program." *Journal of Music Therapy*, 10(3) (Fall, 1973), 141–155.

McDermott, Elisabeth. "Music and Rhythms: From Movement to Lip-Reading and Speech." *Volta Review*, 73(4) (April, 1971), 229–232.

Mendum, Catherine. "A Study in the Use of Psycho-Movement Drama as a Group Counseling Technique." Master's thesis, University of Wisconsin, Madison, 1952.

Meredith-Jones, B. "Moving and Living: Elderly People." *Laban Art of Movement Guild Magazine*, 27 (May, 1961).

Mettler, Barbara. "Creative Dance: Art or Therapy?" Jan., 1973. Unpublished paper.[f]

Miller, A. "Growing with Music: Program for the Mentally Retarded." *Exceptional Child*, 20 (April, 1954), 305–307.

Monsky, Millie. "A Program of Dance for Visually Handicapped Young People." *International Journal for the Education of the Blind*, 7(3) (March, 1958).

Montague, Mary. "The Effects of Dance Experience upon Observable Behavior of Women Prisoners." Ph.D. dissertation, New York University, New York, 1961.

———. "Women Prisoners Respond to Contemporary Dance." *Journal of Health, Physical Education and Recreation*, 34 (March, 1973), 25–26.

Monzani, A. "Dance Therapy and the Origin of Wheel-Chair Dancing." *Dance Gazette*, 132 (1973), 5.

Morris, Margaret. "Movement and Art for the Handicapped." *Creation and Dance and Life*. London, 1972. Pages 116–120.[g]

Morrison, John. "Never Lose Yourself." *Reaching Out*, 3(2). Springfield, Ill.: Department of Mental Health, 1972. Pages 22–29.

Mosey, Ann. "Treatment of Pathological Distortion of Body Image." *American Journal of Occupational Therapy*, 23(5) (Sept.–Oct., 1969).

Mossman, Maja, and Linni Silberman. "Movement—the Joyous Language." *Children's House Magazine*, 3(5) (Spring, 1976), 11–15.

Muller, Stephanie. "Teaching the Emotionally Disturbed Child." *Ballroom Dance Magazine* (May, 1965).

Music Educators Journal. "Dance Therapy Initiated in Israel." Vol. 51 (Feb., 1965), 130.

Music Educators National Conference. "Music in Special Education." *Music Educators Journal,* 58(8) (April, 1972), 5–143.

Nagel, Charles, and Fredricka Moore. *Skill Development through Games and Rhythmic Activities.* Palo Alto, Calif.: The National Press, 1966.

Neale, Marie. "The Effects of a Broad Art and Movement Programme upon a Group of Trainable Retarded Children." *International Copenhagen Congress on Scientific Study of Mental Retardation: Proceedings.* Copenhagen, Denmark: Det Berlingske, Boytrykkeri, 1964. Pages 294–302.

New York Times. "Dance Therapy Is Used to Help the Mentally Ill." Aug. 7, 1973. Page 46.

North, Marian. *Personality Assessment through Movement.* London: Macdonald and Evans, 1972.

Obenauer, Heidi von, and Victoria Huckenpahler. "Dance Books." *Dance,* 49(5) (May, 1975), 98–99.

Offner, R. "Dance as an Adjunct to Therapy with Psychotic Patients." Master's thesis, New York School of Social Work, Columbia University, 1953.

Pawlowski, Miriam. "Movement Assessment of Perceptually Handicapped Children by Means of Modified Labanotation and Effort Notation." Master's thesis, Smith College, Northampton, Mass., 1972.

Perlmutter, Ruth. "Dance Me a Cloud." *Children's House,* 6(6) (Winter, 1974), 15–19.

Pesso, Albert. *Experience in Action: A Psychomotor Psychology.* New York: New York University Press, 1973.

———. *Movement in Psychotherapy: Psychomotor Techniques and Training.* New York: New York University Press, 1969.

Philp, Richard. "It's Not that Woodpeckers Are Repulsive . . . Toward Breaking a Bad Response." *Dance,* 44(3) (March, 1972), 34–36.

Pierson, Nancy. "A Study of the Use of Dance as Therapy for Psychotic and/ or Emotionally Disturbed Children." Master's thesis, University of Colorado, Boulder, 1967.

Pilates, Joseph. *Return to Life through Contrology.* Boston, 1960.[9]

———. *Return to Life through Contrology: Exercises Transcribed into Labonotation.* New York, 1960.[9]

Plitt, Norna. "Modern Dancing as an Aid in Psychotherapeutics." Master's thesis, New York University, New York, 1948.

Polk, Elizabeth. Presentation. Proceedings of First State-wide Conference on Physical Education for Handicapped Children and Youth, University of State of New York, State Education Department, Albany, N.Y., 12234.

Pomeroy, Janet. *Recreation for the Physically Handicapped.* New York: Macmillan, 1964.

Powell, Richard. "Psychological Effects of Exercise Therapy upon Institutionalized Geriatric Mental Patients." *Journal of Gerontology,* 29(2) (March, 1974), 157–161.

Puder, Miriam. "Dance Therapy for Emotionally Disturbed and/or Neurologically Impaired Children." Master's thesis, Newark State College, Newark, N.J., 1972.

Puretz, Susan. "A Comparison of the Effects of Dance and Physical Education on the Self-Concept of Selected Disadvantaged Girls." Abstracts of Research Papers (Anaheim, 1974). Washington, D.C.: American Alliance for Health, Physical Education and Recreation.

Puttock, Denise. "Dance Therapy." Nursing Times, 68 (Aug. 3, 1972), 960–961.

Rathbone, Josephine, and Carol Lucas. Recreation in Total Rehabilitation. Springfield, Ill.: Charles C Thomas, 1959.

Razy, Varda. "Dance Therapy in a Community Mental Health Center." Impulse (1970), 71–75.

———. "The Value of Dance and Percussion in the Treatment of Emotionally Disturbed Children." Social Casework (Dec., 1961).

Rebel, Gunther. "Gestaltete Bewegung und deren Praktische Anwendungsmoglichkeit in der Sozialarbeit." Das Tansarchives Hamburg. Heft 9,21 (Jan.–Feb., 1974), 289–291, 298–299.

Recreation Literature Retrieval Project. "Selected Bibliography on Recreation for the Mentally Retarded." Therapeutic Recreation Journal, 3(4) (1968), 14, 41–42.

Reich, Wilhelm. Character Analysis. New York: Orgone Institute Press, 1949.

Reiland, Robert. "Dance Workshops Explore Body Awareness." ICRH (Information and Research Utilization Center in Physical Education and Recreation for the Handicapped) Newsletter, 3(21) (1969), 4.

Resnick, Rose. "Creative Movement Classes for Visually Handicapped Children in a Public School Setting." New Outlook for the Blind, 67(10) (Dec., 1973), 442–447.

Revue Therapie Psychomotrice. 7 Rue Godot de Mauroy, Paris 9th CCP, France. Quarterly journal published in French.

Ridenour, Norma. "Dancers in the Dark." The Woman, 21 (Dec., 1948), 45–48.

Riess, Bernard. "Developments in Dance Therapy." Current Psychiatric Therapies, 9 (1969), 195.

Riordan, Jennifer. They Can Sing Too—Rhythm for the Deaf. Springfield, Va.: Jenrich Associates, 1971.

Riviere, Joan. "Magical Regeneration by Dancing." International Journal of Psychoanalysis, 11(3) (July, 1930), 340.

Robbins, Ferris and Jennet. Educational Rhythmics for Mentally and Physically Handicapped Children. New York: Association Press, 1968.

———. Educational Rhythmics for Mentally Handicapped Children. New York: Horizon Press, 1965.

———. Supplement to Educational Rhythmics for Mentally and Physically Handicapped Children. Zurich, Switzerland: Ra-Verlag, Rapperswil, 1966.

Robinson, Luther. "A Program for Deaf Mental Patients." *Hospital and Community Psychiatry*, 24(1) (Jan., 1973), 40–42.

Robinson, Violeta. "The Effects of Psycho-Dance with Neuro-Psychiatric Patients." Master's thesis, MacMurry College, Jacksonville, Ill., 1957.

Roche Medical Image. "Dancing Back to Reality," 1 (Spring, 1959), 5–7.

Rolf, Ida. "Structural Integration: Gravity, an Unexplored Factor in a More Human Use of Human Beings." *Systematics*, 1(1) (June, 1963), 67–83.

Rosen, Elizabeth. "Dance as Therapy for Mentally Ill." *Teachers College Record*, 55 (Jan., 1954), 215–222.

――――. *Dance in Psychotherapy.* New York: Teachers College, Columbia University, 1957.

――――. "Dance in the Therapy of Psychotic Patients." Ph.D. dissertation, Columbia University, New York, 1956.

Russel, Rhoda. "Motion and Emotion." *Dance Magazine*, 32(8) (Aug., 1958), 48–51+.

――――. "The Wisconsin Dance Idea—Tribute from a Movement Therapist." *Impulse* (1970), 68–70.

Ruttenberg, B. A., Beth Kalish, C. Wenar, and E. Wolf. *Behavior Rating Instrument for Autistic and Other Atypical Children.* Forthcoming, 1977.

Sabin, John. "Helping Mental Patients." *American Squares* (Jan., 1953), 4–5.

――――. "Square Dancing as Mental Therapy." *American Squares* (Feb., 1945), 4–6.

Salkin, Jeri. *Body-Ego Technique: An Educational and Therapeutic Approach to Body Image and Self-Identity.* Springfield, Ill.: Charles C Thomas, 1973.

Samoore, Rhoda. "A Rhythm Program for Hearing Impaired Children." *The Illinois Advance* (Jan., 1970), 1–3, 15–20.

Samuels, Arlynne, Stephanie Katz, Irene Marsh. *Listing of Academic Programs in Dance Therapy, Fieldwork Placement, Non-Academic Training or Apprenticeships, and Academic Internship Affiliations.* Columbia, Md.: American Dance Therapy Association, 1974.

Sandel, Susan. "Integrating Dance Therapy into Treatment." *Hospital and Community Psychiatry*, 26(7) (July, 1975), 439–441.

Sare, Dawn. "Changes in Body Image and Self-Concept: A Modern Dance Experience." Master's thesis, University of California, Los Angeles, 1969.

Schade, Maja. "Relaxation." Master's thesis, University of Wisconsin, Madison, 1948.

Schattner, Regina. *Creative Dance for Handicapped Children.* New York: John Day, 1967.

Scheerenberger, Richard. "Description of a Music Program at a Residential School for Mentally Handicapped." *American Journal of Mental Deficiency*, 57 (1953), 573–579.

Schilder, Paul. *The Image and Appearance of the Human Body.* New York: International Universities Press, 1950.

Schlichter, Joseph. "Movement Therapy." *Recognitions in Gestalt Therapy.* David Pursglove, ed. New York: Funk and Wagnalls, 1968.

————. "Psychodance Therapy." Master's thesis, Mills College, Oakland, Calif., 1964.

————. "Sequence." *Impulse* (1970), 76–79.

Schmais, Claire. "The American Dance Therapy Association." *Research in Dance: Problems and Possibilities.* Patricia Rowe, ed. Conference Proceedings of Committee on Research in Dance, New York, 1967.

————. "Dance Therapy as a Profession." *Journal of Health, Physical Education and Recreation,* 38 (Jan., 1967), 63–64.

————. "Learning Is Fun When You Dance It." *Dance,* 40(1) (Jan., 1966), 33–35.

————. "Movement in Expression and Communication: A Survey of the Literature." Unpublished article.[a]

————. "What Dance Therapy Teaches Us about Teaching Dance." *Journal of Health, Physical Education and Recreation,* 41(1) (Jan., 1970), 34–35+.

Schneider, Marius. *La Danza de Espadas y la Tarantela.* Barcelona, Spain, 1948.[g]

Schoop, Trudi, with Peggy Mitchell. *Won't You Join the Dance?* Palo Alto, Calif.: National Press, 1974.

Schullian, Dorothy. *Music and Medicine.* New York, 1948.[g]

Schuman, B. "Dance Therapy for the Emotionally Disturbed." *Journal of Health, Physical Education and Recreation,* 44 (Sept., 1973), 61–62.

Schutz, William. *Here Comes Everybody (Bodymind and Encounter Culture).* New York: Harper and Row, 1971.

Sellers, Jo Anne. "A Bibliography for the 1973 American Dance Guild Conference: Multi-Disciplinary Approaches to Dance in the Elementary Education." American Dance Guild, 1973.

Sender, Sarah. *Rhythm, Movement and Dance as Adjuncts to Psychotherapy.* New York, 1952, IV, 20.[g]

Sexton, Anne. Poetic description of Norma Canner in "Eighteen Days without You" from *Love Poems.* Boston: Houghton Mifflin, 1969. Pages 59–60.

Shallenburg, Myrtle. "Value of Rhythm in the Training of the Subnormal Child." Master's thesis, Ohio State University, Columbus, 1939.

Shaskan, Donald. "Group Psychotherapy: Present Trends in Management of the More Severe Emotional Problems." *Psychiatric Annals,* 2(4) (April, 1972), 10–15.

Shaw, R. "Teaching the Handicapped." (Letter) *Dance Gazette,* 134 (1973), 7.

Sheridan, Nina. "Dancer's Doctor." *Dance,* 36(9) (Sept., 1962).

Siegel, Elaine. "About Emily—A Movement Therapist Responds." *Voices,* 8(2) (Summer, 1972), 44–46.

————. "Movement Therapy as a Psychotherapeutic Tool." *Journal of the American Psychoanalytic Association,* 21 (1973), 333–343.

————. "Movement Therapy with a Group of Autistic Preschoolers." *Psychoanalytic Review,* 60 (Winter, 1973), 141–149.

————. "Psyche and Soma: Movement Therapy." *Voices,* 6 (Special Issue, 1970), 29–32.

Siegel, Marcia. "Describing an Elephant." *Dance Magazine,* 43(1) (Jan., 1969), 92–93.

———. "Effort-Shape and the Therapeutic Community: Sessions at Bronx State Hospital." *Dance Magazine,* 46(6) (June, 1968), 56–59+.

Slama, Linda. "The Foundation of a Body Image: A Theoretical Model." Master's thesis, University of California, Los Angeles, 1968.

Spero, Ruth, and Carole Weiner. "Creative Arts Therapy: Its Application in Special Education Programs." *Children Today,* 2(4) (July–August, 1973), 12–17.

Spraker, Lana. "Movement and Mental Health; The Value of Movement as a Therapeutic Tool." Master's thesis, University of California at Santa Monica, 1972.

Stephenson, Susan. "To Dance Is to Speak." *Dance,* 31(3) (March, 1959), 56–57, 88–89.

Stern, Edith. "Dance of Release." *Coronet Magazine,* 45 (Jan., 1959), 96–100.

———. "She Breaks through Invisible Walls." *Mental Hygiene,* 41 (July, 1957).

Stetcher, Miriam. "Concept Learning through Movement Improvisation." *Young Children* (Jan., 1970).

Stevens, Olga. "Dance as a Basic Need." *Music Therapy,* 8 (1958), 123–125.

Tavares, Marilyn. "An Experimental Investigation in Rhythmic Movement of Institutionalized Mongoloid Children." Master's thesis, Ohio State University, Columbus, 1958.

Taylor, Joyhope. "The Function of Real Joy in Affective-Cognitive Learning and Development through Creative Movement Curriculum. A Basic Concept in Primary Prevention of Mental Health Crises." Master's thesis, University of California, Los Angeles, 1972.

Taylor, Lucille. "Developmental Dance in the Education of the Educable Mentally Handicapped Child." Master's thesis, University of Illinois, Champaign, 1964.

Terry, Peter. "Square Wheeling." *American Journal of Occupational Therapy,* 4 (July–Aug., 1950), 164–168.

Terry, Walter. "Hazards and Healths of Dance." Phonotape, 1967. Audio materials available at the Performing Arts Residential Center, New York Public Library.

———. "Interview with Ted Shawn on the Dance and Therapy." Phonotape, 1967. Audio materials available at the Performing Arts Residential Center, New York Public Library.

Theeman, Margaret. "Rhythms of Community." Ph.D. dissertation, Harvard University, Cambridge, Mass., 1973.

Thieler, Virginia. "A Study of Behavior in a Boys' Dance Therapy Group at St. Elizabeth's Hospital." Master's thesis, Catholic University of America, Washington, D.C., 1950.

Thom, Rose. "A.D.T.A. Conference: Renewal through Art." *Dance,* 49(1) (Jan., 1975), 6–7.

————. "Dance Therapy: A Different Bouquet." *Dance*, 49(12) (Dec., 1975), 77.

Thomas, Deborah, ed. *Journal of the American Dance Therapy Association*, 1(1) (Fall, 1968).

Thompson, Myrtle. "The Arts in Therapy: Part 2." *Parks and Recreation*, 1(10) (1966), 858, 860, 881.

Time magazine. "Dance Therapy," 73 (Feb. 23, 1959), 60–62.

Toombs, Mary. "Dance Therapy in the Ward Music Program." *Music Therapy* (1957), 139–144.

————. "In Memoriam—Marian Chace." *Journal of Music Therapy*, 7 (Winter, 1970), 144.

Tucker, Dorothy, Barbara-Jeanne Seabury, and Norma Canner. *Foundations for Learning with Creative Art and Creative Movement*. Boston, Mass.: Massachusetts Dept. of Mental Health, Division of Mental Hygiene, 1967.

Tula. "Therapeutic Dance Rhythms." *Dance Observer*, 19(8) (Oct., 1952), 117–118.

Urbina, Louise. "The Effects of Body Awareness Therapy on Autistic Children." Master's thesis, California State University at Long Beach, 1973.

Van Krevelen, D. A. "Judo in the Framework of Movement Therapy: Results of an Inquiry." *Acta Paedopsychiatrica*, 40(6) (1974), 221–229.

Van Tuyl, Marian, ed. *Impulse: Extensions of Dance*. San Francisco, Calif.: Impulse Publications, 1970.

Vernazza, Maracelle. "What Are We Doing about Music in Special Education?" *Music Educators Journal*, 53(8) (April, 1967), 55–58.

Vistocky, Dorothy. *American Dance Therapy Association Bibliography*. Columbia, Md.: American Dance Therapy Association, 1970.

————. "Notes on a 'Moving' Experience." *Discovery—Newsletter Australian P.E.A.*, 3(1) (1970), 13–15.

Wadeson, Harriet. "Combining Expressive Therapies." *American Journal of Art Therapy*, 15(2) (Jan., 1976), 43–46.

Wall, Su. "Dance as a Thermostat." *Impulse* (1951).

Weigl, Vally. "Music as an Adjunctive Therapy in the Training of Children with Cerebral Palsy." *Cerebral Palsy Review*, 15 (Oct., 1954), 9–10.

Weiner, Carole. *Dance-Movement Therapy Bibliography*. Helmuth, N.Y.: Gowanda State Hospital, 1973.

Weisberg, Karen. "Dance Therapy." *Off Our Backs*, 11(3) (Nov. 24, 1971).

Weisbrod, Jo Ann. "Rubella and Aphasic Children: Experimental Movement Analysis and Therapeutic Techniques." Master's thesis, University of California, Los Angeles, 1971.

————. "Shaping a Body Image through Movement Therapy." *Music Educators Journal*, 58(8) (April, 1972), 66–69.

Wells, Alan. "Rhythmic Activities on Wards of Senile Patients." *Music Therapy* (1953), 127–132.

Wethered, Audrey. "The Enigmatic Oneness of the Living Being." *Journal of the Analytical Psychology Club*, 11 (1965).

————. *Movement and Drama in Therapy: The Therapeutic Use of Movement, Drama, and Music*. Boston: Plays, Inc., 1973.

————. "Movement and Personality Difficulties." *Laban Art of Movement Guild Magazine*, 21 (Nov., 1958).

————. "Movement Therapy in a Residential Psychotherapeutic Setting." *Laban Art of Movement Guild Magazine*, 34 (May, 1965).

Wheaton, E. "Teaching the Blind." *Square Dance*, 28(8) (1973), 13–14.

White, Elissa Queyquep. "Children Development Movement Studies: Part 1, 1969." Unpublished manuscript.[a]

————. "Effort Shape Movement Analyses and Comparison of Eight Children." 1968. Unpublished paper.[a]

Whitehouse, Mary. "Reflections on a Metamorphosis." *Impulse* (1970).

Wisher, Peter. "All God's Chillun Got Rhythm." *Discover*, 5(4) (1972), 35–37.

————. "Creative Dance for the Deaf." *Music Journal*, 23 (1965), 36–37.

————. "Dance and the Deaf." *Journal of Health, Physical Education and Recreation*, 30 (Nov., 1959), 68–69.

————. "Dance and the Deaf." *Journal of Health, Physical Education and Recreation*, 40(3) (1969), 81.

————. *Psychological Contributions of Dance to the Adjustment of the Deaf*. Washington, D.C.: Gallaudet College, undated.

Wolman, Benjamin. "Creativity and Mental Health: Are They Related?" in Myron Nadel's *The Dance Experience*. New York: Praeger, 1970. Pages 68–73.

Wood, Kinder. "A Case of the Dancing Mania." *Curiosities of Medicine*. Berton Roueche, ed. Boston: Little, Brown, 1958.

Woody, Regina. *Young Dancer's Career Book*. New York: Dutton, 1970. Illustrated by Arline Thompson.

Wooten, Betty. "Movement Therapy in England." *Journal of Health, Physical Education and Recreation*, 30(6) (Sept., 1959), 75–76.

Yocum, Louise. "The Art of T'ai Chi Ch'uan." *Feminine Fitness* (Oct., 1973).

Zaretsky, Sondra. "A Survey of Dance Therapy among Selected Mental Hospitals in the United States." Master's thesis, University of Illinois, Champaign, 1957.

Zegart, D. "Dance Groups for Psychotic Patients." Master's thesis, Smith College for Social Work, Northampton, Mass., 1956.

[a] Copies available from Dance Notation Bureau, New York.

[b] Reprints available from the Dance Therapy Section, St. Elizabeth's Hospital, Washington, D.C., 20032.

[c] Copies available from author, 2121 Broadway, New York, 10032.

[d] Copies available from Developmental Center for Autistic Children, 120 N. 48th Street, Philadelphia, Pa.

[e] Copies available from Flat 14, 30 Crescent Rd., N8, 8DA, London, England.

[f] Copies available from author, 3131 N. Cherry Avenue, Tucson, Ariz.

[g] Listed in New York City, Public Library, Dance Collection. *Dictionary Catalog of the Dance Collection*. New York: New York Public Library, Astor, Lenox and Tilden Foundations. Boston: Distributed by G. K. Hall, 1974. Supplement, 1975.

Contributors

MAUREEN COSTONIS, M.A.
Former Assistant Professor, Department of Dance and Department of Recreation and Park Resources, University of Illinois.

ADAM KENDON, Ph.D.
Former research psychiatrist, Project in Human Communication at Bronx State Hospital, and author of "Some Functions of Gaze-Direction in Social Interaction," *Acta Psychologica,* 26 (1967), 22–47.

JANET ADLER BOETTIGER, M.A.
Faculty of Hampshire College, Amherst, Mass.

JARL DYRUD, M.D.
Professor and Associate Chairman, Department of Psychiatry, University of Chicago.

MARIAN CHACE
First President of the A.D.T.A., movement therapist at St. Elizabeth's Hospital in Washington, D.C., and author of numerous articles.

RAY BIRDWHISTELL, Ph.D.
Professor, Annenberg School of Communication, University of Pennsylvania.

ARLYNNE SAMUELS
Movement therapist, The Sheppard and Enoch Pratt Hospital, Baltimore, Md.

MARTHA DAVIS, Ph.D.
Author of *Understanding Body Movement: An Annotated Bibliography* (New York: Arno Press, 1972).

FRANZISKA BOAS
Editor of *The Function of Dance in Human Society,* reprinted in 1972 by Dance Horizons.

PHILIP R. A. MAY, M.D.
Former research director, Camarillo State Hospital, Camarillo, Calif.; Professor of Psychiatry in Residence, Neuropsychiatric Institute, California State Department of Mental Hygiene.

MILTON WEXLER, Ph.D.
Consulting psychoanalyst, Camarillo State Hospital.

JERI SALKIN
Former research specialist, Camarillo State Hospital. Presently director of body ego therapy program, Cedars-Sinai Community Mental Health Center, Los Angeles, Calif.

TRUDI SCHOOP
Movement therapist at Camarillo State Hospital and a number of other institutions; co-author of *Won't You Join the Dance?* (Palo Alto, Calif.: Mayfield Publishing Co., 1974).

HELEN CHRISTRUP, M.A.
Graduate of George Washington University in 1958.

SEYMOUR FISHER, Ph.D., and SIDNEY CLEVELAND, Ph.D.
Collaborators on *Body Image and Personality* (Princeton, N.J.: Van Nostrand, 1958). Dr. Fisher is also author of *Body Consciousness* (Englewood Cliffs, N.J.: Prentice-Hall, 1973).

NORMA CANNER
Faculty of Lesley College in Cambridge, Mass.

HELENE LEFCO
Movement therapist, Delaware Valley Mental Health Foundation, Doylestown, Pa.

ALBERT PESSO
Director of Psychomotor Institute, Inc., in Boston, and author of *Experience in Action: A Psychomotor Psychology* (New York: New York University Press, 1973).

KINDER WOOD, M.D.
An early nineteenth-century English physician.

PEGGY MITCHELL
Movement therapist in Los Angeles who specializes in private practice and has trained extensively with Trudi Schoop; co-author of *Won't You Join the Dance?*

Index